The Erewash V

The Landscape of D H Lawrence

'The Brangwens had lived for generations on the Marsh Farm, in the meadows where the Erewash twisted sluggishly through alder trees, separating Derbyshire from Nottinghamshire'. – D H Lawrence The Rainbow

The River Erewash, the meandering stream which separates the counties of Derbyshire and Nottinghamshire, celebrated by D H Lawrence (*Author*).

First published in Great Britain in 2017

British Library Cataloguing-in-Publication Data.
A CIP record for this title is available from the British Library.

ISBN 978-1-5272-0866-7

COPPICE BOOKS
Little Orchard,Townsend,
Chittlehampton, Umberleigh,
Devon EX37 9PX
Tel: 01769 540271 or 07732 212937
Email: brenda68brian@hotmail.com

Printed and bound in the UK by
The Amadeus Press
Ezra House, West 26 Industrial Estate,
Cleckheaton, West Yorkshire, BD19 4TQ
Tel: 01274 863200.

By the same author

Local history and topography
Erewash Valley Portrait
Swimbridge – a North Devon Village in the 20th Century
St Francis of Assisi Long Eaton – A History
St Francis of Assisi Long Eaton – A pictorial celebration of the first 100 years

Sports history
Nottingham and Long Eaton Speedway 1928-1967
The Golden Age of Speedway
Speedway – the Classic Era
Classic Speedway Venues

Contents

Front Cover: top, The restored tandem headstocks at the site of Brinsley Colliery, near Eastwood (*Author*); centre, D H Lawrence as a young man (*Manuscripts and Special Collections, The University of Nottingham*); bottom, Shipley Aqueduct, carrying the Erewash Canal over the River Erewash (*Tina Cordon*).

Back Cover: The truly rural and industrial aspects of the Erewash Valley meet in Sandiacre. The parish church of St Giles stands on a hill overlooking the valley, above farm buildings with an almost medieval appearance (*Author*)

AUTHOR'S NOTE

Just in case any reader should question my qualification to write about the Erewash Valley, I will set out my links to the district at the start.

Although born in Derby, like so many of my fellow baby boomers first seeing the light of day in the Nightingale Maternity Home, I grew up amidst the lace and textile mills, the upholstery workshops and the complex system of railway lines that was Long Eaton.

For ten years I travelled on each school day along the lower part of the valley, through Sandiacre, Stapleford and Trowell to Ilkeston, passing over a River Erewash that, seen through the grimy window of a Barton double deck bus, was obviously unattractive and grossly polluted. What a change for the better has come over the river in the 21st century.

After attempting (with meagre success) to gain a few paper qualifications at what was then Ilkeston College of Further Education (now a supermarket), I persuaded the editor of the *Long Eaton Advertiser* and *Stapleford and Sandiacre News* that I had a nose for a story.

For six very happy years I visited most corners of the Erewash Valley, combing the streets of Long Eaton, Sandiacre and Stapleford for news, attending the weekly magistrates court at Ilkeston Town Hall, and spending Saturday afternoons reporting football matches at Heanor, Eastwood, Alfreton and Sutton in Ashfield.

There was true media competition in the valley in that era, especially in the towns of Stapleford and Sandiacre, which were covered for the now defunct *Ilkeston Pioneer* and the *Nottingham Post* newspapers by the blind journalist George Miller. George, whose list of contacts and local knowledge was formidable, was a familiar figure at meetings with his Braille shorthand machine. He later turned to politics and became chairman of Nottinghamshire County Council.

In the era before the ancient institution of the Assizes was abolished and replaced by the less ceremonious Crown Court, I watched the robed and bewigged judges process from Derby Cathedral to the historic court house in St Mary's Gate to hear a murder trial, in the very place where the leader of the Pentrich Rebellion, Jeremiah Brandreth and his fellow conspirators were sentenced to death.

When I did leave the valley for a while, it was to work as a journalist in South Wales, an area which shared many things in common with industrial Derbyshire and Nottinghamshire, notably coal mines, iron and steel works, foundries, and down-to-earth working people.

Altogether, I have spent two thirds of my life living in the Erewash Valley. During the rest of the time, the area was never far from my mind, with the evocative descriptions of the district in the novels and short stories of D H Lawrence always able to exert a soothing influence or induce nostalgia.

During my research for this book I visited virtually every settlement in the valley big enough to rate a place on an Ordnance Survey sheet. I still find each and every visit to these fascinating and friendly towns and villages a deeply satisfying experience and I have no hesitation in dedicating this volume to the people of the Erewash Valley.

PHILIP DALLING
2017

Acknowledgments

Researching and writing this book has indeed been a labour of love, but would have been a more difficult and less pleasant task without the help provided by so many people I encountered travelling around the valley. My thanks go to the following individuals and organisations for information, illustrations, permission to reproduce photographs, and general advice and guidance. Without them this book would not have been possible.

Linda Shaw, Senior Archivist (Collections), and Jayne Amat (Archives Assistant),
Manuscripts and Special Collections, The University of Nottingham
Margaret and Brian Bailey, Waingroves Methodist Church
John Beckett, Professor of English Regional History,The University of Nottingham
Donald Brookes, Coal Industry Social Welfare Organisation (CISWO).
Chris Brookes, Long Eaton RFC
Nick Tomlinson and Paul Darby of *Picture the Past*
Tim Carter of The Environment Agency
Tina Cordon
Anna Soubry MP and Sean Coley
Kenneth Clarke MP, Gloria de Piero MP, Maggie Throup MP
Colston Crawford
Helen Martinez, Museum Manager and Kate Crossley, Collections Officer, Erewash Museum
Andy Croft of Smokestack Books
Stuart Danvers, Long Eaton
Elspeth Langsdale of Oundle School
Mark Drakeley, Eastwood
Steve Footitt
Tim Fryzer-Smith, Long Eaton
John Grace, Waingroves
Simon Harvey, The University of Nottingham
David Lowe, Stapleford
Michael Lucking, Long Eaton Chamber of Trade
Robert Mee Treasurer/Webmaster, Heanor & District Local History Society
Andrew J Mitchell, Artistic Upholstery
Shaun McLoughlin, Head of Engagement and Collections, National Coal Mining Museum for England
Nicole Morris and Tony Simpson, Spokesman Books
Sheila Mason, Ian Palfreyman, Pete Sewell and Tim Johnson of Cluny Lace, Ilkeston
David Murdoch, East Midlands Trains
Edward Perfect, Stapleford
Debbie,Colin, and Alison Reid and Richard Ward of Springfield, Sandiacre
Bruce Richardson, Leek Books
Bryan Rudkin, Alfreton Town Football Club
Selstonia Living History Archive
Staff at Derby, Ilkeston and Long Eaton Local Studies Libraries
Stuart Saint www.codnor.info
Andy Smart
Rob Smyth Public Relations Officer Central England Co-operative Limited
John Sumpter of JMS Photography
Steve Waddington, Richard Lambert and David Crossland of The Amadeus Press for their expertise and patience
Stan Wilton, Smalley

Special thanks to Keith Thomas of Barbrook, Exmoor, for creating the map at the start of the colour section.

Last, but certainly not least, to Brenda Dyer, for wise advice, inspired suggestions, infinite patience and most welcome companionship on my travels in the Erewash Valley.

An A-Z of the Erewash Valley

The exact boundaries of the Erewash Valley, from the river's source just to the south west of Kirkby-in-Ashfield, to the point where the stream joins the River Trent at Attenborough, will perhaps always be a matter of some dispute. Starting at the source and travelling south, several factors have been taken into consideration when attempting to define what is and is not a part of the valley. For the purposes of this book, the towns, villages and hamlets along the Derbyshire/Nottinghamshire border that lie along the banks of the river, or stand on the slopes and ridges above, have been deemed to qualify.
Some 70 individual communities have been visited during the course of research for the book. In every instance the listed communities are mentioned later in the text of this book or are the subject of photographs.

A

Aldercar, Derbyshire. Described in his autobiography by former government minister Kenneth Clarke, who lived there as a child, as the rural end of Langley Mill. The name reflects the alder trees which are common along the Erewash

Alfreton, Derbyshire.

Abraham Lincoln Memorial Library, Alfreton

The main road through the town is lined with the benefactions , including a church, housing and a park, of Robert Watchorn. He was a local boy who started work down the pit at the age of 11, continuing his studies at night. He later emigrated to the United States, where he made good, made a fortune, and never forgot his home town.

Attenborough, Nottinghamshire. An attractive village close to the River Trent, with extensive gravel pits now forming a nature reserve. St Mary's churchyard contains mass graves of victims of the 1918 fatal explosion at the nearby Chilwell shell filling factory.
Awsworth, Nottinghamshire. A village closely linked to two major railway viaducts. Awsworth had a station on the Great Northern Nottingham-Derby line which crossed the Erewash Valley to Ilkeston over the still extant Bennerley Viaduct. Nearby, at Awsworth Junction , a branch line to Pinxton crossed a now demolished viaduct almost half a mile long across the Giltbrook valley, known locally as 'Forty Bridges'.

B

Bagthorpe, Nottinghamshire. The village is believed to have originally been settled by Danish invaders. Bagthorpe and Lower Bagthorpe together form the only conservation area in Selston parish.
Beauvale, Nottinghamshire. The Roman Catholic Diocese of Nottingham annually organises a pilgrimage to the ruins of the Carthusian Priory at Beauvale, suppressed by King Henry VIII. Two Priors, John Houghton and Robert Lawrence were executed in 1535 for refusing to acknowledge Henry as Head of the Church of England. Visitors can enjoy the high quality facilities of The Gatehouse tea rooms on the site.
Blackwell, Derbyshire. A former pit village where the old Miners' Welfare sports ground at Primrose Hill saw the establishment of a cricket world record in 1910, when John Chapman and Arnold Warren of Derbyshire scored 283 runs in three hours against Warwickshire. The ground is little changed to the present day.
Bramcote, Nottinghamshire. Essentially now a part of Greater Nottingham suburbia, but still with much of the feel of a village. A former country house estate on the north side of the village, is now Bramcote Hills Park, from which access can be gained to the Hemlock Stone, an outcrop of New Red Sandstone on Stapleford Hill, deposited more than 200 million years ago in the Triassic Period.
Breaston, Derbyshire. A large village, separated from Long Eaton by the M1 Motorway. One of its public houses, The Navigation Inn, stands by the abandoned Derby Canal, which enthusiasts hope to renovate.

Brinsley, Nottinghamshire.

Brinsley miners being paid.

A village on the River Erewash and the now abandoned Nottingham Canal. The tandem headstocks from the colliery, where D H Lawrence's father Arthur worked, have been preserved and now stand in a country park setting, with good quality information boards available to interpret the area, the mining industry, and the Lawrence connections.

Butterley, Derbyshire. At the foot of Butterley Hill stands the abandoned site of Butterley Engineering Ltd, a successor to the original Butterley Company. Among the last jobs to be fabricated on site were the Falkirk Wheel canal lift in Scotland and Portsmouth's Spinnaker Tower. The surviving gatehouse defied the Pentrich revolutionaries when they laid siege to the works in 1817. The station at the nearby Midland Railway Centre preservation site has an excellent example of that company's architecture.

C

Codnor, Derbyshire. Codnor Castle is a ruined 13th-century fortification, established after the Norman Conquest by William Peverell. The castle comprised a stone keep and bailey fortress, overlooking the Erewash valley. It is today a fragile ruin, privately owned, but with public access managed by The Codnor Castle Heritage Trust.

Cossall, Nottinghamshire.

Cossall Church

Attractive hillside village which attracts many visitors to view the memorial in the churchyard to three local men who fought at the Battle of Waterloo and the dwelling that forms the original of the honeymoon cottage in D H Lawrence's novel *The Rainbow*.

Cotmanhay, Derbyshire. One of many examples of a former village which has become in many ways indistinguishable from the nearest major town, in this case Ilkeston. Nevertheless, Cotmanhay retains a strong local identity. It was for a brief period in the mid to late 19th century a mining centre, and later had a textile industry.

Crosshill, Derbyshire. Crosshill and Codnor railway station was opened in 1890 by the Midland Railway on its branch between Langley Mill on the Erewash Valley mainline and Ripley. Passenger services were considered incidental to coal traffic. Services were suspended during World War One but revived temporarily in 1920, finally being withdrawn in the General Strike year of 1926.

D

Dale Abbey, Derbyshire. Noted for the remains of its ruined abbey and its combined parish church and dwelling house under one roof. Despite its rural setting, Dale had a colliery, a drift mine, owned by the Stanton Iron Works company and linked to Stanton works by a tramway. The pit was known locally as the 'Treacle Mine' due to the tar-like coal it produced. The mine closed in 1921.

Denby, Derbyshire. A former mining village on the western fringe of the Erewash Valley, today world famous for the quality kitchenware and other items manufactured at Denby Pottery, established in 1809.

E

Eastwood, Nottinghamshire.

Former miners' housing in Eastwood in 2017

The birthplace and home until the age of 23 of novelist, poet and artist David Herbert Lawrence. Although Lawrence was largely scorned or ignored by the town for many years, the excellent birthplace museum and the innovative Blue Trail, linking sites related to the writer and his family, today amply repays a visit.

F

Felley Mill, Nottinghamshire. Felley Mill Farm, now largely demolished, and surviving pond with evidence of the former mill race, formed the principal setting for D H Lawrence's novel *The White Peacock*, in which it was named Strelley Mill.

Felley Priory, Nottinghamshire. A former Augustinian Priory, located in the village of Felley, established in 1156 and dissolved in 1536. A private domestic house was then built upon the former monastic site.

G

Giltbrook, Nottinghamshire. The village of Giltbrook is close to junction 26 of the M1 motorway. The name is believed to stem from the old English Gylden Broc, meaning golden stream, or brook. The Gilt Brook is a tributary of the River Erewash. Today the village is the site of a retail park, which has developed around an IKEA store . Giltbrook saw the end of the Pentrich rising in 1817, when soldiers at this point broke up the march on Nottingham.

Golden Valley, Derbyshire. The site of some of the earliest houses built for its workers by The Butterley Company, which still exist today. Situated between Codnor and Riddings, and near Ironville and Codnor Park, Golden Valley was traversed by the now derelict Cromford Canal,and was the site of the eastern portal of Butterley Tunnel, from which the canal emerges into Codnor Park Reservoir. The Pinxton arm of the canal, also derelict, starts at Golden Valley.

Greasley, Nottinghamshire. One of Lawrence's favourite spots in the rural area near Eastwood that Lawrence dubbed 'The Country of My Heart'. Extensive views from the churchyard across to the hills of the Derbyshire Peak District.

H

Heanor, Derbyshire. Former coal mining and hosiery centre with a hilltop market place that in the twilight of an autumn evening can still evoke the atmosphere of previous times in the Erewash Valley. Heanor was the home of World War One Victoria Cross winner Sergeant William Gregg. In 1970, in honour of his gallantry the town's new swimming pool was named the William Gregg VC Swimming Baths, now the William Gregg VC Leisure Centre.

I

Ilkeston, Derbyshire. Traditionally the largest town in the Erewash Valley, with one of the steepest shopping thoroughfares in Great Britain – Bath Street – and noted for its annual Charter Fair in October, one of the largest street fairs in Europe.

Ironville, Derbyshire. A classic example of a 'company town', with housing, schools, a church and other facilities built for its workers by The Butterley Company. The abandoned course of the Pinxton Arm of the Cromford Canal skirts the settlement.

J

Jacksdale, Nottinghamshire.

Jacksdale Miners Welfare in 2017

A classic mining settlement , complete with surviving miners' welfare institute, bordered to the west by the River Erewash, a section of the Cromford Canal and nature reserves.

Jubilee, Nottinghamshire. Part of Selston parish, the hamlet of Jubilee is believed to have been established in 1897, at the time of Queen Victoria's Diamond Jubilee.

K

Kimberley, Nottinghamshire. Famous for its twin breweries, Hardys and Hansons, which later merged. The company was taken over in 2006 by Greene King. The surviving brewery was closed but Greene King still brew ales to the Hardy and Hansons recipe at their traditional site in Bury St Edmunds.

Kirk Hallam, Derbyshire. Once a small agricultural parish, Kirk Hallam's population expanded dramatically in the 1950s and 1960s when large housing estates were developed by Ilkeston Borough Council and the major local employer, Stanton and Staveley Ltd.

Kirkby-in-Ashfield, Nottinghamshire. Cricketing giants stalk the streets of this former mining town. In a series of stunning statues in the town centre, local men and former miners Harold Larwood and Bill Voce face Australian legend Donald Bradman in a replay of the controversial 1932-33 Australia v England 'Bodyline' Ashes series.

L

Langley Mill, Derbyshire. Langley Mill is right on the border with Nottinghamshire. For many years it was a major industrial centre, producing sectional buildings, pottery, hosiery, and engineering products. The restored Great Northern Basin is at the junction of the Erewash, Cromford and Nottingham Canals, whilst Langley Mill railway station, closed in 1967, was re-opened in 1986. International Superbike champion Ron Haslam, who won many titles in the 1970s and early 1980s, comes from Langley Mill.

Leabrooks, Derbyshire. A small urban community linked to the village of Somercotes . It is named after a stream, the Lee Brook.

Long Eaton, Derbyshire.

Erewash Georgian: The Hall, Long Eaton

Once noted for the manufacture of the highest quality decorative lace, it is now world renowned for the excellence of the furniture and upholstery produced in the town.

Loscoe, Derbyshire. The economy here was dominated by coal mining for almost a century and a half. Three mines operated in the village – Old Loscoe (early 1830s – 1933), Bailey Brook (1847–1938) and Ormonde, the last pit in the Heanor area, opened in 1908 and closed in 1970. A landfill gas explosion in 1986 led to the introduction in Britain of legislation and government guidance into the operation of landfill sites.

M

Mapperley, Derbyshire. Mapperley, although just two miles from Ilkeston, is situated for local government purposes in Amber Valley and is an access point to Shipley Country Park. Mapperley Colliery, which was in operation from 1871 until 1965, was formerly a major employer. After this time extensive open cast coal mining took place in the area.

Marehay, Derbyshire. This small community near Ripley has a Community Trust, founded in 2008, which organises a popular annual show and is working with other agencies to redevelop the local recreation ground.

Marlpool, Derbyshire. Part of Heanor, but with a strong individual identity, Marlpool was home to many of the miners who worked at the nearby Shipley Coppice and Shipley Woodside collieries.

Moorgreen, Nottinghamshire. Once the home of a colliery described by D H Lawrence as 'Minton, a large mine set among cornfields', Moorgreen is now noted for the excellence of the Colliers Wood Country Park created on the site of the demolished pit

N

New Brinsley, Nottinghamshire. Unlike the neighbouring village of Brinsley, which is in Broxtowe district, New Brinsley is in Ashfield. New Brinsley was developed during the 19th century expansion of the coal industry.

Newthorpe, Nottinghamshire. A village closely linked to Eastwood, which previously had a railway station on the former Great Northern Railway branch from Nottingham to Pinxton. John Bamford from Newthorpe became in 1952 the youngest person, at the age of 15, to be directly awarded the George Cross for bravery. He was badly burned rescuing two younger brothers from a fire at their home.
Nuthall, Nottinghamshire. A village divided into two areas, Old Nuthall and New Nuthall, the latter area consisting mostly of 1960s and 1970s housing. Nuthall Temple (now demolished) was built in 1757 in the Palladian style and was the home of the Holden family. The parish church at Nuthall is dedicated to St Patrick.

P

Pentrich, Derbyshire. The Derbyshire village of Pentrich, situated close to Ripley and Alfreton, is celebrated far beyond the borders of the Erewash Valley as having given its name to the rebellion of 1817. Much of the planning for the ill-fated rising undoubtedly took place in the village, but the action occurred elsewhere.

Pinxton, Derbyshire.

Pinxton Parish Church

The terminus of a branch arm of the Cromford Canal and the starting point for the first passenger-carrying railway in the Erewash Valley.

Pye Bridge, Derbyshire. Historically this tiny settlement on the River Erewash has been a major communications hub, traversed by the original east-west road from Nottingham to the crossroads of Newhaven in the Derbyshire Peak District, the Cromford Canal and the Midland Railway's Erewash Valley mainline. Pye Bridge was also a centre for iron production and coal mining.

R

Riddings, Derbyshire. Site of an extensive foundry owned by the Stanton Ironworks Company.
Ripley, Derbyshire.

Roman Catholic Church, Ripley

Another hilltop town, with a market place dominated by a Town Hall built in the style of a French chateau. Noted too for its autumn Charter Fair, held on the market square. Pop legend Cliff Richard made his professional debut at a local dance hall in 1958.

Risley, Derbyshire. The home of the Hooley family, consisting of a lace magnate, his son who became an international financier and friend of King Edward VII, and the three children of the magnate's second marriage. A daughter became a well known poet, writer and left-wing firebrand, and a son became a Great War hero, only to die tragically just weeks before the conflict came to an end.

S

Sandiacre, Derbyshire. A typical Erewash Valley blend of the industrial and rural, with a massive former lace mill mirrored in the waters of the canal and, above the valley, one of the finest churches in the area, forming an almost medieval tableau when seen towering above the buildings of an adjacent farm.

Sawley, Derbyshire.

Sawley Baptist Chapel and parish church spire

A Trentside village, which for centuries was more important than neighbouring Long Eaton, until the latter expanded rapidly through industrialisation and became dominant. The village was the birthplace of Baptist leader and radical politician John Clifford. His birthplace, near the Baptist chapel, is marked with a plaque.

Selston, Nottinghamshire. The western boundary of the sizeable Selston parish, one of the largest in the country with an area of more than 3,000 acres and a population of around 12,500, follows the River Erewash, and is bounded on the east by the M1 Motorway. It was a major centre of both coal mining and textiles. In the 1960s textile firms employed more than half the female population.

Shipley, Derbyshire. Shipley derives from the Old English scëap (sheep) and lëah (open ground), meaning sheep-clearing or sheep-pasture. The present-day Shipley Park was extensively open-casted for coal after deep mining ceased but has now been transformed into a publicly-owned country park. The Park includes a large reservoir which fed the Nutbrook Canal.

Smalley, Derbyshire. A roadside village on the main A608 from Heanor to Derby, Smalley's parish church of St John the Baptist's bell tower was built to house a chime of five bells, said to be the heaviest in England with the largest bell weighing over 2 tons. Fittingly the village pub, a previous winner of Derbyshire's Best Pub competition, is named The Bell.

Somercotes, Derbyshire. A former mining village once surrounded by pits, but now noted as a growing centre for industrial estates, a retail park and modern housing developments. Somercotes has provided Derbyshire with several notable cricketers, including the England batsman Denis Smith. The combination of George Beet and Fred Root in the early 1920s provided Derbyshire with instances of 'caught Beet, bowled Root!

South Normanton, Derbyshire. On the north-eastern boundary of the valley, South Normanton was just a small farming hamlet until the 20th century development of coal mining. The East Midlands Designer Outlet, owned by the McArthur Glen Group, is situated on the edge of the settlement, near the M1 Motorway.

Stanley, Derbyshire. Once the home of a colliery nicknamed by the men as 'Nibby' or Nib'lem Pit', an ironic reference to the bad reputation the owners had for reducing or 'nibbling away' at the miners' wages. On the road leading to the neighbouring village of West Hallam, at the point where the pit and the railway station shared by the two villages once stood, are the one-time pithead baths, now in industrial use.

Stanley Common, Derbyshire. A village on the A609 main road between Ilkeston and Derby, part of the same civil parish as Stanley, a mile or so to the south. It incorporates Smalley Common, once part of the neighbouring village of Smalley. The majority of residents worked at pits such as Shipley Woodside, the 'Nibby Pit', at Stanley, and Mapperley Pit.

Stanton by Dale, Derbyshire. One of the most attractive villages in the Erewash Valley which, thanks largely to a screen of trees, kept its identity despite for decades being located above the Iron Dale of Stanton and a major ironworks.

Stapleford, Nottinghamshire. The 'twin town' of Sandiacre across the border in Derbyshire, the two industrial centres shared a railway station until 1967, situated at the northern end of Toton marshalling yard. Stapleford appears in Domesday with, unusually, the same spelling as today. It was an important centre of the stocking trade. Arthur Mee, editor of the *Kings England* series of guides to the English counties, was born here.

Strelley, Nottinghamshire. The village of Strelley is on the eastern borders of the Erewash Valley geographical area. Coal mining was a significant industry in Strelley as early as the 16th century and the village was the upper terminus of the earliest railway lines, on which horse-drawn wagons carried coal to Wollaton.

Swanwick, Derbyshire. The Hayes has been a leading Christian conference centre since 1911. Poet Laureate John Betjeman and C S Lewis, Christian apologist and author of the *Narnia* books, attended a Student Christian Movement event there in July 1939. Built in the 1860s, The Hayes was the home of Fitzherbert Wright, maternal great, great grandfather of the Duchess of York.

T

Toton, Nottinghamshire. Formerly an agricultural village on the eastern bank of the Erewash, Toton is a name forever associated with the railway system. It is close to the now semi-derelict Toton Marshalling Yard, which has been chosen as the site for the HS2 High Speed Train's East Midlands station. The parish is the terminus of Line Two of the Nottingham Express Transit tramway system, which it is intended will eventually be extended to serve the transport hub that the HS2 station will provide.

Trent Lock, Derbyshire.

Narrow boats on the Erewash Canal

The spot where the Erewash Canal, flowing down from Langley Mill, enters the River Trent. Trent Lock is a major meeting of waterways, where the Cranfleet Cut, built to avoid a weir on the Trent, and the River Soar, also diverge. A paradise for boaters and a magnet for pleasure seekers, with pubs, a tea room, boating and yachting facilities.

Trowell, Nottinghamshire. A village mostly of ribbon development along the roads from Ilkeston to Nottingham and Stapleford, once famous, indeed notorious, for being chosen as Britain's Festival Village, at the time of the Festival of Britain in 1951. The Festival Inn commemorates the event.

U

Underwood, Nottinghamshire. A hilltop village in a former coal mining area in the Hidden Valleys section of Nottinghamshire, with extensive views across the Erewash Valley towards the Southern Pennines. Underwood Miners Welfare has survived the demise of the coal industry. The Welfare Cricket Club, founded in 1894, has a ground on Church Lane .

W

Waingroves, Derbyshire

A modern-day Methodist Church, at Waingroves

A former pit village close to Ripley, where the unemployed miner Walter Brierley wrote his best-known novel *Means Test Man* in the 1930s. The village shares with Swanwick the distinction of being the only two villages in the Erewash Valley to carry on the Peak District tradition of well dressing.

Watnall, Nottinghamshire. Watnall is part of Greasley civil parish, and is located one mile north of Kimberley. It is home to many businesses, including a large bakery. The Royal Air Force's fighter command for the Midlands was situated in bunkers in the village during World War Two.

West Hallam, Derbyshire. The village existed at the time of Domesday in 1086 and until the early 20th century was largely agricultural. In the 16th and 17th centuries the village was known for the Roman Catholic adherence of its leading families, at a time of persecution. It became a mining centre, but after the rundown of the industry extensive housing development transformed West Hallam into a commuter village.

Westhouses, Derbyshire. The valley's other great railway centre, after Toton. Westhouses had a locomotive depot in the Toton group and a vestige survived in the form of a traincrew depot until 1987. The Midland Railway and later the London Midland and Scottish Railway (LMS) was the main employer , and the company originally built and maintained the school. The very last Westhouses man in railway service worked at Toton Depot.

Westwood, Nottinghamshire. Part of the civil parish of Selston, Westwood, like so many Erewash Valley villages, expanded dramatically in the 19th century, with its population rising from 120 in 1837 to 1,700 60 years later. The village now links with neighbouring Jacksdale, sharing many amenities and community activities.

Chapter One

Defining the Valley

'D H Lawrence was born at Eastwood, a Nottinghamshire mining village on the hills above the Erewash Valley. There the natural beauty, the remaining fragments of Sherwood Forest, comes up against the industrial ugliness, those collieries that thrust their headstocks and their smoke above the farm fields' – Harry T Moore in The Intelligent Heart, The Story of D H Lawrence, 1954.

How to define the Erewash Valley?

It is at one and the same time a literary landscape, a vital artery of communication, a beacon of hope for environmentalists, and a classic example of how swiftly the face of Britain has changed in the post-industrial age.

Its rich heritage as an early cradle of the Industrial Revolution and its later status as an industrial powerhouse of the first rank, its coal mines, blast furnaces and towering lace and hosiery mills tied together by a complex network of canals and railway lines, forms the backcloth to the finest novels and short stories of David Herbert Lawrence, one of England's greatest writers.

Lawrence, although often deploring the grime of the valley's industrial towns and what he saw as the plodding and unimaginative lives of the miners, furnace men, twisthands and their families, yet was able to capture the strange but undeniable romance of heavy industry, with a skill matched only in Arnold Bennett's chronicles of the Five Towns of the Potteries, fifty miles to the west of the Erewash.

The author's prose lifted onto a higher plane of perception even something as mundane as a grouping of collieries on the edge of his home town of Eastwood. *"New mines were sunk, so that soon there were six pits working; six mines like black studs on the countryside, linked by a loop of fine chain, the railway."*

No less memorable is Lawrence's account, in the short story *Fanny and Annie*, of the smart and worldly-wise lady's maid returning by train from a metropolitan life to marry her fiancé, patient but lacking in ambition and content to live his life in what she sees as a small and stifling coal and iron community. On arrival at her home town, looking out through the open door of her train for the man, she sees *'the pulse and darkness of red fire from the furnace towers in the sky, lighting the desultory industrial crowd on the wayside station."*

Lawrence showed equal skill in depicting the softer side of a valley which, even at the height of its industrial heyday, and outside the heavily concentrated clusters of mines, furnaces and mills, was still predominantly rural.

The Past and The Present One: Horses graze on reclaimed land by the River Erewash, transformed from the polluted waterway of the past, in the shadow of the abandoned Bennerley Viaduct, a relic of the valley's industrial past (*Author*).

The Past and The Present Two: Former pit tips, a reminder of Eastwood's old reliance on coal mining, are today transformed into a sheep pasture, whilst in its shadow, 21st century residents, no longer reliant on the trams and trains of D H Lawrence's day, fill their cars with fuel at a giant supermarket that dwarfs the old market place (*Author*).

The sometimes curious juxtaposition of heavy industry and agriculture, not always so apparent in other coal and iron regions of Britain, was recognised early on in his life by politician Kenneth Clarke, who grew up in the valley in the 1940s, in Aldercar and Langley Mill, on the Derbyshire side of the Erewash.

In his autobiography, *Kind of Blue*, Clarke looks back to the landscape of his childhood and describes the contrast between the dirt, dust and noise of the collieries and the calm of the farmland which surrounded the pits as 'strangely bucolic'.

Clarke, born in 1940, was educated at the infant school at Aldercar and the all-age Langley Boys School before moving on to Nottingham High School and eventually to Gonville and Caius College, Cambridge. He is a barrister-at-law, becoming Queen's Counsel in 1980. He first became active in politics at Cambridge, where he was President of the Union, and Chairman of the University Conservative Association.

Clarke came from a genuinely working class background. His grandfather was a Communist-supporting toolmaker and his father, also Kenneth, was a colliery electrician for a time, working at Moorgreen Colliery near Eastwood, before buying a watchmaker and jeweller's business in the Nottingham suburb of Bulwell.

D H Lawrence, to Kenneth Clarke, was someone who had 'lived on the next hill'. The politician's family, like so many local people, had their own particular view of the author, which will become apparent in Chapter Three of this book, *The Valley as a Literary Landscape*.

The area to the north and west of his home town of Eastwood was especially dear to Lawrence. He described it as '*The Country of my Heart*', and returned to it in his imagination and in his prose no matter where in the world he was living, during his restless and nomadic later life.

That the Erewash Valley was a distinct geographical entity was acknowledged by Lawrence in both his published work and in his letters to, and conversations with, friends and collaborators.

The collapse of the coal mining and iron and forging industries, and the decline of textile manufacturing, notably the once mighty lace trade, might have rendered the valley faceless, reduced to a bland series of anonymous industrial estates, retail parks, and dormitory estates for commuters to the nearby cities of Nottingham and Derby.

It is somehow fitting and poetic that the very identity of a district that initially won fame for its polluting industries, and at the same time attracted bitter criticism from Lawrence for its ugliness, should now be based upon the sterling efforts made in recent years to restore the landscape and restore it wherever possible to the pastoral beauty it enjoyed before large-scale and largely unregulated industrialisation.

The valley, from its source near Kirkby-in-Ashfield in Nottinghamshire, in the heart of the former coalfield, to the point some 30 miles later where it meets the River Trent near Attenborough, effectively in the outer suburbs of the City of Nottingham, has benefitted enormously from the efforts of both local authorities and the Derbyshire and Nottinghamshire Wildlife Trusts to develop its surviving natural assets.

Industrial Prosperity One: The riches of the valley awaiting delivery to the markets of the midlands and the south. Coal traffic at Toton Sidings in Midland Railway days (pre-1923), with the locomotive depot to the right of the picture. In the distance are the towering chimneys of tenement lace mills in Long Eaton (*Derbyshire Local Studies Libraries and www.picturethepast.org.uk*).

It is ironic, too, that the canals, the transport arteries that made it practicable and commercially viable to exploit the valley's mineral wealth at the end of the 18th century, now form a major component of 'green Erewash'.

Whether operating or abandoned, the man-made waterways provide green and easy-to-follow trails either north-south, as in the case of the Erewash and Nottingham Canals, or roughly east-west, in the case of parts of the mainline of the Cromford Canal and in particular the now wholly disused Pinxton Arm.

The River Erewash rises in a now-decayed setting formerly occupied by industry and railway sidings, south of the former pit town of Kirkby-in-Ashfield. Its early life as a river is utterly undistinguished, being culverted for a distance before surfacing definitively near Kirkby Woodhouse and flowing west towards the neighbouring county of Derbyshire.

Between Pinxton (Derbyshire) and Selston (Nottinghamshire) the two former mining settlements which form the first townships of the Erewash Valley proper, the river becomes the county boundary between Nottinghamshire and Derbyshire – a role it plays for much of its journey to the Trent.

As the river begins to curve south, it is bounded to the north and west by a series of Derbyshire towns and villages once dominated by coal and iron - Alfreton, Somercotes, Riddings and the Victorian town of Ironville, built for its employees by the once powerful but now sadly extinct engineering giant, The Butterley Company.

High above the Erewash, in the foothills of the Peak District and on the ridge that separates the hinterland of the border

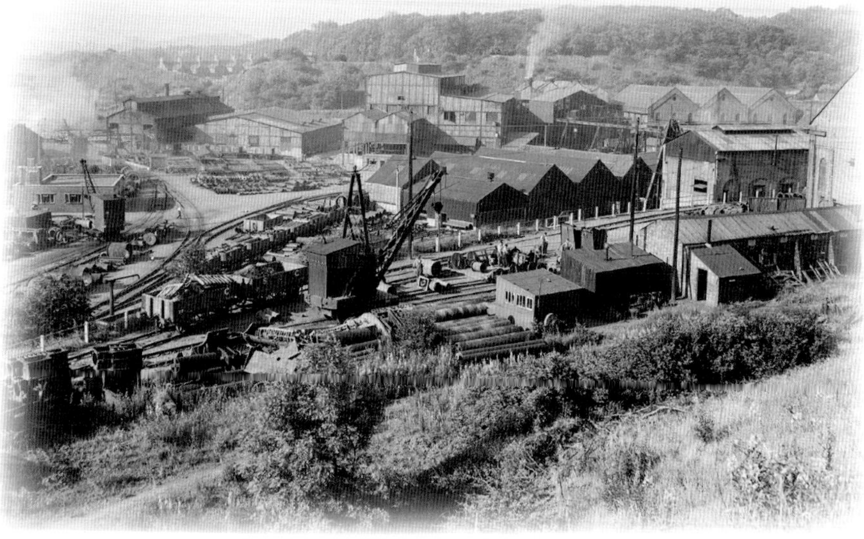

Industrial Prosperity Two: Riddings Foundry, owned by the Stanton Ironworks Co Ltd, in full production in the 1920s. (*Derby Museum and www.picturethepast.org.uk*).

Industrial Decline One: Moorgreen Colliery awaits demolition after closure in the 1980s. D H Lawrence described Moorgreen (or Minton, as he re-named it) as 'a large mine among cornfields'. The photograph, with a ploughed field in the foreground illustrates how mining and agriculture existed side by side in the Erewash Valley (*Derbyshire Local Studies Libraries and www.picturethepast.org.uk*).

river and valley from its westerly neighbour, the Derwent, positioned at a height of 1,000 feet, is Crich Stand, the lofty tower that forms one of the strongest links binding together the sometimes disparate counties of Derbyshire and Nottinghamshire.

For the people living on the Nottinghamshire bank of the Erewash, the high country on the western horizon was an ever-present part of their daily life. One of D H Lawrence's favourite views, described in the autobiographical novel *Sons and Lovers*, was from the family's second home in Walker Street, Eastwood, across the gently sloping farmland of the valley sides, '*to Crich and the hills of Derbyshire'*.

Walker Street is today undergoing considerable change, with the demolition of older buildings and the redevelopment of industrial sites. But by standing in the spot Lawrence loved, in the street where the most formative years of his Eastwood upbringing were spent, you can still quite clearly see Crich.

The Crich tower itself is the permanent memorial to the men of the historic Notts and Derbys regiment of the British Army, the Sherwood Foresters, that recruited mainly from the two counties. At night the beam of its powerful searchlight sweeps across both Erewash and Derwent valleys, and is visible for a radius of 40 miles.

One of the best-known chroniclers of the Derbyshire countryside, Roger Redfern, writing in his 1970 book *Peakland*

Industrial Decline Two: With the demise of mining and ironmaking in the valley, the vast railway marshalling yard at Toton is semi-derelict, largely used to store redundant locomotives and rolling stock. The diesel maintenance depot on the site is still active. The proposed station at Toton for the HS2 High Speed Train project would rejuvenate at least part of the yard (*Author*).

Black scars on a once pastoral landscape. New Selston Colliery in 1946. (*Courtesy of Selstonia Living History Archive*).

Days, acknowledged that from the commanding height of Crich, virtually the very end of the Pennine Chain, the views towards the west and the Derwent Valley were overshadowed.

He wrote: *"The eye is drawn particularly towards the north-east and the wooded lands about Hardwick Hall. Roving the eye southwards are the little ridges cluttered about the Erewash, in the vicinity of Riddings, Codnor, Westwood and Eastwood".*

Redfern implicitly recognised that the defining characteristics of the upper and central Erewash Valley were the hilltop market towns, standing slightly above the strange blend of grimy industry and pastoral landscape that characterised the valley's slopes and the narrow level ground on both banks of the river.

Lower down, where the valley (although not the river itself) widens substantially, the coalfield came to an end and the landscape, previously with a distinctly northern feel, softened as it met the Trent Valley and the Midland Plain.

A tower of some kind has stood at Crich since the middle of the 18th century, when a wooden structure was built to provide a landmark and a viewpoint for the panoramic views of the surrounding countryside. Beacons were traditionally lit at the site and in June 1856 crowds gathered to mark the end of the Crimean War.

When after World War One the search began for a suitable site for a lasting memorial to the Sherwood Foresters, it was suggested that Crich, visible from large tracts of both Nottinghamshire and Derbyshire, was the ideal location.

A new 64ft stone tower, with a dome weighing forty tons, was erected, using the stone from a demolished predecessor, which had been carefully stored. The new memorial was opened on August 6 1923, by the Colonel of the Regiment, General Sir Horace Smith-Dorrien.

During the general retreat of the British Expeditionary Force in France in August 1914, Smith-Dorrien gained everlasting fame (and some censure from his senior officer) by turning to meet the enemy. Smith-Dorrien's famous message to his Sherwood Foresters, 'Gentlemen, we will stand and fight', is commemorated at Crich.

As it flows south, the Erewash continues to skirt the industrial villages which look down on the river from both banks. Waingroves, Somercotes, Swanwick, Codnor, Loscoe, Aldercar and Langley Mill are in Derbyshire. Jacksdale, Westwood, Underwood and Brinsley are on the Nottinghamshire side of the river.

The larger centres of population are the distinctive hill towns, of Alfreton, Ripley, Heanor and Ilkeston on the western, Derbyshire bank, and Eastwood on the Nottinghamshire side to the east. All five centres are traditionally grouped

Transformation One. The Colliers Wood Country Park now occupies part of the site of Moorgreen Colliery and is a magnet for family groups. Another part of the former colliery is now an industrial estate, with the buildings visible in the background (*Author*).

around their market places and parish churches, and the general plan of the Derbyshire towns is unchanged, with more modern development taking place on the fringes of the urban area.

Lawrence's birthplace, Eastwood, is the most altered in character, with a modern road system, primarily built to serve a large superstore and its attendant car parking areas, completely dominating the centre and obliterating the little market place lovingly described in *Sons and Lovers*.

For many years (for reasons related in more detail in Chapter Three, *The Valley as a Literary Landscape* Eastwood was decidedly lukewarm about Lawrence. Today the situation is substantially different. The town now boasts a Birthplace Museum, an excellent Lawrence collection at the public library and a well-defined trail linking sites of interest to fans of the author.

If the local authorities and other public bodies now do their best, given limited resources, to celebrate the Lawrence connection, commercial businesses have equally realised the benefits of making the most of the steady flow of literary pilgrims.

The market at Heanor, like those in many other small towns, is now regarded as being a mere shadow of its former self. Yet the hilltop market place, occupying a rare piece of level ground can, on a gloomy autumnal or winter afternoon with the dusk settling in, retain something of the feel of the atmosphere generated by Lawrence in his descriptions of the shopping habits of the wives of the colliers.

It is not difficult to visualise the women, especially during the times of strike or short time, when household budgets were even tighter than usual, bantering and haggling with the traders in the flickering glare of the napha flares illuminating the stalls, making the limited contents of their purses stretch as far as possible.

The feeling survives here in a way that the re-ordering of Eastwood town centre, although obviously more practical, has effectively destroyed.

South of Heanor is the former Shipley estate of the Miller-

Transformation Two: A heron in the rushes around the lake at Colliers Wood (*Author*).

The Old Order Disappears One. Shipley Hall, the home of the coal-owning Miller-Mundy family, The building, ironically, was demolished after being affected by mining subsidence (*Heanor & District Local History Society*).

Mundy family, originally a manor mentioned in Domesday and later a heavily-afforested hunting ground, with a lodge at its centre on Shipley Hill.

Coal mining came early to Shipley and was pursued on the estate for three centuries. Ironically, the industry that enriched the Miller-Mundy family and helped pay for Shipley Hall, the mansion which replaced the hunting lodge, was also the cause of its eventual downfall.

During the heyday of the hall, the family entertained King Edward VII at a house party. But the noise and pollution of the nearby collieries, and the damage to the structure wreaked by subsidence, first led the family to seek more agreeable locations and, eventually, to the demolition of the hall.

Today the Shipley estate is a country park, opened in 1976. It took ten years after the final demise of the Woodside and Coppice collieries on the estate in the mid-1960s for the spoil heaps that littered the area to be contoured, the polluted lakes to be cleansed and the abandoned shafts sealed, with trees planted and fields and meadows seeded, before Derbyshire County Council was able to open the land to the public.

The local authority had the valuable idea of marking out the foundations of the hall, to at least give the many visitors to Shipley Hill an idea of its dimensions.

On the eastern fringe of the Shipley estate, close to the site of the former Woodside pit, the authority agreed to the creation of a theme park. The first attempt to establish a rival to Alton Towers failed, although the second, in the shape of The American Adventure, completed with Wild West Town and a polystyrene Boot Hill, initially thrived but closed in 2007 after interest had declined.

Across the river in Nottinghamshire, south of Eastwood, are the villages of Newthorpe, Greasley, Nuthall, Giltbrook and Awsworth, and the former brewery town of Kimberley. The old hilltop village of Cossall, which maintained its attractiveness throughout the 96-year life of its colliery, from sinking in 1870 to closure in 1966, provides the backcloth for the Erewash Valley novels *The Rainbow* and *Women in Love*.

The fields between the Erewash Valley Railway line and the former Nottingham Canal formed the site of the Marsh Farm, home of the Brangwen family, the predominant characters in *The Rainbow.* Lawrence used the etymology of the name Erewash (the meandering stream) to introduce the family to the reader, describing how the Brangwens had *'lived for generations on the Marsh Farm, in the meadows where the Erewash twisted sluggishly through alder trees, separating Derbyshire from Nottinghamshire'.*

Today, although the Marsh Farm itself disappeared long ago, there is plenty of interest for the Lawrence enthusiast who can spare an hour or so in the area. Up the hill from the Marsh is Cossall Village itself. Here the most evocative sense of stepping out of the real world into the atmosphere of *The Rainbow* is sparked by the road that leads up to the village proper, passing the old Vicarage.

It is the path trodden by Tom Brangwen of the Marsh Farm, leading his horse with a cartful of seed from Nottingham downhill from the village, past the vicarage and meeting, on their way back home, the vicar's Polish housekeeper, who Tom was later to marry, and her daughter Anna, the heroine of *The Rainbow* and the mother of the heroines of the sequel, *Women in Love*.

It is still possible to imagine, as described in *The Rainbow*, the shock to the system of a long-established farming family whose small, isolated rural world was suddenly invaded by canals, railways and a colliery. The canal aqueduct survives, helping to pinpoint the location of the Marsh Farm.

The town of Ilkeston, with its church tower on the hilltop as freely visible today on the broad skyline as it was when it was the sight that met the eye when the Brangwens lifted their heads from their work, provided a ready market for the family's produce, turning them almost from farmers into tradesmen.

Cossall village, one of the most attractive in the entire Erewash Valley, still has its almshouses, its church, with a memorial to local heroes of the Battle of Waterloo (see Chapter Eight *A Valley at War)* and the house which acted as the model for the honeymoon cottage where Anna Brangwen and her new husband walked after the wedding celebrations at The Marsh depicted in *The Rainbow.*

An attempt at providing a leisure facility on the site of Cossall colliery, this time in the form of an illuminated ski slope, was short-lived.

Ilkeston, the largest town in the Erewash Valley and the third largest in Derbyshire, behind Derby and Chesterfield, also features prominently in *The Rainbow*.

Urban Continuity: Ripley Market Place, pictured here in 1903, still stages a weekly market, serving a wide area. The horse and brake in front of the White Lion public house (left) belonged to Worthington's of Jacksdale, who ran a passenger service from Ripley to Jacksdale on market days (*Courtesy of the Wood Collection and www.picturethepast,org.uk*)

Urban Change: The Gate Inn at Codnor Gate has been demolished and replaced by dwellings. The original Daybrook-based Home Brewery, pictured on the pub sign, was itself a victim of rationalisation in the brewing industry (*Stuart Saint www.codnor.info*).

Although the town's borough charter dated from the reign of Queen Victoria, being granted in 1887, the charter for the annual street fair, one of the oldest and largest in Europe, dates back much, much further, having been granted by King Henry III in 1252, making the fair older than Nottingham's more famous Goose Fair.

Ilkeston needed to be very much on its dignity in 1953 when the German-born Dr Nikolaus Pevsner, scholar of the history of art (and of architecture in particular), first published the Derbyshire volume in his monumental 46-tome series of guides to the English counties.

The series is officially entitled *The Buildings of England*, but its identification with the German-born, later British academic, is so total that the guides as a whole are generally referred to simply as 'Pevsner'. Whether or not Pevsner himself wrote the guide's section on Ilkeston, or merely signed the work of a researcher, is difficult to tell at this distance in time (the author died in 1983).

Pevsner wrote off Ilkeston as 'a town singularly devoid of visual attractions'. He made no attempt to enlarge upon the reasons why he, or someone acting on his behalf, had decided to be so crushingly dismissive.

Many people felt the Pevsner put-down to be grossly unfair and, allowing for local pride, wholly inaccurate.

The current writer, some 30 years after Pevsner, had declared a belief that Ilkeston's central market place was a supreme example of the buildings and institutions essential to the social and cultural life of a north midlands town.

My belief then, and it remains the case today, although the market place and the buildings have suffered decline in the intervening years, is that everything one would expect in a town of Ilkeston's size and role was securely in place.

Urban Change: The centre of Eastwood is today dominated by a large superstore (*Author*).

The wetlands along the banks of the once severely polluted River Erewash, seen here close to Jacksdale, can be followed on footpaths and now offer a variety of wildlife and different vistas according to whether the river is in drought or flood conditions (*Author*).

My list of buildings of interest ranged around the boundaries of the market place, starts with the parish church of St Mary – Pevsner grudgingly accorded it some faint praise but added insult to injury by incorrectly ascribing it to the patronage of St Mark, rather than St Mary.

Just off the market square in Market Street is a fine example of a Victorian mill built for hosiery and glove manufacture – the former Rutland Garments building. On the southern boundary is the Carnegie Free Library, donated by the Scots philanthropist who made a fortune in steel after emigrating to the United States, whilst to the west of the rectangle is the range of Co-operative Society buildings once considered such an important part of life for both working class and middle class residents, together with the Town Hall, and a clutch of (equally essential) public houses.

As far as I can gather, no-one had the courage to upbraid the influential Pevsner on his dismissive opinion, either at the time of the guide's publication (I excuse myself from criticism, as I was only six years old at the time), or subsequently. Perhaps they felt unqualified to argue with such a distinguished personage as Pevsner on the technical merits or otherwise of the individual buildings.

Pevsner's approach was often (and not just in the case of Ilkeston) unforgivably cold and bloodless. Although unarguably a man of great learning, he appeared to lack much warmth and any understanding that buildings are not simply stone, bricks and mortar, but places where people must live both their private and communal lives.

Ilkeston's central buildings added up to the sort of urban ensemble one instinctively feels *belongs* at the heart of a typical North Midland industrial town.

Pevsner was not without equally distinguished critics in his lifetime, Another accomplished writer on architecture and a pioneer conservationist, Sir John Betjeman, carried on a long feud with the academic.

Betjeman called him 'a dull pedant from Prussia', continually mocked him as 'the Herr Professor Doktor', and wrote a hostile review of *The Buildings of England*. Betjeman contended that much of what appeared in the Pevsner guides had been written by researchers who 'have gone around getting things out of directories and sometimes using their own eyes but not, I suspect, often'.

The end result, he claimed, was that the Pevsner guides were impersonal and often incomplete 'catalogues' and failed to tell the reader what a place was really like.

D H Lawrence, in *Sons and Lovers*, was also fairly dismissive of Ilkeston. When the hero of the book, Paul Morel and

The Old Order Disappears Two: The footprint of the rooms at Shipley Hall has been laid out in brick to give visitors to the site an idea of the building's size and interior layout (*Author*).

friends go on an Easter excursion to the Hemlock Stone near Stapleford (probably the most southerly point in the valley to gain a mention in a Lawrence novel or short story) they pass through the town in mid-morning.

The book records that '*the colliers were waiting in gangs for the pubs to open. Ilkeston was a town of lounging and idleness*'. Given that it was a Bank Holiday and a rare opportunity to spend a weekday at leisure, it is not really surprising that the miners had decided to celebrate their day off with a drink or two.

South of Ilkeston, the countryside on the Derbyshire flank flattens out somewhat before descending to the Trent Valley. The major settlements in this area are the former mining villages of Mapperley (perhaps more properly linked with the Shipley estate), West Hallam (now greatly expanded by modern housing), Stanley and Stanley Common.

The now greatly diminished Stanton Ironworks industrial site is earmarked as the site for a virtual new town. Erewash Borough Council has plans for 2,000 new homes, a 25-acre business park, a 25-acre industry park, a neighbourhood centre and a wildlife park on the brownfield site. The plans also envisage a possible extension of Nottingham's tramway system to the new development, utilising a disused rail link that formerly served the Stanton works complex.

Flanking the former works, but largely shielded from it even in its heyday by a barrier of woods, are the highly attractive rural settlements of Stanton-by-Dale and Dale Abbey.

Pevsner's dubious reputation in the Erewash Valley at the time of publication of his guide was slightly retrieved by his entry for Dale Abbey. The village contains a hermit's cave cut into the local sandstone rock, the ruins of a 12th

Rural Erewash One. The Cat and Fiddle post mill at Dale Abbey (*Author*).

An attractive house in Dale Abbey village, reputed to be partly built of stone from the ruined abbey (*Author*).

century abbey, initially founded by Augustinian monks and later associated with Praemonstratensian Canons, and one of Britain's most unusual current places of worship.

The hermit's cave lies in an area of woodland to the south of the village, believed to have been hewn out of the sandstone cliff by a 12th century baker from Derby who had seen a vision of the Virgin Mary and vowed to live the rest of his life in prayer, as a recluse. The cave measures some six yards by three yards, with a door opening, two window openings, a peephole and a niche to hold a light.

The abbey flourished for almost 350 years until the Act of Dissolution in 1539, in the reign of Henry VIII. The furnishings and fittings of the abbey church were either sold or stripped out and installed in other churches, and some of the stonework was built into houses around the village.

Shown by excavations to have had transepts 100 feet in length, a crossing tower, nave and a cloister 85 feet square, all that today remains is a still-impressive 40-foot-high chancel window, standing isolated in a field.

The abbey church font was returned to the nearby church of All Saints in the village of Dale Abbey in the late 19th century.

All Saint's, at just 26 by 25 feet, was described by Pevsner or his researchers as not only one of the smallest in the country but also one of the oddest, in that it shares a roof with a dwelling house which may, at one time, have been used as a pub.

South from Dale is the large industrial village of Sandiacre, which possesses in Springfield Mill, situated on the eastern bank of the Erewash Canal, one of the finest examples of a Victorian lace factory in the entire district. Built in 1888 for Terah Hooley, who both developed mills to let to manufacturers and was a lace maker in his own right, the four-storey,

41-bay mill, with a towering chimney reflected in the waters of the canal, had a total capacity of 160 lace machines, and dominates the local scene to this day.

On the Nottinghamshire bank of the river south of Ilkeston is Trowell, which in 1951 was rather mysteriously chosen as the Festival of Britain Village. At the time blending residential ribbon development with proximity to the blast furnaces and spoil heaps of the Stanton works, the choice raised eyebrows across the more obviously attractive rural settlements of the country.

The point where Trowell meets the substantial Nottinghamshire town of Stapleford marks the southernmost extent of the Erewash Valley coalfield. It was the site between 1881 and 1928 (with some evidence of earlier workings) of Trowell Moor Colliery, also sometimes known as Stapleford Colliery.

Stapleford is generally associated with its 'twin town' of Sandiacre, which lies across the county boundary in Derbyshire. The two small industrial centres shared a long-vanished railway station on the Erewash Valley main line, and a newspaper, also sadly a thing of the past.

The two towns lie at the northern end of the now virtually redundant Toton marshalling yards. Although the yards are now semi-derelict, a victim of the run-down of the coal industry and the decreasing demand for even imported coal, the Erewash Valley main line which passes through the sidings is still very much in existence, and the Toton site also still has a flourishing maintenance depot for diesel locomotives.

Change is in the air here, as the proposed HS2 High Speed train will pass between Stapleford and Sandiacre and the station to serve the North Midlands, with connections to Derby and Nottingham, will be located within the old yards.

The old adage maintained that successful manufacturers, merchants and professional men in the Victorian and Edwardian eras, after launching their careers in the industrial valleys of the north, 'rose above the smoke' to live on higher ground unpolluted by the prevailing wind, to the west of their workplaces.

Risley, lying above Sandiacre, is perhaps the Erewash Valley's best example of a small village effectively colonised by the middle classes anxious to escape the grime of industry.

Moving south from Sandiacre, Long Eaton, with its neighbour, the formerly independent Trentside village of Sawley, is the last settlement in the Erewash Valley.

Long Eaton's heritage is essentially that of a once-thriving centre of high quality lace manufacturing in the heyday of that industry, with a large proportion of the delicate, decorative Levers Lace actually produced in the Derbyshire town, rather than in Nottingham, which specialised in the less complicated nets.

The town has been fortunate in that, as the lace industry declined, the upholstery and furniture trade for which Long Eaton is also notable, thrived.

Although in many respects closely related to its neighbours to the north, particularly since being merged for local government purposes with Ilkeston, Long Eaton has traditionally had something of an identity problem.

Geographically it belongs almost as much to the flood plain of the River Trent and although the town was and is very firmly in Derbyshire, on the western bank of the Erewash, it is also part of Greater Nottingham suburbia.

At times of local government reorganisation, Long Eaton has more than once been fortunate to survive being swallowed up by a territory-greedy city.

Fortunate in the sense that, in the 20th century at least, a majority of inhabitants would almost certainly have preferred to remain in Derbyshire rather than see their town's individual identity lost as part of a city administration not always renowned for efficient or enlightened governance.

The Nottingham (NG) postcode allotted to the town when such things were introduced (Ilkeston, just as close to the city in terms of miles as Long Eaton has a Derby DE code) has not helped matters although, in truth, confusion reigned before the code development.

Long Eaton's main interface with the River Trent is at Trent Lock, a major waterways junction where that river meets the River Soar Navigation, giving access to Loughborough and Leicester. At this point two canals also meet the Trent - the Erewash Canal, coming south-east from Long Eaton, and the short Cranfleet Cut, which provides a route for boats heading downstream on the Trent to Nottingham, avoiding a weir.

Some way further to the west on the Trent is the Sawley Cut and not far west of that is Derwent Mouth, where the River Derwent and the Trent and Mersey Canal join the Trent.

The River Erewash itself, after flowing through the railway yards, turns east near the Nottinghamshire village of Toton, flowing through the former gravel pits and modern-day nature reserve at Attenborough, by now truly in Nottingham suburbia, to join the Trent.

Lest anyone should imagine that the virtual disappearance of heavy industry in the Erewash Valley (although regrettable in many respects) is essentially a story of gloom, let it be understood that there is a very definite silver lining.

Nearing the end of our word portrait of the geographical valley, it is time to return to the theme of conservation.

Here the story to be told is one of a quite magnificent renaissance.

In the mid-1990s, at a time when the valley's heavy industry had already seen considerable decline, but before most of the pollution it had left in its wake was yet to be eradicated, the National Rivers Authority, a body now subsumed into the Environment Agency, published a damning report on the state of the river.

The survey noted how a valley once predominantly rural and agricultural had been transformed once the previously minute effects of small-scale mining had been replaced by industrial-scale collieries, gas and tar works, and blast furnaces and the development of equally polluting major railway yards and associated depots and works.

Although the survey accepted that much had been achieved in the period between the end of the 1960s and its publication date in 1995, with some of the land occupied by some of the worst colliery and ironworks spoil heaps reinstated under successful reclamation schemes, the river itself was still in many aspects an open sewer.

In the mid-1990s the water quality of the Erewash was dominated by the discharge of treated sewage. In addition, there were the effects of both premature and legitimate storm sewage overflows into the river, whilst the Erewash's upper reaches were highly coloured by trade effluent from the dyeing and finishing industry, most noticeable near Pinxton and Pye Bridge.

Rainfall-generated run-off occurred from surviving colliery spoil tips and opencast workings, with the latter often having succeeded deep mining operations.

The 1995 survey, although identifying the problems that still existed, was positive about the potential for a cleaned-up Erewash. The river, it said, already contained stretches, particularly in the vicinity of Ilkeston and Eastwood, which were still largely natural in character, with their attractiveness marred only by the poor water quality.

The downstream extremity of the river flowed through the Attenborough Site

The River Erewash today falls just short of an actual meeting with the River Trent. It now flows through one of the flooded former gravel pits that form the Attenborough Nature Reserve. The mingled waters then flow over a weir into the Trent. In the background is the parish church of St Mary, Attenborough (*Author*).

Crossing to the other bank. A ferry once operated across the Trent, not far from the spot where the river that marks the boundary between southern and northern England takes in the waters of the Erewash (*Author's Collection*).

of Special Scientific Interest, and the valley as a whole was of high quality for breeding birds and as an important migration route.

Since the publication of the survey, much work has been carried out by the river authorities and by voluntary bodies.

The compilers of the report in 1995 foresaw that an improvement in water quality and the other effects of a decline in industrial pollution would enhance the existing potential of natural green routes through the valley.

In the early years of the present century the River Erewash saw much needed conservation work which helped to clean up the water, removing much of the pollution. Much of the work was carried out by a voluntary body, the River Erewash Foundation, and as a result the fish population has experienced a slow recovery.

Although the River Erewash is not in any part navigable (although occasionally used by canoeists) the fact that it is paralleled for much of its length by the Erewash Canal has helped to create a greenway running through, and relieving the monotony of, urban surroundings.

The Erewash Canal is the only one of the man-made waterways which previously served the valley to survive in its entirety (despite attempts in the 1960s to effectively close it to navigation) but sections of the valley's other historic canals are accessible to the public.

Open air amenities like Shipley Country Park and the facilities the canal towpaths where available provide for walkers, cyclists and fisherman, not to mention the many who cruise the Erewash Canal, together with schemes like the Erewash Wetlands, comprise something of an environmental miracle.

The cleansing of the River Erewash has helped to drive several exciting environmental and leisure projects. The partnership between the Wildlife Trusts of the two counties and the local councils has helped to make both the natural assets of the valley and its industrial heritage accessible to all, through clear but not intrusive signage and well-produced descriptive leaflets and maps.

In pre-industrial times the banks of the river formed a floodplain, with marshland (as suggested by the name of the Brangwen's farm in *The Rainbow*), wet woodland and grassy pasture.

Wildlife once considered common in the valley, including otters in the river and bitterns in the reedbeds, was driven out by the pollution that was a largely avoidable but, given the tenor of the times, an inevitable by-product of industrialisation.

The areas of the valley which mirror its pre-industrial era state are now much reduced, and the river itself has in places been excavated and re-aligned. But enough remains to give a good indication of the area in former times.

The wildlife trusts are keen to encourage sustainable farming and to encourage birds, fish and other wildlife to return to suitable habitats. An ambition, well on its way to being fulfilled, is for the valley to be a place where people can experience the excitement of seeing wildlife on their own doorstep, whilst at the same time it is believed that an improved environment could attract investment into parts of the valley that are still in economic decline.

The development of the Erewash Valley Trail, which takes in the entire length of The Erewash Canal and sections of the Nottingham Canal, involved many organisations and statutory bodies in addition to the local authorities and the wildlife trusts, including the Environment Agency, British Waterways, and the East Midlands Development Agency.

Beginning in the higher reaches of the valley, the Trail includes the Jacksdale Nature Reserve, a mixture of woodland and scrub bordered to the west by the River Erewash. It is a fine example of how remains from the valley's industrial heyday have been incorporated into the conservation project, as the area available to walkers includes part of a redundant railway embankment.

Travelling south, the Jacksdale reserve links with the Erewash Meadows reserve, part of the largest area of floodplain grasslands and wetlands surviving in the valley, which merges with Brinsley Meadows in the central portion of the reserve and Aldercar Flash to the south. A small section of the Cromford Canal leads off from Brinsley Meadows.

The fact that Erewash Meadows straddles the River Erewash means the site can be viewed in various stages of flood or drought depending on the time of year.

The area is a haven for birdwatchers and in the 1980s the Erewash Valley Birding Group, demonstrated to great effect how important the site was for birds, staving off the threat of opencast mining. A hotspot for migration along the valley, nearly 200 bird species have been recorded,

Other significant sections of the Trail take in Bramcote Hills Park Woodland, believed to be the southernmost area of typical Sherwood Forest habitat based on the underlying sandstone rock, and the Attenborough Nature Reserve, a complex of flooded gravel pits and islands into which the River Erewash now empties.

The Broxtowe Country Trail has large sections in common with the Erewash Trail, but extends further to the east, into the Leen Valley and the City of Nottingham.

One result of the efforts of the various organisations working in partnership has been the current classification of the wildlife of the Erewash valley as diverse. The local authorities and conservation organisations credit the efforts of the often-criticised Environment Agency for the significant improvement in river quality. As fish stocks improve, so many other species benefit.

The area also sustains an important population of water voles, foxes, weasel, grass snakes and amphibians, with butterflies and insects.

The greening of the valley is not the only evidence of good management in the valley's transition from heavy industrial to post-industrial status. Some traditional industries, such as upholstery, have not only survived but have thrived, with active measures being taken to promote their importance to not only the local but also the national economy.

The development of industrial estates throughout the valley has brought new trades and service industries and helped to lessen the impact on jobs of the decline of heavy industry.

The scenes of manufacturing grandeur (and, it has to be admitted, of industrial squalor) brought to life in the prose of D H Lawrence, are gone beyond retrieval.

But the prosperity once confined to the relative few is now more equally shared and not even the most nostalgic, if the truth is known, would want to return to the conditions of the Erewash Valley of yesteryear.

Chapter Two

Revolution in the Valley

'Some sixty years ago a great change took place. The little gin pits were elbowed aside by the large mines of the financiers. The coal and iron field of Nottinghamshire and Derbyshire was discovered' – Sons and Lovers.

Revolution came to the Erewash Valley in the late 18th and early 19th centuries in two very contrasting forms.

The Industrial Revolution changed Britain from a mainly rural, agricultural society into the manufacturing powerhouse of the world, and in so doing utterly transformed the borderlands between Nottinghamshire and Derbyshire.

Whilst small extractive and manufacturing pursuits had been followed in the area for centuries, they had failed to make much of a mark on the landscape.

The workings of the primitive coal mines, powered by horses plodding round a capstan or gin, had hardly been noticeable amid the cornfields and pastures of the valley, whilst lace and hosiery manufacture was simply a cottage industry.

Technological advances, allied to growing markets for coal as the population mushroomed in the industrial towns of the midlands, brought rapid change. Growing demand could only be satisfied by more efficient communications and first canals and later railways made it possible to fully exploit the Erewash Valley's abundant reserves of coal.

The scars of deep mining, the night time glare and fumes of blast furnaces, the roar of foundries, and the 24-hour clamour of railway shunting yards, turned sleepy market towns and rural villages into thriving but grimy centres of extraction and manufacture.

Alongside coal, iron and heavy engineering, the textile manufacturing once carried out by the wives and children of miners and farm labourers in the relatively peaceful and safe upper rooms of their cottages transferred to huge red brick tenement mills, where thousands laboured for long hours (and small wages) in noisy, hot and often dangerous conditions.

Change on such a large scale was bound to arouse opposition; Arkwright's mills in the neighbouring Derwent Valley were built in a location chosen largely for its relative inaccessibility to potential rioters, whilst in South Wales the iron masters of Merthyr Tydfil created private armies and a virtual fortress (complete with cannon) to which they could retreat if their downtrodden employees turned to real violence.

Widespread industrial discontent, fanned into a flame by the threat to the livelihoods of traditional textile workers by the development of mechanisation in the textile industry in the Nottingham region, brought revolution of a more lethal kind, real and bloody, to the Erewash Valley.

The Industrial Revolution viewed as a positive development. This illustration of Stanton Ironworks new works (circa 1909), seen from the canal towpath near Hallam Fields, Ilkeston, originally appeared in a publication entitled The Beauties of Derbyshire (*Derbyshire Local Studies Library and www.picturethepast.org.uk*).

The gatehouse at the entrance to the former Butterley Company site at Butterley Hill, near Ripley, is a solid stone construction that once repulsed the Pentrich revolutionaries. Like the Arkwright mills at Cromford, the structure was purpose-built as a defensive strongpoint for use in times of civil and industrial unrest (*Author*).

The effects of mechanisation and harsh industrial conditions were exacerbated following the end of the Napoleonic wars by a severe economic depression and mass unemployment, whilst the Corn Laws massively increased the price of bread. Industry in the Erewash Valley was badly affected, with one of the major industrial employers, The Butterley Company, formed 27 years earlier, suffering from the decline in production of war materials, an important element of its engineering business, and problems in two other of its many areas of interest – a slump in the price of iron ore and a steep reduction in the production of coal.

In addition, the valley's hosiery trade had also experienced several difficult years.

Politically, the movement for parliamentary reform was strenuously opposed by a government afraid that the violence of the French Revolution would be matched in Britain. Secret revolutionary committees were formed across the country and men met covertly to plan revolt in the village of Pentrich, between Ripley and Alfreton.

The actual revolt broke out in June 1817 when a gathering of some two or three hundred men, stockingers, miners, quarrymen and iron workers, led by Jeremiah Brandreth, known as ' the Nottingham Captain', set out from South Wingfield near Alfreton to march on the city.

They were only lightly armed, with pikes, scythes and just a few guns. With their plans betrayed by an informer, they were met en route by troops and easily subdued. Those identified as the ring-leaders, Brandreth (an unemployed stockinger himself), Isaac Ludlam and William Turner, were tried for treason, convicted and hanged and beheaded at Derby.

During the course of their march, the Pentrich rebels had attempted to storm the gates of The Butterley Company's Ripley complex, but were successfully repulsed. The solid stone gatehouse before which a scene of revolution was enacted still stands four square today, at the entrance to the derelict and largely demolished works.

The founders of the Butterley empire, just like Arkwright and the Merthyr ironmasters, had prepared for every eventuality in a tense era for Britain.

Revolt, whether it was confined to breaking up machinery or escalated into treasonable rebellion, could never hope to halt the advance of industrialisation. As the 19th century progressed the Erewash Valley became an industrial hotbed, producing millions of tons of coal, iron and other foundry products, and hosiery, knitwear, and lingerie of the highest quality.

The economy of the valley actually benefitted from industrial unrest in Nottingham, where lace manufacturers, particularly those involved in the production of higher quality decorative material, moved out of the city to the Erewash towns, where trade union activity was, at least in the early days, less organised and effective.

The valley became the centre of the Levers (occasionally spelled Leavers) lace industry, creating a trade that was in some ways more democratic than other occupations. To a degree perhaps

Jeremiah Brandreth, recognised leader of the Pentrich Revolution, executed together with two fellow ringleaders (*Derby City Council and www.picturethepast.org.uk*).

Children in the valley still play in the shadow of gaunt tenement lace mills and towering chimneys *(Author).*

only matched by the self-employed craftsmen of the Sheffield cutlery industry, the famed 'little mesters', the Erewash Valley lace trade offered opportunities for a thrifty and ambitious employee to become his own master.

The huge tenement lace mills which line the Erewash Canal in Long Eaton and Sandiacre were usually occupied not by just one or two large manufacturing combines. The speculators who built them rented out space in the mills – and sometimes let out the actual machinery as well – to multiple operators, often operating on a small scale.

An operative who could save a modest amount of capital could rent space and acquire (often on credit from the same speculators) a few lace machines. In some cases the new capitalist thrived, whilst in others his business acumen failed to match his ambition and he soon found himself back on the factory floor.

When the lace trade was at its peak, Harrington Mill, in Leopold Street, Long Eaton, housed 26 separate business ventures. Constructed by a consortium of manufacturers in 1885, it is well over a quarter of a mile in length (557 yards), contains one and a quarter million bricks, and has 224 cast iron windows down one side.

Lace making has disappeared from Harrington Mill, but the huge building is still busy, housing a variety of businesses.

Despite the early outbreaks of machine-smashing, strikes and even open armed rebellion, the Erewash Valley has, in truth, always been adaptable. This virtue is as strong in the 21st century as in the preceding decades.

Over the years, as the scale and the prospects of the coal and iron industries inexorably declined, the valley turned to alternative industries. Today, it is one of the main centres of quality upholstery production in the UK, maintaining and developing a tradition of excellence that includes the furnishing of the great Ocean Liners of the first half of the 20th century.

Light industrial estates have replaced winding gear, pit tips, and blast furnaces and the valley's gaunt mills, where still standing now, as in the case of Harrington Mill, offer a home to a multitude of different trades and businesses or, in some cases, have been converted into desirable apartments.

The retail sector too, is of importance to the valley, and at least one large former textile mill is now devoted to several floors selling clothing and allied goods, rather than to manufacturing processes.

Adaptability has allowed the Erewash Valley to survive and even prosper in the 21st century, whilst the existence of many jobs, both of a traditional manufacturing and service nature in the nearby cities of Nottingham and Derby, has seen a great increase in commuting from the valley towns and villages.

The reports drawn up for parliamentary constituencies by the leading polling organisation YouGov go a long way towards accurately summing up the present-day state of the Erewash Valley. The dominating terms in descriptions of the Erewash (Ilkeston and Long Eaton) and Broxtowe (Stapleford and Toton) seats are 'affluent' and 'commuter' – tags that would astonish earlier generations of valley residents.

Amber Valley's three former coal mining towns (Heanor, Ripley and Alfreton) are seen as being balanced electorally by the Conservative-voting rural areas, with light industry and the service and retail sectors replacing mining as the main economic activity.

Ashfield (Eastwood), also once predominantly a mining area, is now 'gradually transitioning towards being more of a commuter area for Nottingham'. The biggest employer today in Bolsover, the fifth of the parliamentary seats to cover a part of the geographical Erewash Valley (Pinxton), is today the East Midlands Designer Outlet complex, just off the M1 motorway at South Normanton.

An ability to adapt has saved the Erewash Valley from the worst aspects of recession on many occasions. West End Mills at Long Eaton is no longer home to lace making but, like the neighbouring Harrington Mill, is now home to a variety of trades *(Author)*.

The relative prosperity and stability of life in most parts of the valley today is to be welcomed, but it would be shameful to reject the industrial heritage of the area in the past 250 years or so. The industrial site that best sums up the rise and fall of the heavy industrial heritage of the Erewash is the former headquarters of The Butterley Company, at Butterley Hill, on the outskirts of Ripley.

It was the development in the late 18th century of the Cromford Canal, as a means of transporting the valley's mineral wealth to markets further south, including the excavation of Butterley Tunnel, that revealed the true extent of the coal and iron reserves in the area. These were to be exploited to great effect by the Butterley Company.

What was to evolve into The Butterley Company was originally titled Benjamin Outram and Company, founded in 1790. It was in 1793 that the canal engineer William Jessop, with the assistance of Outram, constructed the Cromford Canal to connect the burgeoning industrial village of Cromford,with the Erewash Canal. (See Chapter Four – *The Valley as a Route to Riches*).

The rise of the company was greatly aided by the outbreak of the French revolutionary wars in 1793, leading to a huge rise in demand for pig iron. By 1796 the company's blast furnace was producing nearly a thousand tons a year and the firm soon expanded, with a second works at Codnor Park, further down the Erewash Valley.

The company, which adopted the title of The Butterley Company in 1805, over the

Butterley Company Masterpiece One: The Falkirk Wheel (*Brenda Dyer*).

Butterley Company Masterpiece Two: The roof of London's St Pancras railway station (*Brenda Dyer*).

years became a prime example of a world-renowned multi-layered industrial combine, owning collieries, ironworks, brickworks and foundries and employing thousands of workers at sites across the Erewash Valley.

It retained the historic name until 1968, when the firm was split into three sections, Butterley Engineering, Butterley Brick and Butterley Aggregates. Butterley Engineering was still a byword for engineering innovation and manufacturing excellence as the 21st century dawned.

In the years immediately following the Millennium it was responsible for designing and constructing the Falkirk Wheel, the futuristic boatlift in Scotland which has reconnected the Forth & Clyde Canal and the Union Canal, taking the place of a derelict flight of 11 locks.

It also fabricated the steelwork for the Spinnaker, the landmark observation tower in Portsmouth, which at 560 feet (170 metres) above sea level is two and a half times the height of Nelson's column.

These modern-day projects were fit to rank alongside the company's earlier achievements in producing the ironwork for the 1914 Vauxhall Bridge in London and its best-known engineering triumph, the manufacture of the roof spans for William Barlow's famous train shed at St Pancras Station.

Part of the Butterley Company empire in the firm's heyday; Brittain Pit, near Ripley. Private owner railway wagons belonging to the company are amongst the trucks in the sidings (*Wood Collection and www.picturethepast.org.uk*).

A sad end for a proud company. Derelict Butterley Company buildings in 2016 (*Author*).

Generations of travellers waiting to return via the Midland mainline to Derby, Chesterfield and the Erewash Valley towns on the western side of the River Erewash have experienced a sense of pride every time they read the plaques at the base of the huge girders bearing the weight of the roof span, proclaiming 'The Butterley Company, Derbyshire'.

The Falkirk Wheel was fully constructed and assembled on the Ripley site. The structure was then dismantled in the summer of 2001, when 35 lorry loads trundled past the Georgian gatehouse en route to Scotland. On arrival the structure was reassembled into five sections on the ground, and lifted into place.

The Wheel was opened in May 2002 by HM Queen Elizabeth II, as part of her Golden Jubilee celebrations. The Spinnaker was completed in October 2005.

But just four years after the completion of the Portsmouth project, more than two centuries of engineering excellence was finally brought to an end by a few strokes of an accountant's pen. On March 5 2009, Butterley Engineering was placed into administration. The administrator's bald statement simply said: "This is a highly specialist business that has proven vulnerable to the economic downturn".

Today the Georgian gatehouse at Butterley Hill which witnessed the Pentrich Revolution guards nothing more than a vast area of industrial dereliction, patterned with rusting railway lines, but fast being obscured by undergrowth.

The creeping neglect of such a solid building, would be sad in any circumstances. The current condition of the grade two listed hexagonal structure, built in pleasant ashlar sandstone, is made even more deplorable by the fact that this is no run-of-the-mill former industrial building but was for two centuries the gateway to the main manufacturing base of an historic organisation responsible for some of Britain's most iconic structures.

Coal Mining

D H Lawrence forgot more about living in a coal mining community than I could ever claim to know.

Growing up in Long Eaton, my main industrial influences were gained from contact with railwaymen, lace operatives, and upholsterers. I ventured down a working pit three times in my life, and the Sunday morning jaunts occupying a couple of hours at a time were, I have to confess, enough for a lifetime.

I did, it is true, go to school in Ilkeston at a time when the Queen of the Erewash Valley was still home to mineworkers, and plenty of my schoolmates had fathers who worked underground , particularly in the Shipley pits.

Winning coal the hard way with a pickaxe (*Erewash Museum*).

Lawrence had plenty to say about the more squalid physical aspects of an industry inseparable from grime, and many of his comments on the lifestyle of the miners appear hostile at first glance. A closer reading of his Erewash Valley novels and short stories nevertheless reveal that the writer possessed a deep understanding of the mining community, an understanding which admittedly did not always translate into sympathy.

This understanding of the forces that drove the miners' way of life, combined with Lawrence's unrivalled gift for describing the attitudes and aspirations of ordinary people, has left behind a picture of life in an early 20th century industrial community unrivalled then and now across the British literary landscape.

Desperate times for miners. Coal picking at Cossall during a strike in 1912 (*Derbyshire Local Studies Libraries and www.picturethepast.org.uk*).

Lawrence might not have agreed with many of the attitudes of the miners he encountered during his most formative years, but he both recognised and recorded what lay at their roots. Some of the most effective examples occur in Lawrence's treatment of strikes in the industry, which if prolonged brought misery and hunger to the wives and children of the colliers.

Despite the fact that in his own personal experience Lawrence must have known the effect a loss of income must have had on the miner's household, in his short story *Strike Pay*, he shows an understanding of both the 'holiday mood' prevalent at the start of the dispute, with the miners unexpectedly liberated from the long hours underground, and also of the fact that the camaraderie that made life at the coalface tolerable translated into a feeling of strength through unity when a dispute occurred.

When the strikers are part of a crowd walking the nine miles from Eastwood to Nottingham to watch Notts County play Aston Villa, the high spirits develop into a feeling of confidence that by standing together, they can achieve their goals.

Prompted by the sight of a local coal owner driving past with his immaculate team of horses, one collier proclaims: "*We oughtna ter go back under a twenty per zent rise. They can do nowt bi-out us, we'n on'y ter stop out long enough*"

To which another striker adds: "*We'n on'y ter stick out, an we s'll see who's gaffer*!

The other side of the coin is illustrated at the end of the story, when the youngest and newly married member of the group around which the narrative revolves returns home to be berated by his mother-in-law for his day of pleasure. "*You're a pretty little jockey, are'nt you? Oh, its a gala time for you, the strike is. That's all men strike for, indeed. They enjoy themselves, they do that.*

Happier times in the industry. Erewash Valley miners finish a shift (*Author's Collection*).

"*Ripping and racing and drinking, from morn till night, my sirs*!

The climax of the story also illustrates an aspect of the recurring major theme in Lawrence's work of the complex relationship between the sexes. When the collier, demanding his tea, abuses the mother-in-law, she tells her daughter that if she gives the man his tea after such an outburst, she is '*a trollops*'.

The daughter quietly prepares her husband's tea. "*She attended to him. Not that she was really meek. But – he was her man, not her mother's*'.

Coal mining in the Erewash Valley

Mining was part of everyday life in the Erewash Valley for at least eight hundred years, from the 13th century onwards, when a handful of men combined their work in the fields with digging out small quantities of coal from the point where the seams touched the surface of the land.

The wheel turned full circle in the closing years of the 20th century and the first decade of the new millennium, when the surviving mineral wealth of the valley was once again extracted by a just a few men, this time driving giant bulldozers on opencast sites, taking out the kind of tonnages which at the peak of the mining industry required the sweated labour of thousands of men.

The Derbyshire and Nottinghamshire coalfield comes closest to the surface on the western bank of the River Erewash, making exploitation of the seams relatively easy and inexpensive.

Deep mining on an industrialised scale started relatively early here, and reached a peak around the turn of the 19th/20th centuries, with 28 pits on the Derbyshire side of the river producing coal in 1896, from Dale Abbey in the south of the valley to Blackwell and South Normanton in the north. The western bank of the Erewash accounted for more than half of the collieries operating in Derbyshire as a whole at that time.

Reckoning up the wages. Colliers often worked on the butty or contractor system with a team paid a lump sum by the pit owners, which then had to be divided up between the men, according to their status and minus various deductions. The piles of coins can be seen on the ground in the centre of the group (*Erewash Museum*).

Across the county boundary in Nottinghamshire, the records of early mining are more precise than those that exist for Derbyshire, and have been interpreted by scholars, notably John Beckett, Professor of English Regional History at The University of Nottingham, and Dr Denise Amos.

Mining activities in Erewash Valley communities from Cossall in the south to Selston in the north are well documented, and coal extraction in Nottinghamshire benefitted over the centuries from the interest of both monastic institutions at Lenton, on the outskirts of Nottingham, and Beauvale near Eastwood, and the aristocratic Willoughby and Strelley families, of Wollaton and Strelley manor respectively.

Until the onset of the Industrial Revolution, coal was sold mainly to domestic customers. The lack of transport other than horse-drawn wagons and pack trains linking the coal-producing areas with the area's larger towns and cities, hampered development of the industry until the development of first canals and then railways.

The need to convey coal speedily (by the standards of the day) and inexpensively prompted surveys for canals, initially the Erewash Canal, from a junction with the River Trent near Long Eaton, and then the Cromford Canal, which linked Arkwright's mills at Cromford in the Derwent Valley with the Erewash at Langley Mill. The Nottingham Canal, connected the city to the Cromford and the Erewash at Great Northern Basin at Langley Mill, whilst the Nutbrook Canal, designed to open up the rich coalfield based on Shipley, West Hallam and Mapperley, also made a junction with the Erewash.

(Full details of the valley's interconnecting canal system can be found in Chapter Four, The Valley as a Route to Riches).

The excavations for the Cromford Canal had revealed extensive seams of coal in the Ripley/Pinxton areas of the valley and their discovery helped to build the empire created by The Butterley Company, an industrial giant for some two hundred years. The Butterley concern owned a dozen of the 51 Erewash Valley pits on the Derbyshire side of the valley, in an 1896 survey by the HM Inspector of Mines for the Midland Counties.

At the nationalisation of the coal industry in 1947, there were 68 collieries in Derbyshire, with 28 of them situated in the Erewash Valley. The very shallowness of the seams on the western bank of the Erewash that had facilitated commercial exploitation meant that workable reserves ran out correspondingly early. The last Derbyshire pit in the valley, Ormonde at Loscoe, opened quite late in 1905, closed in September 1970.

Across the river in Nottinghamshire the 2000 square miles of deep coal veins were a tempting resource for the mining companies In the 1850s collieries were opening in the Eastwood area, at Kimberley and Babbington, and at Trowell Moor, near Stapleford, the furthest south on the eastern bank of the Erewash Valley that coal was mined.

Major development of the coal industry in Nottinghamshire, after the first phase of pit sinkings, occupied two distinct periods. The years between 1870 and 1910 saw more than 40 collieries start producing in the Mansfield and Nottingham areas, with 35,000 men and boys employed in the industry in the county in 1907.

The second major phase of expansion came after World War One, with the development of the Dukeries coalfield, including what were to be some of the UK's last deep mines to operate.

From the 1960s onward, with the Derbyshire Erewash Valley pits defunct, Nottinghamshire became the major supplier to the power industry, with Ratcliffe-on- Soar Power Station to the south of Long Eaton consuming 65 per cent of the output of the South Nottinghamshire pits.

In later years it was Nottinghamshire's turn to experience a lack of workable and viable reserves and this, combined with the effects of imported coal, led to the end of the UK mining industry.

The closure of Thoresby Colliery in 2015 brought down the curtain on mining in the county.

The memory of the coal industry will endure for a long time in the Erewash Valley. Talking to men who worked in the industry up to its eventual demise and would baulk at any attempt to glamourise the life of the miner, the theme of camaraderie and what it meant to be part of a close-knit community, dominate reminiscences.

Newthorpe-born Mark Drakeley's experience of the coal industry in the second half of the 20th century, a period of decline and closure but yet with an overall expectation that deep mining would survive, albeit in a reduced form, mirrored that of thousands of mineworkers in the Erewash Valley and across Britain.

Hard labour for man and beast. Colliers and a pit pony transport coal to the shaft at Brinsley Colliery (Nottinghamshire County Council and www.picturethepast.org.uk).

With collieries on both banks of the River Erewash gradually exhausting their viable coal reserves or becoming unprofitable to exploit, the work – and those miners who wished to continue in the industry – were forced to move north and east to the more modern deeper pits in Nottinghamshire and Yorkshire.

With the closure in the mid-1980s of the Erewash Valley's last pits – Moorgreen, Underwood and Pye Hill, Mark and his fellow mineworkers effectively became industrial commuters.

Mark joined the industry in 1970, straight from school. He recalled: "I was actually only 14, finishing a week before my 15th birthday. With I suppose about another 300 lads I started at the National Coal Board's Moorgreen Training Centre, near Eastwood and not far from home.

"I didn't have any close relatives in the industry and going down the pit was just one of the jobs on offer locally at a time when the future of coal mining still looked good, and the newspaper advertisements were talking about bright prospects for the future. The money was good and conditions underground and the safety aspect had improved since the old days."

Mark was at the training centre at Moorgreen for around two years, with his time there interrupted by the national miner's strike of 1972. When the period of training was completed he began work at Underwood Colliery and eventually became a highly-skilled face-worker, driving cutting machinery, including trepanners and shearers.

The enduring picture often retained by people outside Britain's mining areas, of men hewing the coal with pickaxes, was at odds with the realities of modern mining. Mark Drakeley has maintained a full record of his employment during his quarter of a century working underground, and his documents include a full record of the extensive training required for him to handle the sophisticated cutting machinery.

Like many of the Erewash Valley mines, the pit at Underwood where Mark worked underwent a change of name periodically, as the underground workings were merged. The pits were also often known by nicknames. New Selston Colliery was known locally as the Bull and Butcher pit after a nearby public house. New Selston merged with Pye Hill Colliery in 1956. Underwood Colliery's official name was Selston Colliery until this changed to Pye Hill No 1 in the late 1960s. In the same way, Jacksdale's pit eventually became Pye Hill No 2.

Mark Drakeley from Eastwood, who worked at Moorgreen, Underwood and Calverton collieries, pictured with the mining memorial in the churchyard of St Michael and All Angels, Underwood (*Author*).

When Underwood, Pye Hill and Moorgreen closed in 1985, Mark and many others were transferred to Calverton, some 15 miles from Eastwood. The pit at Calverton had first been planned in 1937 but work was held up by World War Two and the colliery was not officially opened until 1952, by which time the industry had been nationalised by Clement Attlee's Labour government.

The shaft at Calverton had actually been sunk in 1946, before nationalisation. At the opening ceremony for the shaft, Claude Lancaster MP, the chairman of B A Collieries Ltd, the private company proposing to open the mine, said that it was estimated that beneath the surface there might be 125 million tons of coal, which if one thousand men were to produce a million tons every year, would provide employment for 125 years.

In 1992, seven years after Mark Drakeley had made his move east, British Coal, the privatised successors to the NCB, announced the closure of seven Nottinghamshire mines, including Calverton, which at the time employed 749 men. Ironically, the announcement came in the week the pit achieved a weekly production record of 450,000 tons – nearly half of the annual production level forecast in 1946, before full-scale mechanisation!

Although the Government later announced a U-turn on the future of Calverton, the work force was drastically reduced to an initial 150 men. For Mark and a great many of his fellow miners, it was the end of their careers in the coal industry.

Calverton, said to be losing money and experiencing deteriorating geological conditions, with no guarantee of a market for the remaining coal, closed for good in 1999 – 78 years short of the working life predicted by Claude Lancaster in 1946.

Mark Drakeley took a job driving before finally retiring from full time work. Today many of his skills are put to good use working with the track maintenance team at the preserved Ecclesbourne Valley Railway, which runs from Duffield to Wirksworth in Derbyshire.

His memories of his years in the coal industry are almost all positive. "What did I enjoy about the job? Everything really, but particularly the comradeship, the crack with the men you worked with. The money was good too, and I came out of the job with a decent pension."

Like many others, and not just in coal mining, Mark was not over keen on the shiftwork, but he accepted that the anti-social hours were part of the job.

Another not-so-happy memory is of the year-long strike in 1984, when Mark and the majority of Nottinghamshire miners left the National Union of Mineworkers under Arthur Scargill to join the newly-formed Union of Democratic mineworkers (UDM), continuing to work during the bitter dispute.

Mark recalls: "They called us scabs and there was a lot of ill-feeling. But the majority of the men agreed with the UDM view that the strike was unconstitutional."

The final two deep coal mines in Britain, Thoresby in Nottinghamshire and Kellingley in North Yorkshire, closed in 2015.

The pay check issued to Mark Drakeley when he was transferred to Calverton Colliery on the closure of the last pits in the Erewash Valley (*Author*).

Mark Drakeley believes the complete destruction of the industry will eventually be seen as a mistake. "People always point to the fact that coal is a dirty fuel, but it doesn't have to be in the modern era. Clean coal-fired power stations have been successfully developed and operated in Germany.

"I believe we could have retained a British industry built around ten or so modern pits, avoiding a complete reliance on imported coal."

The Mining Community

Anyone familiar with *Sons and Lovers* will appreciate the lengths to which the miner's wife, Gertrude Morel, in real life D H Lawrence's own mother, Lydia, will go in order to keep her sons from a lifetime in the pit, a much more arduous, dangerous and relatively ill-paid life at the time the novel was written than in later years.

Just as the plot of *Sons and Lovers* reflected the real life fate of the sons of the Lawrence family, it is not difficult to discover similar stories of an equal determination in more recent years to prevent sons from working underground.

Retired schoolteacher John Grace has lived in the former pit village of Waingroves all his life. His father was a miner, working successively at pits in Ripley, Denby and at Ormonde Colliery, Loscoe, near Heanor, the last working colliery in the Ilkeston/Shipley/Heanor area when it closed in 1970.

Mr Grace senior eventually became a deputy, a role which combined supervision with safety responsibilities, something for which, as captain of the rescue team, he was admirably suited.

John Grace recalls: "He had always been reluctant to become a deputy, but in the end the manager of the pit offered him the stark choice of taking the job or taking his cards. He was better off eventually; being a deputy meant he earned less, but his pension was better."

Fred Grace, like virtually every miner, enjoyed the comradeship engendered by the team work so vital underground. His son says: "Mining, no doubt about it, was not only dirty and smelly but also extremely dangerous. My dad knew this as well as anyone, through his work on the safety team.

"So yes, in many ways he enjoyed the life. But having said that, he and my mother were both equally determined that I should not follow him down the pit. In fact I never knew a miner who wanted his son to follow in his footsteps."

John Grace does have happy memories of the fringe benefits of living in a mining community such as Waingroves.

"For most years of my childhood we went as a family to the Derbyshire Miners Holiday Camp at Skegness. Ripley railway station had lost its regular passenger services in 1930, but was re-opened each summer for holiday trains, which annually carried up to a thousand mineworkers and their families to the Lincolnshire coast.

"When we arrived at the holiday camp I always found that all my mates were there as well. There was certainly no problem making up sides for football matches between the boys from the various pit villages!

D H Lawrence's novels and stories generally depict the life of the mining community from the point of view of the ordinary colliers themselves and their families, or describe (and often caricature) the lives of the upper strata of local society, the mine-owners.

The owners divide for the most part into the older, aristocratic and gentry families, such as the Miller-Mundys of Shipley Hall and the Drury-Lowes of Locko Park, and on the other hand into the men of business, who had risen to positions of power and influence in the industry on their merits, once coal mining had become fully commercialised and capitalised.

Lawrence as a writer made enemies among both the ordinary colliers and the owners, producing unflattering portraits of both classes in general and as individuals.

He often seems less concerned with the middle strata of local society, although he successfully reflects the scorn with which a fair number of colliers often held those who had risen from the lowest level to positions of responsibility and had become regarded as ' bosses' men'.

There is a memorable scene in *Sons and Lovers* in which Walter Morel, the miner based on Lawrence's father, abuses and guys the pit manager. Morel, described as being '*blab-mouthed*' and a '*tongue wagger*', holds court at the bar of his favourite public house, regaling his drinking partners with an account of how the manager had complained that (Morel's) stall in the pit was unsafe, claiming that the wooden pit props holding up the roof were inadequate.

When the manager warns Morel that the roof will fall in, the miner replies: '*Tha'd better stan' on a bit o' clunch (solid fireclay). then, an' hold it up with thy 'ead.*' Morel imitates the manager's *'fat, squeaky voice, with its attempt at good English.*

The Derbyshire Miners' Holiday Camp at Skegness, pictured shortly after it opened in 1939. The camp enabled miners and their families to have a week's holiday by the sea. It closed in the late 1990s *(Norman Grogan)*.

When the manager retorts by asking the miner, '*who knows more about it, me or you*', Morel replies:"*I've never fun out how much tha knows, Alfred. It'll appen carry thee ter bed an' back*', causing the other miners to laugh.

Morel's skills as a collier mean he avoids outright dismissal, but the manager gets his own back by hitting the miner's pocket, allocating him poor and unproductive stalls in the pit.

A rare glimpse into the middle strata of the mining world in a later period than that covered in *Sons and Lovers* is afforded by the autobiography of John Rimington, a native of the Erewash Valley who became a distinguished civil servant, reaching the rank of Permanent Secretary. From 1984 for eleven years he was a highly influential Director General of the Health and Safety Executive, and was closely associated with the modern approach to regulating major industrial hazards.

John Rimington was born in Marlpool, Heanor, in 1935. His grandfather, Thomas Rimington, was once a farmer who had 'gone down-t pit' as a surer way of earning a living in hard times. Like many of his type, he was keen to see his own son do well in life, using his contacts to find him a job in the offices of the Shipley Colliery Company, which had been formed to run the pits at Coppice and Woodside formerly owned by the Miller-Mundy family.

Major Godfrey Miller-Mundy was still a director of the company at nationalisation in 1947, at which time the Coppice and Woodside pits, which closed in the mid-1960s, were producing around one and half million tons of household, manufacturing and steam coal, and employed more than 2,700 men.

Rimington's father became first chief accountant to the Shipley Company and later the firm's finance and commercial director and a member of the company's main board, by the age of 32. Following nationalisation he became finance director of the Scottish Coal Board and effectively number two in the industry north of the border. In his book, John Rimington paints a fascinating picture of life in an area offering a microcosm of the classic Erewash Valley blend of rural tranquillity and industrial clamour.

Like Lawrence and former cabinet minister Kenneth Clarke, Rimington was educated at Nottingham High School and later at Jesus College, Cambridge where he read history. He was made a Companion of the Order of the Bath in 1987 in recognition of conspicuous services to the Crown.

John Rimington's autobiography is titled *Erewash to Radegund*, the latter name being a veiled reference to St Radegund, the patron of his alma mater, Jesus College, Cambridge.

John Rimington's father, pictured at Shipley, rose to become a director of the colliery company where he had worked since leaving school.

The iron industry

The novels and short stories of D H Lawrence have helped ensure that coal mining has generally claimed the lion's share of attention whenever the Erewash Valley and its working class communities come into focus.

Coal mines and colliers have usually tended to overshadow the contribution made to the life and the economy of the valley by other industries and occupations, particularly ironmaking and the associated foundry and heavy engineering trades, which embraced similarly arduous and often equally dangerous ways of earning a living, and were arguably as essential a contributor to the local economy as the pits.

It occasionally seems, at least to this writer that, undoubtedly unintentionally, Lawrence could not help himself in attaching a certain amount of romance to the way of life of the miner. It is not difficult to find references to many other industries in his work, including iron making, lace and hosiery manufacture, and the pottery trade, but the theme in so many novels and short stories, sooner or later, centres around the underground worker.

In a wider sense, the fact that coal was absolutely inseparable from the everyday life of most of Great Britain for many generations may also be a contributing factor. Steam, generated from coal, drove British industry and provided the motive power for the railways, for long the almost exclusive means of long distance passenger travel and freight haulage.

Perhaps even more important, it was coal that directly warmed the hearths of millions, cooked their meals, and made possible the production of gas and electricity.

Whatever the reasons for the supremacy of 'King Coal', iron making was of major importance in the Erewash Valley.

From the Alfreton and Ripley districts in the north, to the Iron Dale of Stanton further south, this area of Derbyshire had been known for its outcrops of iron ore from the middle ages onwards.

The Butterley Company, mentioned earlier in this chapter for the excellence of its engineering and the tragedy of its ultimate demise, and a major player in the valley mining industry, was for long also at the forefront of iron production.

Coal and iron were discovered when William Jessop and Benjamin Outram excavated Butterley Tunnel during the construction of the Cromford Canal. Both men, with John Wright, whose family owned the Butterley Park estate, developed what became The Butterley Company.

At the peak of the French Revolutionary Wars, in 1796, the Butterley concern was producing nearly a thousand tons of pig iron a year and by the second decade of the 19th century the company owned four blast furnaces, two each at Butterley and Codnor.

The long years of industrial development and prosperity in the 19th century saw the company thrive and become not just the largest coal owner but also the second largest iron producer in the Midlands. Butterley produced an extensive range of goods, from rails to castings for machinery.

The company quickly recognised the new Bessemer process for steel manufacture in the mid-19th century, being one of just four businesses that obtained a licence from Sir Henry Bessemer once his method had been perfected.

Notable patents taken out by the company's manager, Sir John Alleyne included a method of producing a load bearing iron beam, and a process for the more efficient and speedy handling of hot ingots, greatly increasing productivity. By 1863 Butterley was rolling the largest masses of iron of any foundry in Britain and was well equipped for such projects as the construction of the 240-foot St Pancras station roof spans.

Alleyne, also invented and patented the two high reversing steel mill in 1870, which used two steam engines to allow metal ingots to be repeatedly rolled to get the correct size and section.

Industrial Revolution survivors. The two remaining primitive blast furnaces from the once extensive Morley Park ironworks, owned by John and Charles Mold. One of the furnaces dates from 1780, the other from 1818. (*www.picturethepast.org.gov*)

A group of Stanton Ironworks Company workmen and boys in 1885 (*www.picturethepast.org.gov*)

At its peak in the 1950s The Butterley Company employed around 10,000 people but a decade later the 1965 closure of the Codnor Park works was a precursor of harder times to come, eventually leading to the eventual collapse of the firm, as described earlier in this chapter.

The Stanton ironworks, situated to the south of Ilkeston close to the village of Stanton-by-Dale, traced their roots back to 1846 when Benjamin Smith and his son Josiah erected three blast furnaces alongside the Nutbrook Canal, which had been built in 1796 to exploit the coal measures in the Shipley area.

Percy Wilson, foundry general manager at Stanton, pictured in 1936 relighting one of the two1928-built blast furnaces at Old Works. Wilson was an important figure in the history of the Stanton Company from the 1920s until the mid-1950s and was particularly associated with the successful introduction of the iron pipe spinning process (*www.picturethepast.org.gov*)

From those original furnaces, capable of producing just 20 tons of pig iron a day, grew an industrial site which at its peak was the district's largest manufacturing concern and its biggest employer, with some 7,000 people on the payroll.

The Derbyshire industrial tradition includes evidence of ironmaking in the area in mediaeval times and of a blast furnace operating in the area between Stanton by Dale and Dale Abbey for a brief period in the late 18th century.

The Stanton business was taken over by the Crompton family in the mid-19th century, who owned the concern for more than 80 years. The business, re-named as The Stanton Ironworks Company Ltd in the early 20th century, benefitted from the demand for iron created by the Franco-Prussian War of 1870 and the works expanded rapidly, extending its boundaries to also line the banks of the Erewash Canal.

The years following World War Two saw Stanton's fortunes fluctuate, with nationalisation, privatisation and

The Iron Dale. Stanton New Works, pictured circa 1954, with the slopes of the Erewash Valley in the background. St Helen's church at Trowell is visible to the right of the three blast furnaces. The centre furnace was taken down in the early 1960s after experimentation with crushed coal as a fuel failed live up to expectations. It was never rebuilt. (Information supplied by Stephen Flinders) (*Derby City Council and www.picturethepast.org.gov*).

Making a template for the manufacture of car bodies, at the Stanton Ironworks Company's Riddings Foundry. Three workmen are pictured in 1946, guiding a sand core into the bottom half of the mould, on the casting floor ((*www.picturethepast.org.gov*)

Finished products from Stanton leaving the works branch to join the Erewash Valley mainline. Stanton Gate station is in the background. The conical slag tips to the top left of the picture gained the nickname of a particular part of the anatomy of a 1950s celebrity (*Derby City Council and www.picturethepast.org.uk*).

re-nationalisation taking place. Nationalised under the Attlee Labour government , the company was privatised when the Conservatives returned to power and eventually was taken over by Stewarts and Lloyds Ltd and merged with the Staveley Iron and Chemical Co Ltd in 1960 to form Stanton and Staveley.

In 1967 Stewarts and Lloyds became part of the nationalised British Steel Corporation, During a second privatisation, Stanton in the early 1980s became part of the French Pont-a-Mousson Group and later part of Saint Gobain. Production wound down during the 1990s and eventually stopped on May 24, 2007, when the last pipe was made.

Another essential component of the iron making and foundry industry in the Erewash Valley was the development of Riddings Ironworks, opened in the early years of the 19th century by Derby ironfounder James Oakes and his partners, utilising the Pinxton Arm branch of the Cromford Canal for transportation.

James Oakes became sole owner of the Riddings works in 1818, buying out his former partners and throughout the 19th century he and his family greatly expanded their industrial holdings to include several collieries. In 1888 they established the Riddings and District Gas Company, in partnership with The Butterley Company, to produce tar, sulphuric acid and other chemicals.

The Riddings works is claimed to be the mid-19th century site of experiments carried out into the behaviour of coke-fired blast furnaces by the German chemist Robert Bunsen, famous for giving his name to the Bunsen burner.

Stanton pipes being loaded into narrowboats at a recently-commisioned wharf on the surviving section of the Nutbrook Canal, in 1938. An Andrew Barclay 0-4-0 crane tank locomotive is lowering pipes into the Grand Union Carrying Company's boat 'Corvus' and Fellows Morton and Clayton boats are also visible. Traffic ceased on this section in 1949 (*www.picturethepast.org.gov*)

Lacemaking and Hosiery

A modern lace mill in Long Eaton, pictured in the early 20th century (*Derbyshire Local Studies Libraries and www.picturethepast.org.uk*).

Colliers occupy a position of vast and unarguable importance in the industrial heritage of the Erewash Valley. Yet the story of a smaller but no less distinctive group of skilled workers is nevertheless well worth telling.

With the complete demise of Britain's deep mining industry, there are today no underground workers in the Erewash Valley. Thankfully, the twisthand, the aristocrat of the lace industry, still clings to his craft. That the skill is still practised in this country is thanks to a prime example of the aforementioned adaptability of the valley's industrialists and entrepreneurs.

Levers (the original spelling, although later the alternative form of Leavers was often used) lace is the branch of the product used in high fashion, the machine equivalent of traditional hand-made lace, previously a luxury product beyond the reach of most pockets.

Although John Heathcoat, from Duffield in Derbyshire, invented the bobbin-net machine, the springboard for transforming a cottage industry into a factory-based trade, his machine produced only plain net and was unsuitable for making the much-coveted patterned lace.

In 1813, four years after Heathcoat's first breakthrough, John Lever invented a lace machine on which net could be formed without the need for a traversing. It then took 20 years to discover a satisfactory method of thread control, essential in the making of patterned lace.

This complementary invention was the work of the Frenchman Jacquard who devised a machinery modification that utilised a punched card device to make possible the mechanically patterned lace which was adopted enthusiastically by the clothing industry.

All the artistry and variety of hand-made lace was now brought within the scope of machine mass manufacture. Mass production of patterned lace for trimmings, dresses and curtains was now possible.

Because most of the development work in the lace industry was carried out in the Nottingham area, machine-made lace as a whole had become widely known by the generic term of Nottingham lace. The warp, plain net and curtain branches of the trade were to continue to be centred in the city but, because manufacturers in Nottingham were plagued by industrial disputes, Levers lace, the product at the fashion end of the market, was to be centred in the lower Erewash Valley.

The great movement of the Levers trade from Nottingham, to Long Eaton in particular, on the Derbyshire bank of the River Erewash, followed major disputes over wage rates in the city, culminating in the damaging strikes of 1873-74 and of 1889.

There was already a tradition of small-scale lace making in the Erewash Valley, and as early as 1830 bobbin lace manufacturers were recorded as operating hand-powered machines in small workshops in Long Eaton.

Lace mending at Long Eaton (*Derbyshire Local Studies Libraries and www.picturethepast.org.uk*)

This small nucleus gradually increased, and by the early 1840s William Bush, who is thought to have moved from nearby Beeston, set up business in Long Eaton and built a lace factory in

Main Street, where his machines were driven by steam power. By the mid-19th century increasing mechanisation helped Long Eaton develop into the true centre of the Levers lace trade. The town prospered on lace, with the population increasing more than tenfold between 1851 and 1901.

Although wages, at least initially, were lower than those demanded in the city of Nottingham, skilled twist hands, card punchers and lace mechanics moved into the town to take advantage of the work opportunities and the ready availability of living accommodation.

In 1891 125 firms were established in Long Eaton, the vast majority manufacturing Levers lace and by 1905 around 800 machines and 1,200 twist hands were at work in the town and its surrounding area. In the years from 1900 to the outbreak of World War One in 1914, lace and the people who earned their living from the trade, generally prospered.

The manufacturers flaunted their wealth by building impressive new houses, often situated on the main roads leading out of the town. One of the finest surviving houses from the era is Red Court, on the Derby Road in the more fashionable west end of Long Eaton. The grade II-listed property was designed by local architect Osborne Moorhouse Thorp in the then fashionable Arts and Crafts style, for lace manufacturer William Johnson, and completed in 1910.

Springfield Mill, built by the Hooley family by the side of the Erewash Canal at Sandiacre (*Author*).

The fundamental process in John Heathcoat's original machine was twisting and the machine operator became known as a twisthand. An Erewash Valley legend was born. Twisthands were true aristocrats of the working class, ranking on a par with coal face workers in the mining industry and locomotive footplatemen (generally known in the Erewash valley as enginemen).

During the heyday of the lace trade the twisthand in the factory was always a man. During that era the employment of women would have aroused serious opposition from the men and, in any case was precluded because of the then legal prohibition of women undertaking night work.

The duties of the twisthand included the supervision of the threading of the Levers machine, work consisting of putting thousands of warp and spool threads through eyelets and their respective guide bars, and in adjusting the pattern cards, prepared by the draughtsman from the original design, which effectively drove the machine.

When the machine was working it required constant supervision; broken threads must be tied, empty bobbins replaced, and any imperfection in the pattern detected and adjusted. The twisthands jealously guarded their craft skills and their privileges, which included exerting a considerable influence on who entered their trade.

When the lace trade was prosperous, the skilled operatives had money to spend as the publicans of the growing towns and villages of the valley found to their benefit. Such was the prestige of a twisthand when the lace trade was on the crest of a wave that some public houses had bars reserved for their use alone, with signs on the doors warning lesser mortals that the room was for 'twisthands only'.

Right up until the last quarter of the 20th century a good twisthand could command a job in any lace centre. His skills were at a premium not just in the Erewash Valley, Nottingham and elsewhere in Great Britain. The United States established a considerable lace industry in the 20th century, often based on machines built in Long Eaton and exported, sometimes when they were made redundant by one of the frequent slumps in the UK trade.

A fine example of a rags to riches story concerned Jim Beattie, employed as a trainee in a local mill in the early 1900s, who became a lace industry tycoon in the United States. He prospered in a fast growing American lace industry, eventually owning several factories and became a major figure in the American horse racing world, training thoroughbreds on the four ranches he owned.

In 1965 Beattie embarked in New York on board the liner Queen Elizabeth. Ostensibly his purpose was to visit family in the East Midlands, but the trip may have also have been designed to test the willingness of skilled lace operatives in the Erewash Valley to follow his lead and emigrate to the States.

Sadly, Beattie, who was 75 years of age, was taken seriously ill just before the Queen Elizabeth docked in Southampton, and was taken to hospital in the south coast port, where he died. Perhaps not quite by coincidence, his trip had coincided with a warning by a major figure in the industry that the lure of high wages for twisthands and other skilled operatives in America could damage the British lace industry.

Bill Pegg, himself a manufacturer, and a scion of a family long established in the industry, was President of the British Leavers Lace Manufacturers Association. At a time when recruitment to the Erewash Valley lace trade was difficult enough, with newspaper advertisements offering top wages to the right men, he told a television interviewer that for a manufacturer with between ten and twelve Levers machines, losing just one twisthand to America would affect the firm's ability to fulfil its orders.

Tim Johnson at Cluny Lace in Ilkeston, working on a Levers lace machine (*Author*).

The very inventiveness that had enabled lace manufacture to become industrialised also produced individuals and companies able to develop and manufacture machinery of the highest standard. These companies, Wallis and Longden, Longmire and Spridgeon, sold their products not only to the local market but also exported to international rivals in the industry - thereby sowing some of the seeds of the international competition which eventually led to the virtual demise of the home industry.

No retrospective look at the Erewash Valley lace industry would be complete without mentioning the small but significant part the trade played in the literary work of D H Lawrence.

Lawrence makes reference to the lace trade in *The Rainbow*, in which a member of the Brangwen farming family breaks away from the land to become first a lace draughtsman and later a fully-fledged designer in Nottingham – a role which, Lawrence says, makes him 'almost a gentleman'.

Lace designers needed to possess both technical knowledge and artistic ability. True to form, the painstaking, intensely-detailed tasks of both draughtsman and designer were not to the taste of the free-spirit in the novelist. He described the work as drudgery, which 'stole the soul of the Brangwen man'.

Lawrence described how Brangwen's hand, when drawing, was naturally inclined to swing in big, bold lines. It was torture for the man to 'pedgill' away at the lace designing, constantly counting and plotting on the squared paper.

The Levers lace trade is still alive in the Erewash Valley, thanks to what amounts to an industrial revolution in reverse.

The last company to manufacture lace of any kind in Long Eaton, Grangers in New Tythe Street, closed down in 2001, Levers lace is still produced in Ilkeston by Cluny Lace Ltd. The firm occupies the old Tatham's factory in Belper Street, built at the turn of the 19th century, and which in the past was shared by Levers lace manufacture and needle-making.

Pete Sewell, the oldest twisthand in Britain, at two weeks older than his colleague Ian Palfreymen. Both men started work in the lace trade on the same day in 1965 (*Author*).

The revolutionary aspect of the company's continued existence lies in the fact that its owners, realising that their firm was unable to match international competition in the popular market, sold its modern equipment and bought traditional machines, some more than a hundred years old, and embarked on a successful new era catering for a niche market in quality decorative lace.

The factory is now owned and managed by the eighth and ninth generations of the Mason family. Director Sheila Mason is acknowledged as one of the leading authorities on the history of the lace trade.

The Mason family was already established as framework knitters and flax dressers by the 1730s and started making lace when this fabric was first produced by machines in the 1760s.

Cluny Lace has built up a data bank of hundreds of lace patterns and by combining the best of old traditions with new technology, the firm is able to produce a wide range of exquisite designs of Levers Cluny style lace. Many of the lace patterns still used today were designed and draughted by Frank Maltby Mason and Francis Bowler Mason, the sixth and seventh generations of the family. No other manufacturer in the world produces the same range of patterns and these patterns are unique to Cluny Lace.

The 16 Levers machines operated by Cluny Lace have an interesting history of their own. When the lace trade modernised many older machines were exported. Machines running in Belper Street, Ilkeston today were, in some cases, repatriated by the Mason family. "We survive by adapting', says Sheila Mason.

The decline of lace making has left employees of Cluny Lace claiming a unique distinction.

In the summer of 1965 two fifteen-year-olds left Derby Road Boys School in Long Eaton to join an industry which had been the lifeblood of the town and of the lower Erewash Valley for more than a century. Pete Sewell and Ian 'Polly' Palfreman were following in the footsteps of thousands of young men and women as they began careers in what was still a thriving industry, albeit smaller in terms of the number of companies and employees than in its heyday.

The two youngsters worked their way up steadily from being trainees to the status of skilled twisthands in the Levers branch of the trade. They were the heirs to a long tradition.

Today, Pete and Ian are no longer part of a large fraternity of craftsman in a flourishing trade. Both past normal retirement age, they are part of a tiny group of seven men and one woman entitled to the name of twisthand, keeping their skill alive and making possible Cluny Lace's unique position in the British textile industry.

Both men, and their younger colleagues at Cluny Lace, are well aware of their rarity value. As Pete Sewell says: "I am two weeks older than Polly, so I suppose that makes me the oldest twisthand in the country. After more than half a century working in the lace trade, I was headhunted by the Mason family when the company decided to go back to traditional methods of making lace."

Like Pete Sewell and Ian Palfreyman, one of the younger twisthands at Cluny Lace, Tim Johnson, lives in Long Eaton. He has been in the lace trade for 20 years, also working for Charm Lace, E & A Reynolds and Grangers. A great-grandfather was a twisthand.

Tim started work as a presser at Grangers at the age of 17 but left the trade for a 15-year period, as the industry started to slip into almost terminal decline. "Cluny Lace has given me the opportunity to return to lace making and now that I am back, I am not planning to be going anywhere else in a hurry.

"The job is really creative and that's what I have always enjoyed the most about lace-making."

Concentrating on Hosiery

A study in employee concentration at hosiery firm Aristoc's Heanor works in the 1950s. Aristoc was founded in 1919 to make fully-fashioned stockings. The company was acquired by Courtaulds in the 1960s and production later moved to Belper. The Heanor factory site was demolished in 2002. Although perhaps lacking the glamour of the lace industry, hosiery and lingerie firms (including Charnos of Ilkeston) employed thousands of workpeople *(Heanor Local History Society)*

Furniture Manufacture

Visitors to Long Eaton are now greeted at entrances to the district by signs proclaiming that it is now the UK Centre of Quality Upholstery Manufacture.

The town's predominant position in the industry, long known to those closely involved in the field, is now being proclaimed to a wider public, courtesy of Long Eaton Chamber of Trade.

Michael Lucking, secretary of the Chamber, says Long Eaton's economy has been fortunate in that the rise of furniture and upholstery manufacture, first established towards the end of the 19th century, really took off at a time when the dominant lace trade was starting its long decline.

The roots of the industry locally can be traced back to the final decade of the 19th century, when the company which became the Lace Web Spring Company was founded in Sandiacre by J E Marshall. The firm used Marshall's patented revolutionary spring units, which supplanted the previously individually attached springs.

Over the subsequent decades a large number of companies were founded, establishing the area's reputation for quality and innovation.

Michael Lucking explains: "When the Long Eaton furniture industry was beginning, a few experienced workers were recruited from Lace Web and elsewhere, but the majority of the operatives were young people, many of them school leavers.

Upholstery, hosiery, knitwear, and lingerie manufacturing skills are cherished in Long Eaton, as demonstrated by Sharon Kokins. *(Long Eaton Chamber of Trade)*.

"While this did not directly help the town's redundant skilled lace makers, it did help to prevent large scale unemployment at a difficult stage in the town's development. Although some of the original companies have either ceased trading or have been sold to new owners, several are now into the second and third generation of family ownership."

Mr Lucking adds: "Today there are no fewer than 50 companies involved in furniture manufacturing or allied industries in the district, and much of what is made locally finds a public through quality retailers that are household names both nationally and often internationally.

"In addition to furniture for private homes, the Long Eaton manufacturers are represented in hotels throughout the world and in many British and foreign embassies."

A significant pointer to Long Eaton's status in the trade is the fact the main trade exhibition to promote high quality furniture staged in the UK, Long Point, takes place twice a year in the town, and attracts buyers from across the globe.

Long Eaton is also home to permanent offices and showrooms created by furniture manufacturers from elsewhere in Britain, taking advantage of the Erewash Valley town's reputation.

Today the upholstery and furniture industry in the Erewash Valley employs up to 6,000 people, with around 2,700 based in Long Eaton.

The annual turnover of the Long Eaton-based companies is more than £250 million.

Prospects for the industry's future continue to be bright, and Long Eaton manufacturers are safeguarding the future supply of skilled workers by maintaining WEBS Training, the main UK training centre for the trade, three miles from the town, in Beeston.

The inauguration of the signs promoting Long Eaton's status as the UK's centre of quality furniture and upholstery production. Pictured left-to right are Michael Lucking, chairman Long Eaton Chamber of Trade, Councillor Michael Powell (Lead member for Regeneration and Planning, Erewash Borough Council), Councillor Chris Corbett , then leader of Erewash Borough Council, and Andrew J Mitchell of Artistic Upholstery *(Long Eaton Chamber of Trade)*

Chapter Three

The Valley as a Literary Landscape

'The most familiar landscape in (Lawrence's) stories lay just above Moorgreen, stretching towards Underwood – the farm fields known as Greasley Haggs and the patch of woodland to the west. This is the true Lawrence Country, the setting of Sons and Lovers and many of the early stories' – Harry T Moore in The Intelligent Heart, The Story of D H Lawrence, 1954.

David Herbert Lawrence, gazing down from the heights of the pantheon reserved for literary giants, would no doubt be bemused and perhaps not a little irritated by the manner in which his home town of Eastwood has belatedly embraced his fame.

Lawrence's literary reputation nationally and worldwide has experienced continual ups and downs since the writer's death in 1930. His present-day status, say the *bien pensant,* has not been helped by feminist criticism of the way he represented women in his work, which is largely taken up with the relationship between the sexes.

Whatever the world at large might have said about Lawrence in the past, for good or for ill, the attitude of the majority of the citizens of the Erewash Valley mining town has quite simply veered from apathy to outright hostility.

In 1963, when Penguin Books were (unsuccessfully) prosecuted under the Obscene Publications Act 1959 for publishing *Lady Chatterley's Lover*, the author's most controversial but by no means his finest novel, the Lawrence admirer on a literary pilgrimage to Eastwood would have had a fairly thin time of it.

At a time when Lawrence's genius, his motives and his morality were daily debated in Number One Court at The Old Bailey, with the court proceedings splashed across the columns of both the serious broadsheets and the tabloids, the literary pilgrim would have had to struggle to find much acknowledgment of his very existence in his home town.

Directions to the author's birthplace and the subsequent Lawrence family homes in the town would have been given, although in some instances grudgingly. Evidence of his years in Eastwood and subsequent fame and notoriety would have been found mostly in the staid setting of the public library.

Compared to the almost cult status accorded to other literary figures on their native heaths, Eastwood did very little to even acknowledge that the small Erewash Valley town had been both the birthplace and the early inspiration for a man widely considered, like him or loathe him, to have been one of the most influential writers of the 20th century.

It is hardly necessary to repeat here the huge changes that have taken place in English society since that autumn of the Chatterley trial, the moment in time

David Herbert Lawrence, as a young man (*Manuscripts and Special Collections, The University of Nottingham*).

Lawrence's birthplace at Victoria Street, Eastwood (*Author*).

immortalised by the poet Philip Larkin when he wrote, *'sexual intercourse began in 1963, (which was rather late for me), between the end of the Chatterley ban and the Beatles first LP'.*

Change has come to Eastwood too, with complete decimation of the mining industry on which the town lived and breathed (or coughed, given the prevalence of bronchial disease among the colliers) throughout Lawrence's lifetime.

The town centre is dominated today by a vast superstore and its attendant car park, from where sheep can be seen grazing on what before reclamation was a grimy pit bank. It is a huge contrast to a town dominated in the late 19th and early 20th century by the all-embracing Co-operative stores and the tiny market at the point where the main roads from Nottingham and Derby, Ilkeston and Mansfield met, and where Lawrence's mother Lydia (and her fictional counterpart in *Sons and Lovers*, Gertrude Morel) loved to shop and haggle with the stall holders.

Today both 'official' Eastwood, in the guise of local authorities and literary societies, and 'commercial' Eastwood, in the shape of a variety of businesses, have decided that 'Young Bert' can bring both kudos and cash to the community.

The writer would probably at least regard with tolerance the concept of the birthplace museum, the murals, the greatly extended collection of material in the public library, and the innovative town trail that links his birthplace, his family's subsequent homes in the town and other sites of Lawrence interest.

He would probably be less impressed with the various cafes, pubs and other businesses which today trade on his name.

The present-day seeker after Lawrence's memory can enjoy a coffee and cake at The White Peacock, close to the birthplace museum, while those in search of a full English breakfast, a juicy steak and a pint of real ale can satisfy their appetites in The Lady Chatterley, the Eastwood branch of the excellent JD Wetherspoon pub chain.

Even so, there is evidence that, outside the relatively undemanding task of attaching the name of the author or one of his literary works to a commercial enterprise, keeping Lawrence's memory fresh in Eastwood can still be a challenge.

The Lawrence family photographed in the Phillips and Freckleton Studio, Market Place, Nottingham. Pictured are back row, left to right, Emily, George and Ernest, front row, left to right, Ada, Mrs Lydia Lawrence, David Herbert, and Arthur Lawrence (*Nottingham City Council and www.picturethepast.org.uk*).

The view across the countryside, photographed in 1960, was little changed from the days when Lawrence was growing up in Victoria Street, Eastwood (*Manuscripts and Special Collection, The University of Nottingham*).

This author's own most recent literary pilgrimage to Eastwood, undertaken after a gap of many years, got off to a disappointing start.

Approaching the town from the direction of the former pit village of Brinsley, where Lawrence's father worked underground, it was with considerable anticipation that I pulled into the car park of Durban House, once the offices of the local coal-owning company, Barber Walker and, since 1998, the home of the Lawrence Heritage Centre.

I was looking forward to re-visiting what at the time of its launch had been regarded as ushering in a new era of appreciation of Lawrence locally, as well as a target for attracting both literary pilgrims and general tourists, from overseas especially, to an area badly in need of a new economic base to replace its rapidly disappearing traditional industries.

Back in 1998 I had been a guest at the official opening of the Centre, representing The University of Nottingham, an organisation that, as a belated acknowledgment to its former student, had donated a significant sum of money to the costs of funding the creation of what was to be Eastwood's major contribution to the then emerging Lawrence heritage industry.

Any feelings of optimism I may have harboured driving into Eastwood soon disintegrated. The car park at Durban House seemed strangely deserted and I began to have my doubts as to whether the place was open for business.

A glance at a notice in a window near the main entrance to the landmark building confirmed my growing suspicion; the Heritage Centre was indeed no more.

Closure was first mooted in the autumn of 2015 by the body running the Centre, Broxtowe Borough Council. The authority claimed it would save £80,000 a year – an important contribution, in an age of austerity, to what was then its overall savings target of £3.5million.

The council's decision caused a considerable amount of embarrassment which, to be honest, is an emotion never very far removed in the Erewash Valley and Nottingham from almost anything to do with the controversial Lawrence.

The red faces were largely as a result of the closure move more or less coinciding with UNESCO's decision to nominate Nottingham as an international 'City of Literature'. Arts Council England duly came up with a cash injection of £20,000 to fund a study to look at the future of the centre and to ascertain whether or not it could be kept open.

The great and the good flocked to support the moves to keep the Heritage Centre open. Oscar winner Glenda Jackson, star of the cinema version of Lawrence's novel *Women in Love* joined Oscar nominee Rosamund Pike in signing a letter criticising the attempt to close it, and the campaign won the backing of local MP Gloria De Piero.

The eventual answer, nevertheless, was negative. In April 2016, shortly before my visit, the Centre closed. The 'talking exhibits' of the life and times of D H Lawrence, unveiled with great enthusiasm and optimism a couple of years before the Millennium, had finally fallen silent after a lifespan of just 18 years.

Perhaps the best-known of the objects previously housed in the centre were the actual copies of *Lady Chatterley's Lover*, used in court during the 1960 trial, court proceedings that many today regard as one of the prime factors which opened the door to extensive social liberalisation in the 'swinging sixties'.

The great irony surrounding the Heritage Centre at Durban House centres around the fact that the building itself was loathed by D H Lawrence himself.

Durban House, built in 1896, a year after Lawrence's birth, is situated on Mansfield Road, just a short walk from the author's birthplace in Eastwood town centre.

The Lawrence family's third Eastwood home, in The Breach (*Author*).

As the headquarters of the colliery-owning company (Barber Walker in reality, Carston Waite and Company in *Sons and Lovers*) that dominated the town, it was the place where wages were paid weekly to the colliers. The novel recounts in detail how the young Paul Morel (Bert Lawrence), suffering as he did from acute shyness, hated having to queue with the bantering miners and their offspring, excited by the prospect of the drinking which for many of them was the inevitable conclusion of pay-day.

After the disappointment of finding the Lawrence Heritage Centre defunct, the author's day in Eastwood improved dramatically. Just a step away from the superstore and its attendant modern road network is what can perhaps best be described as a D H Lawrence quarter.

Situated in a block of terraced streets clustered on the hillside on which the town stands, with similar views of the surrounding countryside (minus the pit tips) to those which would have been available in the author's days in Eastwood, the compact district contains the D H Lawrence Birthplace Museum, which incorporates the writer's actual birthplace at 8a Victoria Street, and an adjoining property which includes a gift shop.

The Birthplace Museum, with friendly and knowledgeable staff, has effectively assumed the mantle of the defunct Heritage Centre and is linked to the three other homes where the Lawrence family lived in Eastwood, and other relevant sites, by what Eastwood can fairly claim as a world first, the blue line trail.

Modelled on the famous red-line Freedom Trail in Boston USA, which links sites connected with the early events in that city connected with the American War of Independence, the blue line on the footpaths of the former mining town leads the visitor to many of the places associated with the author's early life.

Many reasons have been advanced over the years for Eastwood's decided coolness towards its most distinguished son. Lawrence's often unsympathetic treatment of the culture of the mineworkers in general and of his father Arthur in particular, in the autobiographical *Sons & Lovers*, which effectively damned the reasons for the town's very existence was not surprisingly, badly received in Eastwood.

The novel's dismissal of Arthur Lawrence, in the character of Walter Morel, as a hard-drinking, half illiterate collier, often teetering on the verge of violence towards his sensitive, southern, educated and pious wife, did not go down well with the neighbours and acquaintances of the writer's family, nor with the wider community.

Many contemporaries of the Lawrence family recalled Arthur Lawrence as being a generally decent man, at least by the standards of the time, and a skilled miner who, far from being feckless, was a good provider.

The offices of Barber Walker and Co Ltd, Eastwood's principal colliery company, which was later the home of the (now closed) D H Lawrence Heritage Centre (*Author*).

D H LAWRENCE – A LIFE

David Herbert Richards 'D H' Lawrence was the fourth of five children of Arthur and Lydia Lawrence. Arthur Lawrence was an Erewash Valley coalminer, who went down the pit at the age of ten and is usually dismissively described as a dialect speaker, a drinker and virtually illiterate.

In contrast Lydia, who spent much of her early life in the south of England, is generally presented as being a superior person, educated, refined and pious, ill at ease among the other miner's wives in Eastwood.

These impressions were certainly fostered by the writer himself, particularly in the autobiographical novel *Sons and Lovers*.

Lydia Lawrence worked hard to prevent her three sons from following their father into the pit. The young David Herbert – 'Young Bert' – first attended Beauvale Board School, before winning a scholarship to Nottingham High School. He left school at the age of 16 to earn a living as a clerk in a Nottingham surgical appliances factory, giving up the job when he contracted pneumonia.

Whilst recovering from the illness, he began visiting Haggs Farm near Underwood, close to Eastwood. This was the home of the Chambers family, with whom Mrs Lawrence was acquainted. Lawrence never returned to the world of commerce, instead studying for a teaching certificate at University College Nottingham, the predecessor institution to the present University of Nottingham. He later taught at a school in Croydon, in Surrey.

Jessie, the daughter of the Chambers family, was a major influence on Lawrence. She encouraged him to draft his first novel, *The White Peacock*, and submitted a short story of his to the *Nottingham Guardian* newspaper. Despite the relationship with Lawrence being a difficult one, Jessie spared no effort to promote his literary career, sending some of his poetry to the editor of *The English Review*, which began to publish his work.

Lawrence's contact with the *Review* opened the door to meetings with other writers and critics. *The White Peacock* was recommended to the firm of Heinemann, who published the novel in 1911, soon after some major events in the author's life; the death of his mother and his final break with Jessie. His second novel *The Trespasser* , attracted the interest of an influential editor, Edward Garnett, who arranged for his own firm, Duckworth, to acquire and publish *Sons and Lovers*, the work that established the author's reputation.

Lawrence's major life-changing event proved to be a meeting with Frieda Weekley, the German-born wife of Ernest Weekley, his former Professor of Modern Languages at University College Nottingham. Six years older than Lawrence and with three children from her marriage to Weekley, Frieda was a distant member of an aristocratic German family, the von Richtofens and her cousin was the German pilot and air ace, Baron Manfred von Richthofen, also known as the Red Baron.

The couple eloped, going first to Germany and then to Italy, where the writer completed *Sons and Lovers*. They were married in 1914, following Frieda's divorce. During World War One Lawrence and Frieda lived in England, in Cornwall, Derbyshire, and in London, often in poverty and under suspicion of espionage.

The war years nevertheless saw Lawrence writing at his best, producing more powerful work, focusing on the complex relationships between the sexes like *Sons and Lovers* and again being mainly set in the Erewash Valley. The work was split into two novels, *The Rainbow,* which was immediately suppressed as obscene, and *Women in Love*, which was not published until 1920.

In 1919 the couple returned to Italy and Lawrence, despite occasional visits, was never again to live in England. A nomadic life saw spells in Ceylon (now Sri Lanka), Australia and, eventually, New Mexico, where the couple settled for a while in Taos. By this time Lawrence had been diagnosed with tubercolosis.

The dying Lawrence moved to the South of France. He died at Vence in 1930 and was at first buried there. His ashes were removed to Taos in 1935.

His most controversial novel, *Lady Chatterley's Lover*, was privately published in 1928. The book had a cat and mouse tussle with the legal authorities in the Anglo-Saxon world, until court cases in New York (1959) and London (1960) made it freely available to the public.

Haggs Farm, home of the Chambers family and Lawrence's retreat from life in Eastwood during his youth (*George L Roberts and www.picturethepast.org.uk*).

One of the most scathing criticisms of Lawrence's attitude to his father in recent years has come from the former cabinet minister and Conservative politician Kenneth Clarke who , as related in Chapter One, *Defining the Valley*, grew up in Aldercar and Langley Mill, just down the hill from Eastwood and across the River Erewash in Derbyshire.

Clarke's published memories of a childhood in an industrial community are reasonably kind to the area. Aldercar, he says, was 'the rural end' of Langley Mill, and young Ken enjoyed watching films at the local cinema, which his father managed, and watched Aldercar Football Club and the Langley Mill Cricket Club.

But although his reminiscences of his early life in a closed, almost entirely working class community are, for the most part positive, considerable vitriol is reserved for Lawrence and in particular for the author's depiction of his parents.

Clarke is doing no more than express, in a more articulate manner, the thoughts of so many people of Eastwood in past generations, when he writes of Lawrence's father: "Old man Lawrence was a marvellous individual and highly popular."

Lawrence's mother Lydia, however, gets both barrels as Clarke adds: "They all deplored (Arthur's) stuck-up and snobbish wife."

Kenneth Clarke's father had friends who knew Lawrence, but regarded him as 'a prickle on their town's history'.

Similar comments were made by a man who knew the Lawrence family particularly well. David Chambers was the brother of Jessie Chambers, Miriam of *Sons and Lovers*, and later became Professor of Economic History at The University of Nottingham.

Interviewed in 1960, Professor Chambers said: "We had very little sympathy for Mrs Lawrence. She felt herself superior to her husband and was jealous of Jessie. Mr Lawrence, although he drank, was a very respected man."

(Left): Jessie Chambers (*Manuscripts and Special Collections, The University of Nottingham*).

(Right): The Chambers family had fields close to Greasley Church, where Lawrence helped with the haymaking (*Author*).

The parish church of St Mary, Greasley, set in what Lawrence described as 'The Country of My Heart. The author cherished memories of the area throughout his life (*Author*).

Another factor in the cold shoulder turned towards Lawrence in Eastwood and the Erewash Valley, both during his lifetime and for decades after, was his extensive use of local characters, usually disguised in only the thinnest of manners, in his novels and short stories.

Lawrence used his work to take revenge on those he disliked, carrying on a particular vendetta against members of the Barber Walker family, the dominant local coal owners.

Moorgreen Reservoir, Nethermere in Lawrence's works (Author).

The idea persisted for decades (and perhaps still persists to a degree today) that Lawrence, despite his protestations that the still highly attractive Nottinghamshire countryside around Eastwood was the true 'country of my heart,' had done little to enhance the reputation of the district.

Lawrence's elopement with Frieda Weekley, allied to the increasingly explicit sexual nature of his work, would also have counted against Lawrence in a tightly nonconformist community.

Despite much national and international critical acclaim, both during his lifetime and after his death in 1930, Lawrence's reputation both as a man and as a literary figure is today not much higher in Nottingham than in Eastwood.

His often unflattering portrait of the commercial and cultural life of the city and his poetic dismissal of the Queen of the Midlands as 'that dismal town where I went to school and college' contributes to the overall feeling that the novelist was not altogether worthy of local worship.

It was certainly not just the slighted inhabitants of Eastwood and the Erewash Valley who had a low opinion of Lawrence. The website for one of the country's premier independent book sellers, the excellent Scarthin Books of Cromford, contains an amusing D H Lawrence gossip column.

Claiming that Lawrence is now little read in England except by literature students, it cites among other evidence the company's own experience at the book fair staged in Nottingham to mark the author's centenary, which attracted just 30 visitors a day.

The original home of University College Nottingham, where Lawrence studied for a teaching certificate. The building is now part of Nottingham Trent University (*Author*).

Lawrence was taught at University College Nottingham by the Professor of Modern Languages, Ernest Weekley, pictured second from right, with his wife Frieda by his side and his parents to his right. Lawrence later eloped with Frieda and eventually married her. The photograph was taken in London in 1910 (*Nottingham City Council and www.picturethepast.org.uk*).

Church Cottage in Cossall, Anna Brangwen's honeymoon cottage in 'Cossethay', in *The Rainbow* (*Author*).

At least the attitude of The University of Nottingham, successor institution to University College Nottingham, where the young Lawrence studied for a teaching certificate in the first decade of the 20th century, has improved substantially. The attitude on campus was, for several decades after Lawrence's death, often rather frosty.

The treatment of Weekley by Lawrence and Frieda certainly grated with the academics at what was then University College Nottingham. Ernest Weekley outlived Lawrence, living until 1954, and was a respected and well-liked member of the academic community.

The University's attitude towards one of its most famous former students (not graduates, as Lawrence was awarded a certificate and not a degree, lacking the knowledge of Latin required at the time to graduate) did eventually thaw.

Lawrence, typically, did not always display a 'how to win friends and influence people' attitude, either towards Eastwood or to his alma mater.

When the University embarked on its move from the city centre to the University Park campus at Highfields in the 1920s – an enterprise largely funded by Sir Jesse Boot, founder of The Boots Company (and another bête noire of Young Bert) – Lawrence wrote a sarcastic poem, with digs at Boot, the College and the City, summed up in the line 'in Nottingham, that dismal town, where I went to school and college'.

The University of Nottingham is now the leading centre for the study of Lawrence, as is entirely appropriate. The D H Lawrence Research Centre was founded in 1991 with the aim of celebrating the work of Lawrence and promoting understanding of his life and legacy both within and outside academia.

One of Lawrence's best-known short stories is *Tickets Please!*, set on the long-closed tramway route from Ripley via Codnor and Eastwood to Nottingham. The car is seen leaving Co-op Square, Ripley (*Wood Collection and www.picturethepast.org.uk*).

Beauvale Priory ruins (*Author*)

The Centre organises academic conferences, exhibitions and public events relating to Lawrence within the University, while also working alongside D H Lawrence heritage providers in Eastwood to showcase his importance for the local area.

Over the years the School of English at the University has led the way in Lawrence research; it has been home to several celebrated Lawrence scholars, including Vivian de Sola Pinto, James T. Boulton, Peter Preston and John Worthen (who remains Emeritus Professor of D H Lawrence Studies).

In addition the University's Department of Manuscripts and Special Collections on the King's Meadow Campus (the former Central Television studios) houses an outstanding collection of Lawrence manuscripts, first editions, letters and research materials.

The collection has been awarded Designated Status by The Museums, Libraries and Archives Council as being of outstanding national and international importance. Through the annual Journal of D H Lawrence Studies, which is edited in-house, the Centre also has firm links to the D H Lawrence Society in Eastwood and to the worldwide community of Lawrence scholars and enthusiasts.

A life-size statue of Lawrence in bronze, sculpted by Diana Thomson, was unveiled at the University Park campus in 1994. The statue, which depicts Lawrence holding a blue gentian flower – a nod to his poem *Bavarian Gentians* – was accepted by the University at a ceremony attended by members of the writer's wider family.

It is perhaps symptomatic of a University attitude to Lawrence that is still ambivalent that the campus authorities, not quite sure what to do with the statue, shifted it from its original home in the Arts Centre, a building open to the general public, to a couple of other sites before giving it a permanent home in a less prominent position.

The author of this volume is not a literary critic and is scarcely qualified to comment on Lawrence's status as novelist and poet, still less his ability as a painter.

It would be an absurdity to regard Lawrence primarily as a regional author; he skilfully used his experience of life in the Erewash Valley as a backdrop to what is often regarded as his central theme - a deep concern with the male-female relationship, in all its many aspects.

Literary appreciation is presumably valid on a variety of levels. It is surely not wrong to enjoy Lawrence's novels and short stories with an Erewash Valley setting for the sheer thrill of recognition, not only of landscape but of the character, mannerisms and attitudes of local people.

The entrance to the D H Lawrence birthplace museum, in Victoria Street, Eastwood (*Author*).

The White Peacock coffee shop, opposite the birthplace museum (*Author*).

Many of these character traits and mannerisms can be found in the district today, despite the huge changes society in general has undergone since the books were written. Sitting in pubs in Ilkeston and Heanor, listening to the conversation of local people, quite often has the ability to transport the listener back several decades.

Not everyone in Eastwood regarded Lawrence as 'that mucky man'. One of his closest friends was William Edward Hopkin, a prominent figure in the town's political and intellectual life, who with his wife Sallie played a role in moulding the views and attitudes of the young Lawrence – perhaps, especially, helping to foster the writer's disdain of local coal owners and landed gentry during an impressionable stage of his life.

Lawrence's commercial value is now fully recognised in Eastwood (*Author*).

Although the identity of the person upon whom the fictional Lady Chatterley was based has not been proven, there are those in Eastwood who believe she could have been linked to the Barber Walker family.

Hopkin was a leading member of the Congregationalist Literary Society and an active supporter of the Socialist Democratic Federation. He was a member of Eastwood Urban District council (the forerunner to the present Broxtowe council) for 45 years, a Justice of the Peace and a Nottinghamshire County Council alderman (See also Chapter Five, *The Changed Face of Valley Politics*)

D H Lawrence's influence is apparent to readers of two other working class authors from the Erewash Valley.

The most prominent of the two was Walter Brierley, who in 1935, when his most famous novel, *Means Test Man*, was published, was an unemployed miner living in the Derbyshire village of Waingroves, between Ripley and Codnor.

Brierley was the middle son of five brothers, who all worked down the pit. His father George worked as a winding engineman at Denby colliery for 45 years. Walter Brierley attended Waingroves school until the age of thirteen, at which age he started work at Waingroves pit, first on the surface and later underground.

In addition to working at the pit he attended continuation classes at Waingroves school, until the strike of 1921. During the strike the pit flooded and never re-opened. Walter was thrown out of work but later found another job underground at Denby. During this period he married and had a son, but by 1931 was once again unemployed.

The 'official' Lawrence Memorial, which echoes the author's Phoenix motif (*Author*).

Surely the ultimate, and perhaps the most inevitable, commercialisation of D H Lawrence. The popular JD Wetherspoon chain's Eastwood pub commemorates the writer's most notorious female character (*Author*).

Brierley was not bowed down by his unemployment, an aspect of his life that, when *Means Test Man* was published, to general acclaim, was to be the cause of a certain coolness on the part of the hard left. He continued as best he could to pursue an education, won a Miners' Welfare Scholarship to University College Nottingham and twice won the Arthur Markham Prize, donated for writing by a miner.

Brierley was helped to achieve publication of *Means Test Man* by members of the Birmingham Group, associated authors from the West Midlands, who wrote from the 1930s to the 1950s.

Although Walter wrote three more novels and many articles, he was unable to make a living as a full-time writer and in 1936 joined the Derby Education Authority as a welfare officer, working there until he retired in 1965. He died in 1972.

Means Test Man has been described as a portrayal of a coal miner humiliated by the means test and the effects of unemployment. The novel explores the effect of such a situation on a sensitive mind, and the pain and outrage experienced by the main character at the indignity of no longer having status or function in the community.

One of Walter Brierley's earlier works was published in a book called *Under Thirty, An Anthology* , edited by Michael Harrison. The book contains stories written by several authors before attaining their thirty first year.

Walter submitted a story called *Transition* which describes a young boy's last day at school and first day working down the pit. The story is based on Walter's own experience and describes life in Ripley (which he re-christens Pirley).

At the time of its publication, *Means Test Man* was considered to have a status and importance comparable to such classics with an economic and social background as Walter Greenwood's *Love on the Dole* and the American writer Upton Sinclair's *The Jungle*.

Whilst the two other works have been almost continuously in print since the 1930s, *Means Test Man* was forgotten and unavailable until re-published in 1983 by a publishing house, Spokesman, based in Nottingham.

The statue of D H Lawrence, holding a blue gentian, on the University Park Campus of The University of Nottingham (*Author*).

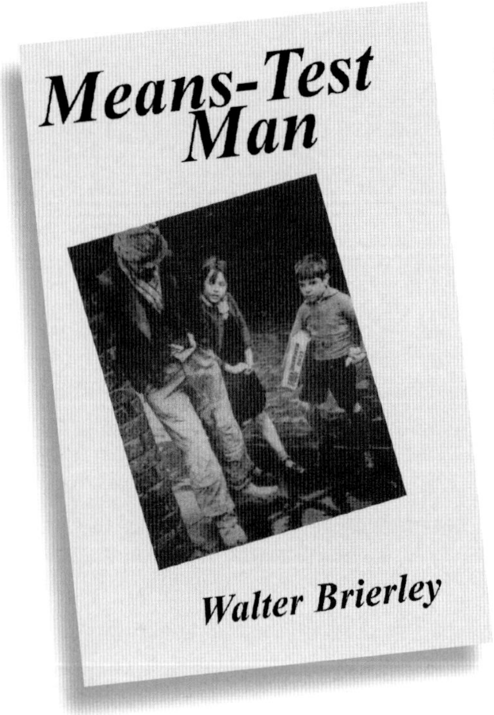

Former miner Walter Brierley of Waingroves near Ripley turned the despair of unemployment and subjection to the means test during the 1930s into a novel highly acclaimed at the time, but now largely ignored (*Author's Collection*).

When *Means Test Man* first appeared in print, it garnered favourable reviews, except from *The Daily Worker*, the communist daily newspaper of the era. The reviewer believed that the stoicism displayed by the main characters of the novel, based on Brierley and his wife, was not the correct attitude for the long-term unemployed.

The reviewer considered that the unemployed worker who sat timidly at home waiting for the investigator (the means test man) was not the rule, as he believed the novel implied, but the exception.

The reviewer's message was that a book which concentrated much more on the fighting spirit of the unemployed would have been of more use to the cause of the working class.

In contrast to the much better known Lawrence, Walter Brierley's achievement has been duly acknowledged in his home village. There is a small housing development named Brierley Court and a Brierley Road, whilst local people are happy to point out the modest house where he grew up.

In 1995, Walter's son John, now deceased, published a reminiscence of his father entitled *In the Shadow of the Means Test Man.* John, like many collier's sons, was encouraged by Walter and his mother Amy to pursue his education, through Bemrose School in Derby, Sheffield University and Queen's College, Oxford, where he obtained a doctorate.

John Brierley taught at Manchester Grammar School and was later a school inspector, spending some time in Derbyshire.

His memoir of his father and comments he made at the launch of the book help to shed some light on the motives behind the criticism of his father in *The Daily Worker*. John said: "My father never burned with political fire, and was concerned with describing life rather than attempting to change it.

"This lack of interest in political or economic forces prevented his writing being taken up by the class warriors. He wrote mainly of his own and his fellow mineworkers' situations, and how to avoid destitution, and not to save his class."

Another working class writer from the Erewash Valley, Leslie Williamson, was born in Eastwood in 1924. Williamson, in his youth, worked as a laundry boy, collecting and delivering washing, ran errands for a local engineering firm, and also found work on the shop-floor at a local hosiery factory.

After service in the RAF he rejoined the hosiery company, rising to become a manager. He also pursued a literary career, with considerable success. He taught himself shorthand and reported for local newspapers, moving on to write fiction and poetry. Williamson

Walter Brierley's home in Waingroves, the setting for Means Test Man (*Author*).

Walter Brierley, wife Amy and son John, pictured in the 1930s (*John Grace, Waingroves*).

wrote three novels with social themes, *The Crowded Cemetery, Death of a Portrait*, and *Jobey*, The latter work is set in 1926, at the time of the General Strike, and was re-issued in paper-back at the time of the 1984-5 miners' strike.

Williamson is also the author of the verse sequences, *D H Lawrence and the Country he Loved*, and *Bread for All*, a dramatic interpretation of the Pentrich Uprising (see Chapter Two, *Revolution in the Valley*).

The novels and short stories of yet another working class author, the Nottingham-born Alan Sillitoe, make reference to the Erewash Valley.

The main thrust of Sillitoe's novels with a Nottinghamshire backdrop, notably his first success, *Saturday Night and Sunday Morning*, are centred on the mean streets of the city's industrial suburbs like Radford and industrial plants such as the Raleigh cycle works.

Sillitoe spent much of his childhood at his grandparents' home close to the Erewash Valley, on the western fringe of Nottingham, and seems in much of his writing to regard the valley as a playground offering a refreshing escape from the grimy urban environment of the city.

Fishing along the banks of the Nottingham Canal near Trowell features in both the novel and in the film version of *Saturday Night and Sunday Morning*, and Sillitoe also makes reference to the dog, motorcycle and horse (trotting) racing at Long Eaton.

In 1994 Sillitoe was given an honorary degree by The University of Nottingham, on the same day that a similar honour was accorded to the Ilkeston-born actor Robert Lindsay. Although the two men were meeting for the first time, Lindsay revealed that in 1959, as a child, he had been an extra on the film set *of Saturday Night and Sunday morning.*

Very different in character to any of the other novelists associated with the Erewash Valley was Eric Malpass, who lived and worked for much of his life in Long Eaton. On his death in 1996, at the age of 85, Malpass was described in his obituary in *The Independent* newspaper as 'a rare creature - a highly successful English novelist who was virtually unknown in England'.

The obituary went on to say: "His reputation and his success were made almost entirely in Europe - in particular in Germany, where he was a household name. More paradoxical still, the setting of his books was always England, often nostalgic recreations of family life in an idealised English countryside, written with a wit and warmth that stopped just short of sentimentality."

Born in Derby, Malpass, while writing in his spare time, worked in a bank in Long Eaton, where he lived for most of his life. He would return home after a day's work and spend the evening writing. He was a regular contributor to *Argosy*, a short story magazine although it took him many years before

Eric Malpass, the Long Eaton bank employee/novelist who won greater appreciation in Germany and elsewhere in Europe than in his native country (*Author's Collection*).

Teresa Hooley as a thoroughly conventional young woman (*Author's Collection*).

he was first published. Many other short story magazines took his work and in 1955 he won *The Observer* short story competition.

His second book *Mornings at Seven* received good reviews in the UK but registered only poor sales, but then rose quickly to the top of the Best Seller List in Germany. It remained there for three years.

This success tempted Malpass to become a full-time writer. His employers at the bank reportedly refused initially to accept his resignation and at one stage threatened to withdraw his pension!

Three of his novels, including *Mornings at Seven*, were filmed in Germany and a six-part television mini-series, also based on the book, was made in France.

Lawrence was not the only literary figure without honour in his own backyard, although for very different reasons than in the case of Eric Malpass, who is remembered in Long Eaton as a gentle and unassuming man, much loved by all who had dealings with him. He lived close to his roots for most of his life and, showing a diplomatic approach to the split county loyalties of the Erewash Valley, was president for more than 40 years of both the Nottingham Writers' Club and the Derby Writers' Guild.

D H Lawrence's reputation as a poet has been overshadowed by the success of his novels and stories, which have over the years been brought to the notice of a non-literary audience by films and television adaptation.

A prominent poet from the Erewash Valley, whose high water mark of reputation came in the 1950s when one of the most prominent critics of the day predicted that she would be one of the few 20th Century women writers whose work would survive into the new millennium, was Teresa Hooley, of Risley.

Born in 1888, she was the only daughter of Terah Hooley, the lace maker and developer of such well-known textile manufacturing units as the iconic Springfield Mill, at Sandiacre. Her half-brother was the financier Ernest Terah Hooley, once described as Europe's greatest fraudster, whilst her brother Basil was a World War One hero whose story will be told in Chapter Eight (*A Valley at War*).

Teresa Hooley established a national reputation in the 1920s when she shared a regular poetry spot in the *Daily Mirror* newspaper with Edith (later Dame Edith) Sitwell.

For many years the critics' belief that Teresa Hooley's work would endure appeared to have little foundation, with her own books going out of print and her verse disappearing from anthologies. The growing interest in the Great War and the publication of a variety of volumes of its poetry brought one of her best known pieces of work, *A War Film*, back into national prominence.

Today it can be found in several 1914-18 anthologies, alongside the great exponents of the genre including Wilfred Owen, Siegfried Sassoon and Rupert Brooke. It appears also in a publication devoted to women poets of the period, a book aimed at introducing war poetry of the era to a young audience, and in a collection illustrated with contemporary news photographs. *A War Film* also featured in a Remembrance Sunday recital by actors at a West End theatre.

Ironically, *A War Film*, unlike most poems about the conflict, was not itself contemporary with the period, but was written in the mid-1920s, inspired by one of the first feature films about the Great War. The graphic re-enactment of battle scenes she witnessed during an afternoon showing of the film at a Derby cinema caused Teresa that evening to

Teresa Hooley's childhood home at Risley Lodge (*Author's Collection*).

smother her young son in what to him seemed a confusing degree of extra affection, driven by her fear that, one day, he too would be involved in war.

Initially published by Jonathan Cape, her books sold well. Occasionally she merited national newspaper headlines, like those generated by her controversial poem *Christ in Woolworths*, which described her mixed emotions on seeing a crucifix for sale in the sixpenny store alongside tawdry trinkets. Her national and international reputation – she was widely published in the United States and in the Commonwealth in her heyday – was based more on her status as a lyrical poet of nature, influenced strongly by and on occasions even compared to, Thomas Hardy.

After the death of her parents, Teresa moved to the West Country and established a new and rather different reputation, this time as a political firebrand. Like her father and her half-brother, she had begun life as a conventional Conservative. After World War One she married and went with her husband to the Middle East. The marriage failed and she returned to England, but her experience of colonial conditions in Egypt had turned her into a fierce radical.

She caused considerable resentment among the gentry in the still almost feudal district of West Somerset. Enraged by the poor housing of agricultural workers, she campaigned long and hard against the neglect of the landlords. On one occasion a member of the local squirearchy threatened to horsewhip her as a class traitor.

Throughout the 1930s she developed artistic and personal friendships with a huge variety of writers, poets and activists from the left of the political spectrum, including the future Poet Laureate Sean Day-Lewis and the novelist, playwright and broadcaster J B Priestley.

Her Derbyshire connections were maintained through links with Vera Brittain and Edith Sitwell, while as the decade proceeded, bringing the political shocks of the Spanish Civil War and Munich, she became close to the revolutionary Tom Wintringham – who despite being suspect for his political views was later to be used by the War Office to train the new Home Guard - and to the rebellious Labour politician Sir Stafford Cripps.

Munich not only prompted a much more active political stance, as Teresa chaired meetings in the West Country for Cripps and other campaigners for a Popular Front of the left-leaning parties, but also inspired some of her strongest, if less well-known work. In a recognisably direct line of descent from *A War Film* was *Peace, 1938*, in which Teresa expressed her belief that Neville Chamberlain's much-trumpeted `Peace in our Time' statement hid a far grimmer mid and long-term reality.

Teresa's emotions over Munich were again driven by her feelings for her own son and, by extension, for all mothers. In *Peace, 1938*, she looks beyond the sense of thanksgiving at the lifting of the immediate threat of war, felt by herself and so many others at that time, to recognise that relief for some would still inevitably mean pain - instant for some, merely delayed for the rest.

You are safe my son, safe,
Sound and whole;
Can see with clear eyes,
Use your limbs,
Hear, taste, talk, laugh,
Breathe sweet air,
When War might have smashed you to
bloody pulp or an idiot's drooling,
But you are bought with a price.
Behind your sight
Are a Nation's tears
Fetters on other feet
Assure your freedom
The anguish of betrayal

She became a member of the Commonwealth Party, founded by the Liberal politician Sir Richard Acland, which enjoyed wartime success in by-elections, largely due to the major political parties having called a wartime truce.

Teresa eventually returned to Derbyshire, living at various locations in and around Risley, and serving as President of the Derby Poetry Circle. She contributed a weekly column to the *Long Eaton Advertiser* entitled *A Poet's Diary*, and for most her image was that of a county lady who opened church fetes and bazaars wearing large hats.

The radical streak, however, continued almost to her death in 1973. A regular Anglican churchgoer, she was nevertheless outraged when the then Bishop of Derby disciplined a clergyman for supporting the nascent Campaign for Nuclear Disarmament, campaigned for voluntary euthanasia, and left her body to medical science.

Ernest Terah Hooley himself just about merits a mention in a chapter devoted to literary matters, through his publication in 1925 of his memoirs, *Hooley's Confessions*, first published in a Sunday newspaper and then issued in book form,

Teresa Hooley's 1944 book of verse, The Singing Heart (*Author's Collection*).

Chapter Four

The Valley as a Route to Riches

'The three children were on the platform at Lethley Bridge, on the Midland main line. Down the line the red and green lights shone ... after two hours they saw the lights of an engine, away down the darkness, and a great train drew up, bound for Manchester, stopping for William's sake at such a small station' – Sons and Lovers.

For almost two and a half centuries the Erewash Valley has been regarded by private sector entrepreneurs and public service officials alike as a route to riches.

First the canal builders, then the railway promoters, then much later the planners behind Britain's fledgling motorway network, all in turn recognised the strategic importance of the valley as a natural route between the burgeoning industries of the north and the ripe markets of the midlands and the south of England.

Today, once again, the valley's status as a vital artery of communication has been recognised.

In the second decade of the 21st century, it is intended to form part of the route of the proposed HS2 high speed rail link, a project regarded by government and much of British industry and commerce as essential to the success of the larger plan to foster a economic renaissance in the nation's former industrial heartlands – the so-called 'Northern Powerhouse'.

The new line (always providing the costly project is not cancelled at a late stage), will penetrate the Erewash Valley at a point favoured in the past by others seeking to exploit its geographical advantages.

First came the canal navigators, seeking a suitable junction on the River Trent for the Erewash Canal to begin its journey north into coalfields ripe for development.

Several decades later virtually the same ground was explored by the surveyors plotting the route of what was to become the Midland Railway's main line to the fast-growing industrial cities of the north of England.

Later, via the company's spectacular Settle and Carlisle line, it became the Midland's direct route to Scotland,

Pinxton Wharf is an important location for both the canal and railway history of the Erewash Valley. The wharf was the terminus of the Pinxton Arm of the Cromford Canal (pictured right). A 4ft 4inch gauge horse-drawn railway line was built from the wharf to Mansfield in 1819, to carry coal from valley pits. In 1832 a passenger service was introduced on market days, tickets being bought from from the Boat Inn (top left). At the time of writing the inn was undergoing refurbishment .(Author).

Solid stone 18th century canal architecture. Pictured is the entrance to the abandoned Pinxton Arm of the Cromford Canal. The Arm, now mostly filled in except at the Pinxton end, left the main line of the Cromford near the northerly end of Codnor Reservoir at Ironville, and terminated some three miles later at Pinxton Wharf (*Author*).

slower than its east and west coast counterparts but immeasurably more comfortable, given the company's renowned rolling stock, and much more scenic.

The Erewash Canal helped Long Eaton, at the southern extremity of the valley, develop as an industrial centre and the town's spectacular growth in Queen Victoria's reign was a further boost to its economy.

The construction of the Erewash Valley railway mainline was followed by the creation of S J Claye's wagon works and the huge Toton complex – marshalling yards, locomotive depot and company wagon repair shops – that developed to the north east of Long Eaton, between the town and Stapleford and Sandiacre.

The Midland company built streets of houses in the centre of Long Eaton for its workers, and over the years railwaymen of all grades played an important part in the civic and public life of the town.

Toton's yards are now largely derelict as a result of the steady demise of its core traffics of coal and iron ore. Trees and shrubs have sprouted and local people now exercise their dogs where previously hundreds of wagons were sorted.

Loose cables swung by the wind against redundant lighting pylons make an eerie noise, in a post-industrial landscape much more desolate than the former colliery sites a few miles to the north, where the bleak spoil heaps have been levelled, contoured and planted with grass and woodland in a way that has transformed them into the type of pastoral landscape once the norm across the whole of the area.

Now the Toton site has the promise of a new birth, by a project that means, depending upon your point of view, either long-overdue and welcome rejuvenation, or disaster. The derelict up yards at Toton are proposed as the site of the High Speed Train station for the region, planned to give Nottingham, Derby and their economic hinterlands a stake in the much vaunted benefits of the new line.

The station will serve not only the high speed lines and services, but will also accommodate connecting rail services from the neighbouring cities. Connections to the road network, and the existence already, close to the proposed station site, of the Nottingham tramway system, now operational on the old rose gardens site at the top of Toton Hill, will create a formidable transport hub.

It has to be said, however, that not everyone in the area backs HS2. After crossing the River Trent into Derbyshire, the new line will largely utilise existing standard tracks and will slice through the centre of Long Eaton, in a manner that is already casting a blight on the housing market in the vicinity of the proposed route.

Just how HS2 will pass through Long Eaton is, at the time of writing, still a matter of some

Pinxton Wharf, bustling in its heyday as an important communications centre, has been restored and is today a sleepy resort for anglers (*Author*).

Great Northern Basin at Langley Mill, restored, busy with narrow boats and home to dockyard facilities, together with a short section of the Cromford Canal, is the southernmost outpost of that historic waterway. The northernmost section of the waterway, in the Derwent Valley, includes the terminal basin at Cromford, a stretch of watered canal along which boat trips are available, and the restored Leawood Pumping Station, built to take water from the River Derwent (*Author*).

debate. Within the town itself, the existing rail lines pass through two level crossings, always the cause of a certain amount of congestion.

The original plans involved the closing of the roads passing over the level crossings. This in itself caused considerable protest and it now appears likely that the new line will pass through the town centre not, as originally suggested, on the level, but on a 50ft high viaduct, instantly condemned by HS2's local opponents as a visual and environmental disaster.

Few have ever denied that the Erewash Canal and the Midland Railway were hugely influential in the development of Long Eaton in particular and the Erewash Valley in general, an influence that was almost wholly beneficial.

The driving of the M1 motorway across the Trent Valley and up the lower reaches of the Erewash in the mid-1960s (and its later widening) undoubtedly caused disruption but there are many advantages to living close to such an important and useful artery.

Considered from the point of view of the aspiration to a 'Northern Powerhouse', it is plain, driving up and down the country, that motorway corridors have prospered economically whilst those areas remote from the network have often stagnated.

Perhaps in time someone will write in similar vein about the effects of the HS2 High Speed railway line. At this point in time, whilst the direct benefits for Long Eaton are difficult to quantify, the likely damage to the environment and the cohesion of the town are potentially dire.

Returning to the onset of the Industrial Revolution, it is interesting to reflect upon the enormous effect canals and railways, both directly and indirectly, had upon the landscape of the Erewash Valley. Directly they altered the shape of the map of the valley; indirectly, they made possible the rapid industrialisation of what had been almost entirely a pastoral landscape.

King Coal, the lifeblood of industry, the prime means of providing energy and power for two centuries, was the reason the canals and their associated plateways and tramways, and later the railways, came to the valley in the first place.

Canals

Canals must be the first channels of communication to be considered, if only because they preceded the railways by several decades. At the same time, it must always be remembered that the history of the canals and the railways, particularly in the Erewash Valley, are closely linked.

It will also become apparent throughout this chapter that in the world of both canals and railways, it is an axiom that the first to be built have usually proved to be the ones to survive.

After the first canals were dug, many subsequent projects were non-essential. Investors foresaw (but never received) large dividends from various ill-conceived enterprises.

The faded sign at Langley Mill is a reminder that the Great Northern Basin was a three-way junction for the Erewash, Cromford and Nottingham canals (*Author*).

The demand for coal created by industrialisation was far beyond the limited tonnages that could be produced by the primitive pits that had been worked in the valley for centuries. Such is certainly the case where the history of both canals and railways in the Erewash Valley is concerned.

The first man-made waterway to challenge the age-old dominance of lumbering carts and packhorse trains in the area was the Erewash Canal. It is the only one of the five canals to be built in the valley to survive in the 21st century as a fully-navigable waterway.

The Erewash, just under 12 miles long from its junction with the River Trent at Trent Lock, (near Long Eaton) to its terminus in the heart of the valley coalfield at Langley Mill, between the towns of Heanor and Eastwood, obtained its act of parliament in 1777 and was completed in 1779 at a cost of £21,000.

The volume of coal it was able to transport from the increasing number of operational pits ensured that it was a commercial success from the beginning. Although coal reserves in large quantities were known to be present in the valley to the north of Langley Mill, transport difficulties prevented their full exploitation. It was no surprise when the success of the Erewash Canal encouraged local business interests to press for a northern extension to that waterway.

The reaction of the proprietors of the Erewash to this proposal was negative, so the interested parties decided to go it alone, commissioning the noted engineer William Jessop to design a waterway between Langley Mill and Cromford in the Derwent Valley, a village becoming rapidly industrialised by Richard Arkwright. A branch off the main line would tap into the coal reserves to the east, around Pinxton.

Coal was not the only prize foreseen by the promoters of the Cromford Canal and the Pinxton Arm. Cotton from Arkwright's mills, limestone (for the growing iron industry) and lead from the Wirksworth area of the Derbyshire Peak District were also there to be carried.

There was little question but that the Cromford would eventually achieve its aim of an end-on

The welcoming sign at Trent Lock near Long Eaton, at the start of the fully-operational Erewash Canal (*Author*).

The Erewash Canal is well maintained throughout its length, typified by the first lock, Trent Lock. The area around the lock is a thriving spot for both boaters, with moorings, sanitary stations and dockyard facilities, and for pleasure seekers from far and wide, who are catered for by two pubs, a tea room, the facilities of a nearby golf club, and plenty of car parking. (*Author*).

junction with the thriving Erewash at Langley Mill. The Erewash management effectively had little choice in the matter; had they continued in their opposition they faced the prospect that a competing canal would be constructed southwards, virtually on a parallel route to their own cut.

A second and competing canal link to the south and midlands, this time direct to Nottingham, was eventually built, as described later in this chapter.

The Cromford's Act of Parliament was granted in 1789, the year that revolution of a different kind broke out across the Channel in France. Construction, in more difficult and hillier terrain than that traversed by the Erewash, was not as simple a matter as the cutting of the earlier waterway.

The contractors soon ran into financial difficulties and, at the end of 1790, walked off the site, with responsibility for completing the project falling to Benjamin Outram.

The Erewash Canal seen in the heart of Long Eaton, towards the end of the waterway's use as an artery for commercial traffic, which came in 1952. The chimneys of some of the town's tenement lace mills are clearly visible, and the bridge in the background carries the main Derby Road. The towpath (right) is in a much better state of repair today (*Horace Holme*).

The work continued to prove problematical. A substantial aqueduct over the River Amber failed but nevertheless Outram persevered, overcoming the challenges posed by the Butterley Tunnel and a further aqueduct over the River Derwent, to complete the project.

Butterley Tunnel was excavated by first sinking 33 shafts, about 75 yards apart and as much as 57 yards deep, to provide a number of working faces. Most of the heading was through soil, with some coal measures and iron ore deposits, the final tunnel being lined through most of its length.

Sandiacre Lock is the home of the Erewash Canal Preservation and Development Association, which in the late 1960s and 1970s saved the waterway from the virtual abandonment envisaged by British Waterways at the time (*Author*).

Locking through at Sandiacre. The Erewash Canal is popular with boaters, walkers, cyclists and anglers. It forms a linear green trail through the central and lower reaches of the valley and links with nature reserves and some well publicised leisure routes (*Author*).

The Derwent Aqueduct needed much modification before the waterway could open for business. The spandrel walls parted due to the horizontal forces imposed by the canal, and a longitudinal split opened up in the arch. Jessop, as engineer, was obliged to meet the cost of remedial work out of his own pocket.

In the end, despite costing almost twice the initial estimate for the work (£42,000), the waterway was finished. It opened in 1794 and, like the Erewash, became a financial success, carrying nearly 300,000 tons a year by 1842.

Railway competition was severe, with first the Midland main line to Manchester through the Peak District and the connecting route from Ambergate to the Erewash Valley at Pye Bridge, which followed in 1875. By 1888 trade had shrunk to 45,000 tons a year.

A major blow came the following year when subsidence closed the 3,063- yard Butterley Tunnel for four years. Further subsidence in 1900 closed the tunnel permanently. Most of the canal was abandoned in 1944 with the exception of a half-mile stretch to Langley Mill which was abandoned in 1962.

After closure, the canal was taken over by the British Waterways Board and acquired by Derbyshire County Council in 1974. Between 1968–69 and 1989 the 5 miles between Cromford and Ambergate were restored either partly or wholly by the Cromford Canal Society together with the beam engine (the Leawood Pump) which was restored to full operation, pumping water from the River Derwent to the Canal above.

Attempts are currently being made to restore the canal and about five miles remains in water. The towpath from Ambergate to Cromford is a popular walking route, with the Derwent Valley railway line running alongside.

The Erewash Canal's commercial success kept it in operation for much longer than any of the other waterways in the Erewash Valley. When the Grand Union Canal Company took over the running of the Erewash in 1932 it was still a going concern and the Erewash was nationalised in 1947.

With the entire canal system in decline the last commercial narrowboat to ply its trade on the Erewash delivered its cargo in 1952. In 1962 the British Transport Commission closed the top section of canal. However, it was kept in water to supply the lower half of the canal and it remained navigable.

Worse news for the canal was to follow when, in 1968, the main line from Long Eaton to Langley Mill was one of seven stretches of canals formally designated as remainder waterways – meaning effective closure as a navigable waterway,

The Erewash Canal Preservation & Development Association was formed in response to the threat of closure and under the dynamic leadership of former senior fire officer Royston Torrington achieved its aim of saving the waterway.

In addition the Association succeeded in re-opening the Great Northern Basin at Langley Mill and putting back into water a short section of the Cromford Canal. Today the Erewash is fully open and actively used by pleasure cruisers and narrowboats. It provides a green spine through the greater part of the Erewash Valley and is heavily used by walkers, cyclists and anglers.

The Association's headquarters are in restored lock-keepers' cottages at Sandiacre Lock and close by is the junction with the former Derby Canal – with a few yards of water the only navigable stretch of that waterway, at least until preservation attempts being pursued for the waterway reach a successful conclusion.

The entrance to the old Derby Canal at Sandiacre 2016 (*Author*).

It was in 1796, a great year for canal openings in the Erewash Valley, and two years after the opening of the Cromford, that the Derby Canal made its own bid to tap the riches of the coalfields. The Derby ran from a meeting with the Trent and Mersey Canal at Swarkestone in South Derbyshire to Derby, where it made a level crossing of the River Derwent, with the towing horses making use of a long wooden bridge over the river.

From Derby the canal split, with one line going to Little Eaton, where it made connection with a tramroad known as the Little Eaton gangway, which enjoyed considerable success until superseded by a railway. The Little Eaton branch of the canal closed in 1935.

The other line of the Derby Canal brought it into the Erewash Valley, to its junction with the Erewash Canal at Sandiacre. The main line of the waterway from Swarkestone to Derby and the Sandiacre line also fell into disuse, although final closure was delayed until 1964.

If the Derby Canal only penetrated to the fringe of the valley, the Nottingham Canal, which opened in the same year of 1796, ran for much of its length on a course parallel to the Erewash Canal, to the east of that waterway.

The Nottingham left the River Trent to first serve wharves in Nottingham and then curved westward to enter the Erewash Valley near Trowell. It rose through 18 locks to reach Langley Mill, where a stop lock connected it to the Great Northern Basin.

Although early dividends were paid to shareholders, the Nottingham faced severe railway competition and in the 1840s sold out to the grandly-titled Ambergate, Nottingham Boston and Easten Junction Railway, which itself eventually sold out to the Great Northern Railway.

The Nottingham end of the canal was still busy at the time of World War One, carrying nearly 125,000 tons of cargo in 1916, but most of this was short-haul traffic between the Trent and the Nottingham wharves. The Great Northern's successor company, the London and North Eastern Railway, had little interest in canal transport and the main line of the Nottingham was abandoned in 1937.

Broxtowe Borough Council bought six miles of the Erewash Valley section of the canal in a bid to retain what was left of the waterway as an amenity.

A plan to re-open the upper section of the waterway for navigation, no doubt inspired by the success of the Erewash Canal Preservation and Development Association in the 1970s, was effectively scuppered both by the construction of the Awsworth by-pass road in 1980 and by opencast coal mining in the upper section.

The latter, like the collapse of the Cromford's Butterley Tunnel due to subsidence caused by mining, was deeply ironic, in view of the fact that both waterways were constructed chiefly to earn money from coalmining.

The local authority has succeeded in transforming remaining sections of the canal into a local nature reserve and the towpath is used by walkers, cyclists, anglers and horse riders. Angling is possible in some spots.

The year 1796 also saw the opening of the Nutbrook Canal, which ran between the heavily-mined Shipley Estate, between Heanor and Ilkeston, flowing through the area that was to become the Stanton ironworks, after which it made a junction with the Erewash Canal, close to the Erewash Valley main railway line at Stanton Gate.

Nemesis eventually brought down the Nutbrook, for like the Cromford and the Nottingham it was a victim of subsidence caused by the very coal mines that it was built to serve. With the mines failing to pay tolls for goods carried on the canal, and in some cases refusing to accept responsibility for the subsidence, most of the waterway closed in 1895, although the final one and a half miles close to the Stanton works remained in use until 1949, carrying ironworks and other traffic during World War Two.

Railways

The through routes opened up to the midlands and the south by the Cromford and Erewash Canals, and later the Nottingham Canal in the late 18th century were to inspire the construction of the Erewash Valley's first railway.

The main line of the Cromford Canal had thrown off a branch arm to exploit the coal reserves around the Derbyshire mining town of Pinxton. In 1817 an Act of Parliament, the first to be obtained for a railway line in the valley, was granted for a line from Pinxton Wharf to Mansfield.

The route, which used horses for haulage, was completed in 1819, carrying stone and lime as well as coal. The railway made possible the sinking of new pits and from 1832 also carried passengers from Pinxton Wharf, where passengers bought tickets at the Boat Inn, to Mansfield market.

Although the line was useful to the local economy, its main claim to fame is through the role it played in the complex railway politics of the first half of the 20th century.

The development of the Erewash and Cromford canals had put the collieries in the Charnwood Forest area of Leicestershire at a commercial disadvantage. This was rectified when, in 1832, the local coal owners opened the Leicester and Swannington Railway.

With the pendulum swinging backwards and forwards, it was now the Erewash Valley pits that found themselves struggling to sell their product in important markets.

The Erewash Valley coal owners, meeting at The Sun Inn in Eastwood, determined to hit back with their own railway line, and at first proposed to expand the Mansfield and Pinxton Railway south down the valley.

The approach of the Railway Mania, with its countless schemes, some sensible and successful, others pure fancy, meant that much more ambitious and less localised enterprises were in the offing.

Several years of proposal and counter-proposal, the constant and often difficult search for the necessary financial backing, all carried out against a background of intense local rivalry between the main cities and towns of the region, eventually produced some concrete enterprises.

The Midland Counties Railway opened in 1839, linking Derby, Nottingham and, via a junction south of Long Eaton, Leicester. From Leicester the line continued to Rugby, where it linked with the recently-constructed London and Birmingham Railway.

In the same year the Birmingham and Derby Junction Railway opened from Derby via Burton on Trent and Tamworth, to Hampton in Arden in Warwickshire where, like the Midland Counties route though Leicester, it also joined the London and Birmingham route, offering a connection to the capital city.

The following year, 1840, another independent company, the North Midland Railway, was completed from Leeds to Derby. The component parts of the railway jigsaw were steadily being put into place, although rivalries at first prevented the puzzle from being completed.

Despite the openings of 1839 and 1840, there was a major snag for the Nottinghamshire and Derbyshire coal owners who, after all, had been the first to press for development of the local railway network.

There was still no line up the Erewash Valley, largely due to bickering between the three independent companies, on the issue of competition. The Midland Counties and the Birmingham and Derby Junction tussled over traffic, both passenger and goods, to London, whilst the North Midland feared that a direct line up the valley to Chesterfield and beyond would adversely affect its own business interests.

The solution came in 1844 when the Midland Counties, the North Midland and the Birmingham and Derby Junction merged, taking the title of the Midland Railway. In 1847 the Midland swallowed the Mansfield and Pinxton and also finally opened the Erewash Valley line, from Trent Junction, near Long Eaton, to Pye Bridge near Ironville and on to Clay Cross, where it joined the tracks of the former North Midland en route for the northern cities.

The Derby-based Midland Railway was an amalgamation of three separate early railway companies. The Erewash Valley main line was opened from Trent Junction, near Long Eaton, to Pinxton in 1847 and extended via Clay Cross to Chesterfield in 1862. The line is still active today for both passenger and freight services. The scene above was pictured in 1962, when long trains of standard 16ton coal trains from valley pits often had to queue for long periods before being accepted into Toton marshalling yard. The coal train is being overtaken by a London St Pancras-bound express, hauled by Jubilee Class locomotive 45562 Alberta. Pictured to the left is the Cadbury Brothers chocolate distribution depot at Gallows Inn, Ilkeston (*Author's Collection*).

The new company turned the original Pinxton to Mansfield line into a standard gauge route, starting at Pye Bridge, which still exists today.

The Midland route from London and Leicester crossed the River Trent just south of Long Eaton, where a complicated layout of lines evolved.

In 1862 the Midland company opened Trent Station, isolated in the fields a mile or so from Long Eaton. Trent acted as an important interchange point, where passengers from Derby and Nottingham could catch services from London to the north of England and Scotland and vice-versa travelling direct up the Erewash valley.

Trent possessed a single island platform, protected by classic Midland canopies of iron and glass. By the time of its closure in 1968 it was used mainly by local services shuttling between Leicester, Derby and Nottingham.

The station had just one vehicular access, via a narrow road from Long Eaton, but could also be reached by a footpath from the town.

Until its latter years it boasted a refreshment room and even in the weeks before closure, when its death warrant had been signed, the coal fires in its capacious waiting rooms were kept burning brightly.

Jubilee class locomotives, including 45593 Kolhapur, pictured above, also worked local passenger trains along the Erewash Valley main line between Sheffield, Chesterfield and Nottingham in the closing days of steam. Kolhapur has been preserved by enthusiasts. (*Roger Barnes ARPS and www.picturethepast.org.uk*)

Long Eaton itself has had no fewer than four railway stations. The first Long Eaton station was built in 1839 by the Midland Counties Railway, and situated on Meadow Lane. In 1847, the opening of the Erewash Valley line north saw a second station constructed, on Nottingham Road. The first station was closed in 1862 and a year later the Nottingham Road station was replaced by yet another, on Station Street, which remained in service until 1967. When this closed Sawley Junction, within the town boundaries, on the line to Derby, was renamed Long Eaton and remains open today, with main line services to London St Pancras.

The first Sawley station was a mile out of the village on Sawley Lane, Breaston. First used in 1839, when the line opened, it closed in 1930.

Travelling north from Trent and Long Eaton along the Erewash Valley's spinal route, the most southerly branch was constructed into the Stanton ironworks. Although a blast furnace on a small scale has been traced to the site during the period of the Napoleonic wars, iron making on an industrial scale began with the completion of three furnaces in 1846, during the period when the Midland's main line up the valley was under construction.

During the 1860s the works began importing iron ore from Northamptonshire, a traffic which was to continue until late in the 20th century. At Stanton Gate, at a point just before the branch to the works diverged from the main line, a marshalling yard was developed to handle the incoming ore traffic, the empties and finished products from the works. The yard acted as a satellite to Toton.

The Stanton branch was extended in 1870 to skirt Ilkeston and serve collieries on the edge of the Shipley estate, at West Hallam and Mapperley.

In 1862, when the Erewash Valley mainline was completed to Chesterfield, the Midland Railway opened Trent Station at the southern end of the route. The station was a couple of miles outside Long Eaton, with only very limited road access. It acted mainly as an interchange point and a complicated series of junctions and loops meant trains from both Nottingham and Derby, and those coming from Scotland and the north of England via the Erewash Valley, could call there. The station closed in 1968 and was quickly demolished (*Derbyshire Local Studies Libraries and www.picturethepast.org.uk*).

North of Trent Station, between the old Long Eaton and Stapleford and Sandiacre stations, was the huge Toton marshalling yard, pictured here in snowy conditions. This view, looking south towards Long Eaton, was taken before modernisation of the yard. The Midland Railway wooden signal box situated in the centre was replaced in 1939 by a brick construction, as part of the mechanisation of the downside marshalling yard (*Mrs P A Brown and www.picturethepast.org.uk*).

Heading north, the Midland main line ran to the east at the foot of the hill on which stood the important market town of Ilkeston. Ilkeston Junction station, actually located on the Nottinghamshire bank of the Erewash, in the parish of Cossall, was more than a mile from the centre of Ilkeston and meant a steep climb in one direction for passengers.

Recognising this, the Midland built a short branch from the Junction to Ilkeston Town Station. This venture was not particularly successful, as the little terminus (now replaced by a Tesco supermarket) also terminated at the foot of the Ilkeston hill.

Passengers still faced a climb and argued that they might as well walk to the Junction in the first place. The subsequent poor receipts prompted the Midland to close the branch to passengers in 1870.

What was seen by many as a half-hearted approach by the Midland, more interested in coal than in passengers, led the towns along the Erewash to welcome the major challenge to the company's domination of the valley, mounted in the 1870s by the Great Northern Railway.

The Great Northern company, already established in Nottingham, was understandably anxious to gain a share of the coal riches of the area, but its attempts in the 1860s to gain a foothold along the Erewash had been thwarted by the Midland.

Increasingly aware that the Midland was unlikely to be a willing collaborator or share the spoils from territory it regarded as its fiefdom, the Great Northern took matters into its own hands by planning and building its Derbyshire Extension.

The Great Northern's bold new line was projected north from Nottingham up the valley of the River Leen (from the very start of its new venture challenging the Midland's existing passenger and mineral interests) before turning west to Kimberley and the Erewash Valley.

At Awsworth Junction, the line divided, with a northern spur running through Eastwood to Codnor Park and eventually to a terminus at Pinxton. The other line continued west to Ilkeston, Derby and Stafford, with a connection to Burton-on -Trent and its valuable brewery traffic.

At Ilkeston the Derbyshire Extension line eventually threw off a passenger and goods branch to Heanor, through the heart of the Shipley mining area, and a line into the Stanton iron complex, giving the works an alternative means of rail access.

Good and mineral services started running to Pinxton in 1875, with the Great Northern reaping the reward for its investment, carrying 115,000 tons of coal in the first six months. Passenger services followed in August 1876.

Mechanisation of Toton included the provision of hump shunting facilities. Wagons like the one pictured were sorted by running down an incline towards sidings. Their speed was reduced by automatic retarders, controlled, like the points for the individual sidings, by the white-painted control tower seen on the left of the picture *(Author's collection)*

Towns in the Erewash Valley had welcomed the Great Northern initiative when it was first mooted, and their optimism was to prove justified. Railway passengers from Eastwood had previously had a steep walk to Langley Mill to pick up a train on the Erewash Valley mainline. Now the town (and Kimberley) had reasonably convenient stations of their own on the GN.

Ilkeston too saw immediate benefit from the Great Northern incursion. Although the GN's new station was hardly closer to the town itself than the Midland depots, the new line offered direct services on an east-west axis to both Derby and Nottingham, whereas the MR's trains to the major centres took considerably longer to make the journeys.

Even in Derby, the proud headquarters of the Midland Railway, there was a feeling that a single company monopoly had led the Midland to become complacent.

The advent of the Great Northern spurred the Midland Railway into furious action. In 1875 the company opened the Radford to Trowell loop, not only allowing better access from Ilkeston to Nottingham but also making it possible for trains from the south to call at Nottingham and rejoin the Erewash Valley line at Trowell. The facility still exists today.

On the same day as the loop opened, the Midland's line from Pye Bridge on the Erewash Valley route to Ambergate, via Butterley, became operational.

In July 1879 the MR re-opened the Ilkeston Town branch from the Junction and a second more direct means of access from Ilkeston to Nottingham, a branch from Bennerley Junction, north of Ilkeston Junction, to Kimberley and Watnall was activated. An existing line built to serve Watnall Colliery gave the Midland access to the city.

Heanor, equally isolated from Langley Mill Station on the Erewash Valley route by the need to negotiate a steep hill, and Ripley, some distance from a mainline station, both became targets for railway improvements.

Between 1890 and 1895 the Midland gradually developed a new route from Butterley on the Pye Bridge-Ambergate line, via Ripley and Heanor, to Langley Mill, on the Erewash Valley mainline. Prior to this Ripley's only rail service had been provided via a branch line from Derby, via Little Eaton and Denby.

This view, again looking south, shows the up yard at Toton to the left of the photograph and part of the steam locomotive depot in the centre. The dominant feature is the concrete automatic coaling plant. The picture was taken in 1965, when steam was on the way out at the depot, which itself was replaced by a new diesel shed and repair facility to the right (*British Rail*).

In the period 1876-78 the Erewash Valley, which the Midland Railway had regarded for some three decades as its exclusive territory, was 'invaded' by the Great Northern Railway Company (GNR). The Great Northern pushed its Derbyshire and Staffordshire Extension west through Nottingham's outer suburbs to the valley at Awsworth, where a branch left the main route for Pinxton crossing the Giltbrook (or Awsworth) viaduct en route. The main line continued over the iron Bennerley Viaduct to Ilkeston, Derby, Burton on Trent and Stafford (*Ilkeston Local Studies Library*).

The Great Northern meantime had opened a mineral branch from Ilkeston to Nutbrook Colliery, Shipley, in 1886 and five years later extended the line to Heanor and opened it to passengers.

Closure of branch and secondary lines is generally associated in the public mind with the Beeching Report of 1962, but many of the lines in and around the Erewash Valley closed long before the former ICI chairman's recommendations were implemented.

The first closures came during World War One. The Ilkeston to Nottingham line, via Bennerley Junction and Basford, closed to passengers in 1917. At the eastern end of the line goods traffic continued to Kimberley (until 1951) and to Watnall (1954). The Langley Mill and Ripley and Ripley to Butterley services were also wartime victims, again having their passenger services withdraw during 1917. Unlike on the Bennerley to Basford line, passenger trains were reinstated in 1920.

Pinxton branch passenger services were withdrawn in 1963. A train bound for Nottingham Victoria station passes the station signal box at the Derbyshire terminus in about 1956 (*Derbyshire Local Studies Libraries and www.picturethepast.org.uk*).

The reprieve was only temporary, as the Langley Mill-Ripley section was finished off by the General Strike in May 1926 and the Ripley-Butterley stub closed four years later. Ripley's remaining passenger service, to Derby, was withdrawn in 1930, although excursion traffic continued on both routes for many years.

It is still possible in the 21st century to travel over part of the Pye Bridge-Ambergate route, courtesy of trains run by the enthusiasts of the Midland Railway Centre, based at Butterley Station.

The Ilkeston Town branch closed for passengers in 1947, and for goods in 1959, whilst the stopping train services on the Erewash Valley line were withdrawn from January 2nd 1967.

Bennerley Viaduct, which crosses the Midland's Erewash Valley mainline, and the Erewash and Nottingham canals, is substantially intact, but is currently inaccessible, with its approach spans demolished. It is pictured here during construction (1877-78), with the contractors' line visible to the right (*Derbyshire Local Studies Libraries and www.picturethepast.org.uk*).

After crossing the Bennerley Viaduct, Derby-bound trains reached Ilkeston GNR Station, renamed Ilkeston North in the British Railways era. The station was the junction for a branch line to Heanor and Marlpool and had three platform faces, a bay platform, and a turntable. A freight only branch also left the mainline to serve a goods depot at Derby Road, Ilkeston and Stanton Ironworks. Passenger trains to Heanor were partially withdrawn except for unadvertised workmen's service in 1928, and restored for a brief period in 1939. The town's Midland Railway Station, on the line between Ripley and Langley Mill, was finally closed in 1926. (*Derbyshire Local Studies Libraries and www.picturethepast.org.uk*).

On the former Great Northern's Derbyshire Extension lines, the advertised Heanor passenger service was the first to officially disappear, in 1928. Unadvertised passenger trains continued to run and an advertised service was reinstated at the outbreak of World War Two, but this lasted for just two months. Goods and coal traffic on the branch continued until 1963.

Services on the section between Awsworth Junction and Pinxton closed in January 1963. The remainder of the Nottingham (Victoria) to Derby (Friargate) services, via Ilkeston and West Hallam, struggled on until September 1964. Colliery services on the Pinxton line and coal, Stanton works traffic and general goods and parcels from Ilkeston on the section to Derby, kept those lines open until 1966 and 1968 respectively.

Today, passenger services run only on the Erewash Valley main line, which has seen considerable investment in track and signalling in recent years. The junction with the Radford loop at Trowell in particular was rebuilt to allow fast running, after the original trackwork had been ripped up when a coal train derailed at the location.

Manners Colliery in Ilkeston (closed in 1949), like Stanton Ironworks, was served by both the Midland and Great Northern railway companies and their successors, the LMS and LNER and eventually the nationalised British Railways. Wagons from both the Midland and the Great Northern stand in the sidings in this photograph (*Erewash Museum*).

The line is used by East Midlands Trains for some of its most important business trains from Leeds and Sheffield to London. The route is also utilised by east-west trains between East Anglia and Liverpool and a Nottingham-Leeds service.

In the late 1950s and up until their withdrawal in January 1967, the author made use of local stopping services on the Erewash Valley route, which served the valley communities of Long Eaton, Stapleford and Sandiacre, Stanton Gate, Trowell, Ilkeston Junction, Shipley Gate, Langley Mill and Eastwood, Codnor Park and Ironville, Pye Bridge and Alfreton,

During a bus strike in 1959 he travelled from his home in Long Eaton to school, using Trowell station, with the inevitable long walk up the hill to Ilkeston in time for the start of lessons.

Long Eaton station, on the Midland Railway's Erewash Valley mainline, pictured in 1965. The lines through the now demolished station still exist and will be used as part of the route of the HS2 High Speed Train (*Author's collection*)

A 2016 shot shows an enthusiasts' railtour heading south through the demolished platforms of the old Long Eaton station. To the right is an extensive residential area of the town, where residents fear their properties have been blighted by the HS2 plans. The High Speed Line is projected to cross the area shown on a lofty viaduct (*Author*).

The Sheffield/Chesterfield locals (via Attenborough and Beeston) were also handier than the bus for travelling to football matches in Nottingham, where the Forest and Notts County grounds were within reasonable distance of the Midland Station.

Before the development of motor bus services, the most effective form of urban and inter-urban transport between the local centres, were tramcars. In this illustration taken at the bottom of Bath Street, Ilkeston, in the early 20th century, two trams have passed on the loop visible behind the nearest car. The other tram is climbing Bath Street towards the Market Place (*Erewash Museum*).

His final rail forays came in the mid-1960s, after starting work as a reporter on the *Long Eaton Advertiser/Stapleford and Sandiacre News* series. The office in Long Eaton was close to the town centre station and after the short hop through Toton Yard, Stapleford and Sandiacre station was a useful starting point for an afternoon of visiting contacts.

At the end of the day, the return trip could be made from Stapleford and Sandiacre or, if the visits had taken him to the far extremity of Stapleford, the diesel railcar could be caught at Stanton Gate.

The final timetable for the valley route's local services advertised a quite generous service of ten trains a day serving all the local stations, with other trains stopping at Chesterfield and Sheffield only.

At that time, as was obvious to anyone passing through on a passenger train, Toton marshalling yard was still very much the Erewash Valley's railway centre par excellence. The complex had grown from a single siding laid down by the Midland Railway in the mid-1850s to become Britain's largest marshalling yard for mineral traffic and one of the most extensive in the world.

At their peak the sprawling yards, situated to the north east of Long Eaton on the Midland Railway's Erewash Valley main line between Trent and Clay Cross, handled a million tons of coal a year and large quantities of iron ore.

The modern light rail image. A tram unit from the Nottingham system waits to leave the present-day western terminus between Toton and Stapleford (*Author*).

Children welcome the first passenger train to serve Ilkeston for half a century. (*Steve Footitt and East Midlands Trains*)

The coal was channelled into Toton from collieries in Derbyshire, Nottinghamshire and Yorkshire, funnelled through smaller satellite yards along the length of the valley.

Both loaded trains from the north for sorting and onward despatch, and services bringing iron ore from Northamptonshire and empty wagons from across the south and midlands for return to the pitheads, had to queue, often for hours at a time, to access the yard.

Few men knew as much about Toton in pre-mechanisation days as Sandiacre man Harry Dawson. He joined the Midland Railway in 1890 as a stable boy, rising to the position of district manager under the Midland's successor, the London Midland and Scottish Railway (LMS) before retiring in 1934.

Although a loyal company servant for 44 years, Harry Dawson had no illusions about the dangers inherent in the long hours and poor working conditions that were the norm in the early part of his career.

He was later promoted to horse shunter and on his retirement recalled how Toton around the turn of the 19th and 20th centuries was widely known as 'the slaughter house', owing to the 'alarming' number of men and horses killed and injured.

The 19th-century railway historian Frederick Williams singled out Toton for attention in his 1883 book *Our Iron Roads*, in which he recorded that in the winter as many as 26,000 wagons a month would be received and despatched.

Williams was intrigued by the role played by horses in the yards, where during severe winter weather, the grease in the wagon axleboxes froze solid, causing wheels to skid along the rails, with two or three animals needed to move a single wagon.

He wrote: "It is very interesting to see the sagacity of the horses, to watch them picking their way among the moving wagons, especially at night. After being suddenly unhooked from a wagon they will be perfectly still where there is only just room for them to stand between two lines of rails, while a squealing engine and a shunt of wagons pass perhaps on each side of them."

It is little wonder that the number of recorded accidents was considerable, with poor lighting at night and lax safety, and little provision was made by the company for an ambulance service.

Mr Dawson was one of the first men at Toton to receive a first aid

A stub of line, abandoned but in relatively good condition, survives within the site of the former Stanton Ironworks. Rail traffic was briefly revived to and from the works in the 1990s. It has been suggested that plans for extensive housing development on the Stanton site could lead to a connection with the Nottingham tramway system at some time in the future (Author).

The M1 motorway was very much the modern transport image in the mid-1960s. Pictured is construction work in 1965 at Junction 26, at Nuthall (*Copyright Nottingham Post and www.picturethepast.org.uk*).

certificate and by the time of his retirement the yard had a well-equipped ambulance, and training courses were provided for all employees.

A new high-level route, built into the Toton Yards from Trent Junction to the south, opened in 1901. The up and down yards were mechanised in the 1930s to accelerate the return of empty coal wagons to the collieries, with the major engineering work completed by May 1939.

Coal traffic was assembled on the "up" or east side of the depot to form trains travelling to various parts of the country in the south, west and east. The return empty wagons were received on the "down" or west side of the depot, where they were sorted and sent to their respective collieries.

This was performed on the gravitation principle on more than 100 sidings, extending over 26 miles and able to handle up to 7,900 wagons. Shunting was now controlled by specially designed clusters of white lights, operated from the hump room.

With the development of the motorways in the 1960s and 70s, tonnages of freight handled by the nationalised British Railways system declined sharply. BR made substantial financial losses and the industry's government paymasters urged economies.

Innovations such as freightliner trains, conveying containers between ports and major cities, and single-load services running from point of origin to destination without the need for marshalling, proved successful.

Now BR management looked for a more economic way of moving wagonload freight and in 1977 launched the Speedlink service, using air-braked wagons. Speedlink covered the whole country, from Penzance and Plymouth in the south west to Keith and Inverness in the north of Scotland. It was based on 12 main marshalling yards, including Toton, each receiving at least one train a day from each of the others.

In addition there were a series of smaller yards located in traffic centres which also provided services for non-Speedlink trains such as crew reliefs, and by 1981 there were about two hundred of these smaller yards, a figure which gradually reduced to under a hundred.

The plan called for each train to spend no more than an hour shunting at each depot, wagons were collected by trip workings in the afternoons and evenings, hauled through the trunk network at night and delivered by trip workings before lunch the following morning.

In spite of early promise and a number of healthy traffic flows, Speedlink failed to achieve a working profit and after a number of rationalisations and cut backs the network was formally closed down in 1991. It was a major blow to Toton, already suffering from a decline in coal traffic.

Toton lost the last of its domestic coal traffic, originating from Daw Mill Colliery in Warwickshire, in the mid-2000s. Now what is left of the yard is primarily a staging point for imported coal from Immingham, Avonmouth and Liverpool docks, for use at Ratcliffe-on-Soar power station.

With the unseemly and potentially disastrous rush to switch to greener energy sources, coal-fired power stations like Ratcliffe are themselves under threat.

The other traffic still handled at Toton is composed of infrastructure services for Network Rail and part of the yard is a 'virtual quarry', the industry's name for what is effectively a stockyard for ballast.

Toton, from the earliest days of the Midland Railway, was also the location for a major locomotive depot. In the 1950s, in the twilight of steam traction, it was the home shed for more than 150 locomotives, although by this time shunting in the yards had largely been taken over by diesel traction.

One aspect of the Toton complex still thriving at the time of writing is the Traction Maintenance Depot, opened in 1966 as the successor to the steam motive power depot.

Since privatisation of the UK rail network, Toton TMD has been operated by English Welsh and Scottish Trains (EWS) now rebranded as DB Schenker Rail (UK).

Changes in the maintenance of locomotives have also meant that Toton is now the only traction maintenance depot within the DBS UK organisation where heavy maintenance is carried out on locomotives.

The summer of 1966 saw final steam-hauled express passenger trains through the Erewash Valley between Sheffield and Nottingham, in the form of the Leeds-Poole holiday service, which ran between June 18th and September 3rd that year.

Fittingly, given the domination the LMS locomotive class had enjoyed over express services through the valley, particularly in the case of the route's main 'named' train, the London St Pancras to Glasgow St Enoch Thames Clyde Express, the job was given to three remaining Stanier Jubilee 4-6-0s, named Alberta, Bihar and Orissa, and Sturdee.

The evocative smell of steam still hangs, at least in the imagination, under the railway bridges of the valley. Despite the controversial nature of HS2, it is comforting to feel that future generations of rail enthusiasts will continue to attach importance to the Erewash Valley as a railway route of importance.

STOP PRESS

At the time of writing the re-opening to passenger traffic of the Pye Bridge to Kirkby-in-Ashfield railway line was being discussed, together with a new station for Pinxton. Local authorities see the possibility of the line providing services to link Mansfield and the Ashfield area to the HS2 project.

Chapter Five

The Changed Face of Valley Politics

'(Clifford) began to get a new idea of his own village. The place had always frightened him but he had thought it more or less stable. Now -? Is there much socialism, bolshevism, among the people? he asked. Oh, you hear a few loud-mouthed ones, but they're mostly women who've got into debt. The men don't take no notice. I don't believe you'll ever turn our Teversal men into Reds.' – Lady Chatterley's Lover.

Those whose familiarity with the Erewash Valley stems mainly from reading the novels and short stories of D H Lawrence could be forgiven for believing that such an industrial hotbed would have an unbroken connection with radical politics.

For decades the radical voice did indeed predominate, until the 1920s through the Liberal Party and then the emergent Labour Party, which for another 40 years or so held sway in most parts of the valley.

Things began to alter significantly in the 1980s, when extensive boundary revisions changed the electoral map and the present-day format was established of the five parliamentary constituencies which still represent the Erewash Valley – Erewash, Amber Valley and Bolsover in Derbyshire, and Broxtowe and Ashfield on the Nottinghamshire bank.

Just exactly how valley politics have changed is perhaps best illustrated by examining the history of the old Ilkeston Parliamentary Constituency, which in its 1950s heyday was one of the divisions where, according to popular legend, the Labour vote was weighed rather than counted.

The very name of the constituency was something of a misnomer, as not just Ilkeston but the other valley industrial and mining centres of Heanor, Ripley and Alfreton were also part of the division, along with many Labour-supporting pit villages.

Then, in 1983, the Ilkeston division was torn apart to create two new constituencies, which would in the years to come produce election results that largely destroyed the old tradition of radical representation.

The new Amber Valley seat (a confusing name in itself, as many of its towns and villages are geographically in the Erewash Valley) took Heanor, Ripley and Alfreton and merged them with the truly rural and Conservative-leaning parts of the old Belper seat, in the Derwent Valley, to the west of the Erewash. The traditional in-built Labour majority produced by the coalfield towns and villages was instantly diluted .

Much the same thing happened in the new Erewash division, where the town

Before extensions to the franchise local politicians were usually drawn from the ranks of the nobility and gentry. Admiral Sir John Borlase Warren, born in Stapleford in 1753, alternated spells as a Member of Parliament with acting as Ambassador to the Russian court at St Petersburg, fighting the French and arguing with the political leaders of the day over their refusal to grant him a peerage.

A Conservative presence in a former Labour stronghold. Erewash MP Maggie Throup, who was re-elected in 2017, has a community office in the former Ilkeston Co-operative Society building in the town *(Author)*.

of Ilkeston now found itself in a parliamentary seat containing not only Long Eaton , once solidly Liberal but much more prone to swing politics in later years, but also a wide swathe of the Tory-inclined South East Derbyshire rural area.

In one swoop the electoral fortunes of the Derbyshire side of the lower and middle Erewash valley were transformed, as will be examined in more detail later in this chapter.

Elsewhere in the Erewash Valley, the wind of change blew in a more moderate fashion.

At the northern tip of the valley, the Pinxton area was (and is) part of the Labour constituency of Bolsover, held for Labour by the former miner Dennis Skinner.

On the Nottinghamshire side of the River Erewash the effects of the parliamentary reorganisation which produced the present-day Ashfield and Broxtowe constituencies, also had repercussions for local politics, although none were perhaps quite as far-ranging as those which transformed the politics of the Derbyshire coal and iron towns.

Since this chapter was first written, the General Election of June 2017 has taken place. Its results were interesting in detail but the overall effect was to leave the political situation in the Erewash Valley unchanged.

The Erewash Valley and its five parliamentary seats emerged from the election in the same shape as it entered a long and fractious campaign, described by political analyst Anthony Seldon, Vice-Chancellor of The University of Buckingham, as ‘the most extraordinary in British history’.

Although the result in the country was a virtual stalemate with Prime Minister Theresa May and her Conservative government clinging on to a semblance of power with the support of the Northern Irish Democratic Unionists, events in the valley suggested that overall, the swing to the right which has characterised local politics in recent times had been maintained.

Tory Maggie Throup quite comfortably retained the Erewash seat and kept the swing from Conservatives to Labour down to just 0.85 per cent.

In the neighbouring Derbyshire seat of Amber Valley, sitting MP Nigel Mills nearly doubled his majority and achieved a swing from Labour to the Conservatives of 4.46 per cent.

The closest to a shock result in the valley came across the county border in Ashfield, where Labour’s Gloria de Piero increased her number of votes but saw her majority of nearly 9,000 at the 2015 General Election shrink dramatically to just 441 votes, with a swing of nearly nine per cent from her party to the Conservatives.

Up in the far north of the valley Dennis Skinner increased his vote in a higher turnout than in 2015 but saw his majority cut by more than half, from 11,778 to 5,288. The swing from Labour to the Tories in Bolsover was 7.70 per cent.

In Amber Valley, Ashfield, Bolsover and Erewash alike there was a common factor; the virtual demise of UKIP as an electoral force, as people supporting Britain leaving the European Union voted Conservative.

In Erewash and Amber Valley UKIP failed to field a candidate, to bolster Conservative (and Brexit) hopes. In Bolsover the UKIP candidate lost three quarters of the support enjoyed in 2015, whilst in Ashfield the UKIP vote slumped from more than 10,000 in 2015 to less than 4,000 in 2017.

All of this leaves just the Nottinghamshire seat of Broxtowe, at the southern end of the valley, to be analysed. Here again,

The wheatsheaf motif of the Co-operative Movement stands proudly on a gable of the former Ilkeston Co-operative Society premises in South Street, Ilkeston. The motto 'Labor and Wait' was originally spelled as 'Labour' but was altered to the American spelling in the 1860s, in tribute to the Northern Unionist side in the Civil War *(Author)*.

UKIP and Brexit was a major, if not quite the deciding factor. Remainer Anna Soubry, a thorn in Theresa May's side since the Prime Minister took on the job, held the seat for the Tories, but saw her majority slashed from 4,287 to 863.

The most famous politician with Erewash Valley links, Europhile Kenneth Clarke, comfortably retained his Rushcliffe seat for the Conservatives, but with a greatly reduced majority.

To best understand the development of politics in the valley over the past two hundred years, we need to examine how not just the make-up of the constituencies but also the vast increase in the numbers allowed to vote, through universal male suffrage and female suffrage, together with changing economic and social conditions, all affected and influenced the political scene.

During the 19th Century the Erewash Valley was transformed from a largely agricultural district with cottage industries and mining and iron-making on a small scale, into a heavily-populated industrial power house.

At the start of the era the various parliamentary divisions in Nottinghamshire and Derbyshire were represented either by members of the aristocracy and gentry, or the monied and propertied new middle classes. Sir John Borlase Warren of Stapleford was a prime example of a gentry politician.

The Reform Act of 1832 retained property qualifications, notably a stipulation in the borough constituencies that the vote for working men was restricted to those who paid a rental of £10 or more. This stipulation meant that the majority of working men were still excluded from the polls.

A second Reform Act in 1867, introduced by the Conservative government led by Benjamin Disraeli, extended the franchise to those who rented rather than owned properties, greatly increasing the electorate.

The second significant round of voting reform coincided with the great surge in industrialisation in the Erewash Valley. Although to get the act through Parliament Disraeli persuaded his MPs that many working men would vote Tory (the legislation was dubbed 'the great leap in the dark'), it was perhaps not too surprising that a district peopled mainly by colliers, blast furnacemen, foundrymen, railway employees, lace industry twisthands, hosiery and knitwear operatives and their families leaned then and for decades after towards more radical candidates.

Although Admiral Sir John Borlase Warren's parliamentary career

Electioneering . Conservative MP for Broxtowe Anna Soubry supported the Remain campaign in the 2016 Referendum on membership of the European Union. She retained her seat, which includes Stapleford and other parts of the Erewash Valley , in the 2017 General Election. *(Broxtowe Conservative Association)*.

occupied the years between 1774 and 1807, before the era of reform, his colourful career qualifies him for a place in any account of Erewash Valley politics and politicians.

Throughout that period he tended to serve a spell at Westminster and then return temporarily to his original calling as an officer in the Royal Navy. He took time off from politics to sink or capture a French warship or two and also served as British Ambassador to the court of the Tsar of Russia, in St Petersburg, but his career, like that of so many politicians, ended in disappointment.

Gloria de Piero was re-elected in 2017 as the MP for Ashfield, which includes Eastwood *(Ashfield Labour Party)*

Although created a baronet in 1775 – the baronetcy had been held until 1689 by his ancestors, the Borlase family, he repeatedly failed to win a Peerage, something he greatly resented.

Towards the end of the 19th century another exceedingly colourful character flashed across the valley's political scene in the form of the financier Ernest Terah Hooley.

E T Hooley was the son of Terah Hooley, lace maker and developer of lace factories in the valley, who resided at Risley Lodge in the village of Risley, after retiring from business to live the life of a country gentleman. E T made a large fortune by floating companies which were to become household names, including Schweppes and Dunlop, and became a friend of the Prince of Wales, later King Edward the Seventh.

For many years E T Hooley lived at Risley Hall, now a hotel and spa. His name returned to the newspaper headlines in recent times when an article recalled his chequered business career and the fact that at one time he owned a second country seat. This was Anmer Hall, the Georgian house in Norfolk which was a wedding gift to the Duke and Duchess of Cambridge from Her Majesty The Queen.

Hooley's eventual financial crash was spectacular, but although he was declared bankrupt and jailed for fraud, he managed to retain Risley Hall, which had been transferred to his wife's name, and continue something of a business career, well into the 1920s.

When he died, in 1947, the *Long Eaton Advertiser* devoted the whole of its broadsheet front page to an obituary.

Seven closely crowded columns of type chronicled his business successes, his qualities as a host, his friendships with royalty and his generosity to charitable causes, but the paper made no mention of the darker side of his life.

If Admiral Sir John Borlase Warren's political career ended, like so many do, in disappointment, Ernest Terah Hooley's never passed the initial hurdle. He was adopted in 1897 as the prospective Conservative candidate for the Ilkeston division and his initial experiences as a candidate served to confirm the hold radical politics had over the valley.

Although a man of consuming ambition, Hooley also possessed a considerable streak of realism and was not over optimistic about his chances of securing a seat in the House of Commons, famously declaring in later years: "They needed almost to have a candle and a lantern to find a Conservative in Long Eaton."

E T Hooley never made it into Parliament, but not because he was defeated at the polls. The year after he lamented the lack of Tories in the area saw him go

Colourful individuals continued to play a part in the political affairs of the Erewash Valley throughout the 19th and 20th centuries. The financier Ernest Terah Hooley of Risley was adopted as the Tory candidate for Ilkeston and said finding a Conservative in certain parts of the constituency almost requires 'a candle and a lantern'. Hooley went bankrupt a year later and was thereby automatically disqualified from standing for Parliament *(Author's Collection)*.

Election stunts were not uncommon in the Edwardian era, even for local borough polls. *(Erewash Museum).*

bankrupt, which automatically excluded him from standing for election.

The industrial towns of the valley generally had a built-in majority for the Liberal Party, until that organisation's virtual collapse as a national force in the early 1920s. The allegiance of the colliers and other industrial workers then passed in the main to the Labour Party.

The boundaries of the parliamentary constituencies covering the Erewash Valley have altered on several occasions during the span of what can be considered to be the era of modern politics (from roughly 1850s onwards).

As we have seen earlier in the chapter, success for Conservative Parliamentary candidates has generally come only when boundaries have been re-drawn to reflect a blend of industrial towns and rural villages. Such changes have, in recent times, helped to create a very different political landscape to that which previously applied.

Political change came to Ilkeston and its neighbouring Derbyshire towns in two stages.

In 1974 re-organisation affected local government, and Ilkeston lost its proud status as an individual municipal borough, formed under the Municipal Corporations Act 1882. Derbyshire had just five towns in total with borough status – Derby (from 1889 a county borough with additional powers), Chesterfield, Ilkeston, Glossop and Buxton.

Under the 1970s re-organisation Ilkeston was merged with the Urban District of Long Eaton, a town which had long coveted borough status but had failed to obtain it on more than one occasion, and with rural parishes which had previously formed part of the South East Derbyshire Rural District.

Heanor, Ripley and Alfreton, together with a number of former mining villages, merged with the politically well balanced town of Belper and a large Conservative-voting area in and around the Derwent Valley to form the new district of Amber Valley.

The new districts were allowed to adopt borough status and appoint mayors, a privilege previously confined to the older municipal boroughs.

Nine years later, in 1983, it was the turn of parliamentary representation locally to be re-organised. Both the Ilkeston and South East Derbyshire constituencies disappeared and the new divisions of Erewash and Amber Valley were created, with boundaries initially generally similar to those established earlier for the new district authorities.

Administrative change brought political upheaval in both of the new seats, which at the 2015 General Election (and again in 2017) maintained fairly comfortable Conservative majorities. The former South East Derbyshire seat had often been marginal, recording the lowest majority recorded for a Tory (12 votes) in the 1959 contest.

Things had been decidedly different in the old Ilkeston constituency, which had existed for almost a hundred years at the time of its abolition and, due again to boundary changes over the years, had become an increasingly strong Labour seat.

Until 1950 the Ilkeston division had consisted of the borough itself, Heanor, Ripley and parishes such as Codnor and Shipley. After that date another mining town, Alfreton, was included within its boundaries. The long-serving Member for Ilkeston, George Oliver, first elected for the seat in 1922, gradually built up a majority which in 1951 totalled 30,398 votes, the fourth largest in the country at the time.

Prior to local government reorganisation implemented in 1974, when the district of Erewash came into being, Ilkeston was proud of its status as an independent borough, one of just four in Derbyshire. Pictured is the incorporation ceremony of the town as a borough, in 1887. A huge crowd gathers outside the Town Hall. *Derbyshire Local Studies Libraries andwww. picturethepast.org.uk).*

The result of the 1980s parliamentary changes was that the majority of the mining and industrial towns and villages of the Derbyshire sector of the valley found themselves, for the first time in modern electoral history, represented by Conservative MPs.

In the 34 years since the new constituencies were first contested, Amber Valley has sent two Conservatives and one Labour MP to Westminster. The Conservatives have held the seat for a total of 21 years to Labour's 13 years in control.

In the case of Erewash, five members have represented the constituency in those 34 years, four Conservatives and one Labour. Again, the Conservatives have held the seat for 21 years, and Labour for 13.

During the 98 years existence of the old Ilkeston constituency, it was very firmly a male stronghold. Not only were all the seven MPs men, but during all that time there were only two women candidates, 40 years apart. Lady Anna Barlow (National Liberal) stood in 1924 and Mrs Peggy Edwards (Liberal) in 1964.

In sharp contrast the modern Erewash seat has had one male MP and four women members since its creation in 1983.

The Conservative Party has planted its standard very firmly in Ilkeston town centre, taking an office, ironically enough, in a shop unit that once formed part of the department store of the now defunct Ilkeston Co-operative Society.

The politics of the past are reflected in Ilkeston by an almost forgotten terracotta plaque, displayed on the gable end of the former Co-operative Society headquarters just off the Market Square.

It proclaims the message of co-operation through the medium of a wheatsheaf, a potent symbol of unity in strength. Whilst a single stalk of wheat can be easily broken, a whole sheaf has greater resilience. The wheatsheaf symbol is flanked by the motto 'Labor and Wait', the original trademark of the Co-operative Wholesale Society, registered in 1863.

The first meeting of Ilkeston Borough Council (*Derbyshire Local Studies Libraries and www.picturethepast.org.uk)*

Kenneth Clarke, who retained his Rushcliffe seat in the 2017 General Election after earlier suggesting that he would retire from Parliament, was another Remain supporter. Clarke grew up in the Erewash Valley and in his early days as an MP his constituency included Stapleford and other parts of the valley *(Rushcliffe Conservative Association).*

The wording of the motto was originally 'Labour and Wait', but was changed to the American spelling to reflect British working class support for the anti-slavery north in the American Civil War.

Given the generally radical political history of the mining and industrial townships of the Erewash Valley, it still comes as something of a shock to read the most recent analysis of the various valley constituencies available at the time of going to print, prepared by the polling company YouGov.

The analysis categorises both Erewash and Amber Valley as marginal Conservative seats, and goes on to describe the former Ilkeston constituency as 'an affluent residential and commuter area'. Accurate, yes, but still enough to cause a flutter to anyone who remembers a landscape of pit stacks, blast furnaces, marshalling yards, and (working) lace mills.

Amber Valley is classified as a marginal conservative seat, with YouGov recording that 'the former coal mining towns of Alfreton, Ripley and Heanor here all tend to vote Labour, but the more Conservative rural sections of the seat balance this out to an extent'.

Few would attempt to argue with the YouGov description of the Broxtowe seat as 'essentially the more affluent owner-occupied western suburbs of Nottingham that lie outside the city boundary. There is a high level of owner-occupation, very little social housing and a high proportion of residents commute into Nottingham for work'.

Ashfield is described as being affected by the economic difficulties associated with the decline of the mining industry. YouGov concludes: "the area is now gradually transitioning towards being more of a commuter area for Nottingham." No doubt the next analysis will factor in the major decline in the Labour vote in 2017.

It is impossible to disagree with YouGov's description of Bolsover 'monolithically Labour', although the polling company qualifies this slightly by recording that Dennis Skinner`s share of the vote has fallen over the years and no longer reaches the heights it did when this was an active mining community. The 2017 results certainly appeared to bear this out.

YouGov's demographics for the four constituencies that cover the vast majority of the geographic Erewash Valley – the proportion of the Bolsover seat that qualifies is too small to be statistically significant – actually offers a fairly consistent picture.

A good proportion of the catchment area of the River Erewash, even at the height of the valley's industrial power, was essentially rural, with the industry relatively tightly concentrated. By the 1990s, with heavy and extractive industry rapidly being replaced by light industry and the service sector, an Environment Agency report concluded that agricultural land (arable, grass and woodland) accounted for 76 per cent of land use, with just 24 per cent of the area classified as urban.

The most recent statistics show that, in Erewash, Amber Valley and Ashfield, around 70 per cent of housing is owner-occupied, unemployment, despite the steady decline of heavy industry, is around the national average of just under five per cent and in terms of ethnicity, between 95 and 97 per cent of the population is classified as white British.

Broxtowe differs from the general demographic trends only in terms of ethnicity, with the figure classified as white British dropping to 88 per cent. The presence of The University of Nottingham, a huge draw for international students, is probably a factor.

Historically, Parliamentary politics in the Erewash Valley over the past century and a half have on occasions exerted a major influence on the direction of government in the United Kingdom. and the area's elected representatives have played a role in many momentous events.

The list of Members of Parliament from both the Derbyshire and Nottinghamshire banks of the Erewash is eclectic, and has included war heroes and Ban the Bomb Campaigners, Jewish refugees and a Nazi sympathiser, doctors and miners,

Local issues are just as important as national concerns for Members of Parliament. Maggie Throup MP for Erewash, campaigned for the re-opening of Ilkeston railway station. She is pictured on the first day trains served the station, with Lawrence Bowman, commercial director of East Midlands Trains and Paul Maynard, the Minister for Rail.. (*Steve Footitt and East Midlands Trains*)

lawyers and railwaymen, party loyalists and men whose activities have helped to topple administrations.

The Ilkeston constituency, in its 98 years of existence, never once elected a Conservative MP. In contrast Long Eaton, although recognised in the early years of the 20th century as a stronghold of Liberalism, was later linked for parliamentary purposes with the rural areas of South Derbyshire. Over the years the constituencies of first South Derbyshire and later South-East Derbyshire elected Liberals, Tories and Labour MPs.

On the Nottinghamshire side of the Erewash the county and the town of Nottingham each returned two members to parliament, in the pre-modern political era. These constituencies were split into two two-member divisions by the Reform Act in 1832. The county was then represented by the North Nottinghamshire and South Nottinghamshire constituencies until the redistribution in 1885.

At this time the Rushcliffe constituency, containing the Urban District of Beeston and Stapleford, and the rural district of Stapleford, together with the Erewash Valley parishes of Awsworth, Cossall and Trowell came into existence.

Eastwood and its surrounding district was part of the Broxtowe constituency for much of the 20th century, until later changes saw the town transferred to the present-day Ashfield seat.

Some of the politicians who represented valley constituencies (and others born or raised locally) have become almost legendary figures through the passing of time, whilst those who have held high office in more recent times may well eventually find their own niche in history.

The Liberal Party's unbroken 40-year tenure of the Ilkeston seat threw up two members of parliament who stood out from the rest, for vastly different reasons. The story of one of these men, J B Seeley, who held the perhaps unenviable position of Secretary of State for War during the run-up to Word War One, and at a time of great unrest in Ireland, is told in detail in a later chapter.

His predecessor as member for Ilkeston, the splendidly-

Sir Walter Foster was Liberal MP for Ilkeston from 1887 to 1910, winning six elections. He became the first medical doctor to hold ministerial office in Britain and is credited with saving the country from a cholera epidemic in 1893. He is pictured, complete with his renowned set of side whiskers, with his wife, circa 1900 *(Ilkeston Local Studies Library)*.

William Ewart Gladstone.

named Sir Balthazar Walter Foster (his first Christian name was rarely used) was born in Cambridge but grew up in Dublin, qualifying as a physician at Trinity College. He later became Professor of Anatomy at Birmingham and one of the leading medical researchers of his time.

Foster first sat in Parliament for Chester but was defeated in 1886. First thought to be leaving politics, and knighted for his past services, he returned to the House of Commons at a by-election at Ilkeston in 1886. Starting with a majority of 1,332, he sat for Ilkeston for 23 years, from 1887 to 1910.

Foster's chief claim to fame lies in the fact that he was the first medical doctor to hold a ministerial post in Britain, winning general acclaim for the role he played in preventing a disastrous worldwide cholera epidemic from reaching the country.

William Ewart Gladstone, in last of his four periods of office as Prime Minister in the 19th century, recognised that Foster's combination of medical knowledge and administrative ability, was ready-made for the cholera crisis.

Foster was appointed to head a three-year-long sanitation campaign, making him the equivalent of the special measures 'Tsars' beloved of more recent prime ministers.

Gladstone and the Liberals lost office during the campaign, not returning to power until 1905. Although Foster had hopes of a Cabinet role, he was overlooked, apparently on the grounds of his age, which was 65 at this point.

Worse was to follow after the General Election of 1910, when after his sixth victory in the Erewash Valley, Foster came under pressure to resign his Ilkeston seat in favour of Seeley, a rising star in the Liberal party who had been defeated in his previous seat.

Foster's consolation prize was an hereditary peerage , as Baron Ilkeston in the County of Derby Sadly, he did not live long to enjoy his new found status in the House of Lords, dying in 1913, at the age of 72.

W E Gladstone himself made at least one appearance in the Erewash Valley before his adoring supporters. Journalist, businessman, sometime Parliamentary candidate and author the late Geoffrey Kingscott, who lived in Sawley, described the occasion in his 2006 book *Last Train from Trent Station*.

Sir Walter Foster was persuaded to step down from the Ilkeston Constituency in 1910, to make way for his fellow Liberal J B Seeley to be returned at a by-election. Seeley, a former Conservative who had earlier crossed the floor of the House of Commons with his friend Winston Churchill, had lost his Liverpool seat in the 1910 General Election. Foster went to the House of Lords as First Baron Ilkeston, and is pictured in his Peer's coronet and robes *(Ilkeston Local Studies Library)*.

Seeley, later ennobled as Lord Mottistone, held the Ilkeston seat from 1910 to 1922, when he was defeated by Labour's George Oliver. Seeley held high political office and was Secretary of State for War with a seat in the cabinet from 1912 to 1914. He was forced to resign following his mishandling of the Curragh Mutiny in Ireland, then redeemed his reputation by gallant military service as a cavalryman *(Erewash Museum)*.

A less flamboyant character than Foster or Seeley, George Oliver enjoyed political triumph and disaster as MP for Ilkeston for nearly 40 years. He still holds the record for the smallest-ever margin of defeat but later established one of the largest majorities in the country. He is pictured in 1959 (*Ilkeston Local Studies Library*).

Trent was an interchange station situated in the countryside a couple of miles from Long Eaton (see Chapter Four *The Valley as a Route to Riches*). In 1886 it was announced that Gladstone would pass through Trent en route from London to Scotland, via the Midland Railway route.

Liberals throughout the midlands decided to stage a show of support, many arriving by rail throughout the hours before the train's arrival in the middle of the day. It was estimated that some 4,000 people gathered to greet the Grand Old Man of British politics, including a party of 150 members of the Long Eaton Liberal Association, led by their President, Joseph Orchard, who marched in procession from the town to the station.

J B Seeley won the by-election that followed Foster's resignation and held the seat until defeated by Labour's George Oliver in 1922. Seeley himself had a chequered career as politician, soldier and controversialist (see Chapter Eight *A Valley at War*).

George Oliver in turn was to be associated with the Ilkeston seat for more than 40 years and played a leading role in one of the United Kingdom's biggest political upheavals of the 20th century.

Oliver retained his seat in 1923, when the Conservatives won a substantial overall majority. The Tory leader, Andrew Bonar Law, then died and was replaced by Stanley Baldwin, who after rejecting his predecessor's electoral pledge not to introduce protective tariffs, sought a fresh mandate from the electorate in 1924.

A this election the Conservatives, although still the largest party, had clearly lost the debate and although Baldwin initially remained Prime Minister (the balance of power was held by the Liberals) he advised the King to send for the leader of the Labour Party, Ramsay MacDonald, as Labour held more seats in the Commons than the Liberals.

MacDonald's first ministry lasted only from January to November 1924. During that brief period Oliver made a name for himself at Westminster, with a motion calling for a national minimum wage.

Re-elected for Ilkeston once again in November 1924, Oliver now set about establishing a parallel legal career. He

A rare photograph of Abraham John Flint, who in 1931 defeated George Oliver in the Ilkeston constituency by a record low majority of just 2 votes. Flint is pictured on the far right of the first row of boys at his public school, Oundle, in 1917. (*Elspeth Langsdale, Oundle School*).

retrained as a trade union lawyer and was called to the Bar by the Middle Temple in 1927. At the 1929 General Election Labour again failed to achieve an overall majority and for the second time took office as a minority government, reliant on Liberal support to pass legislation. In the summer of 1931, the government was faced by a political and financial crisis as the value of the pound and its place on the Gold Standard came under threat over fears that the budget was unbalanced.

During August 1931 MacDonald and his ministers attempted to produce amendments to the budget that were politically acceptable. They failed to find a solution that would prevent mass resignations and a split in the Labour Party.

The straw that broke the camel's back as far as the Labour movement was concerned was a proposal to reduce the amount of benefit paid to the unemployed. The Cabinet split and in August 1931 the Labour government resigned. MacDonald remained at the head of a National Government, made up of a rump of official Labour Party members, Conservatives and Liberals.

Ramsey MacDonald, regarded as a traitor to the cause of the working classes, was expelled from the Labour Party and ever after remained a controversial figure in Labour circles.

In what has been described as the most astonishing vote in the history of British politics, the Conservatives won 470 seats, reducing Labour from 287 to 52. Six parties contested the election, with the National Liberals, supporters of the National Government, securing 35 seats, the mainstream Liberals, headed by Herbert Samuel securing 33, Ramsey MacDonald's National Labour winning 13, and former Prime Minister David Lloyd George's Independent Liberals gaining just four.

George Oliver, who in 1929 had secured a majority of nearly 12,500 in Ilkeston – a huge advance on his 1924 figure of less than 2,000 - stayed loyal to the official Labour Party during the election campaign. Given the size of his majority and local popularity, Oliver was favourite to retain his seat, but in the biggest single upset of a sensational poll, was defeated by the man parachuted into the contest by MacDonald's backers.

In a straight fight between Oliver and the National Liberal candidate, Derby barrister Abraham John Flint, generally known as Bob, and with the Conservatives and Liberals standing aside to give MacDonald's nominee the chance of victory, Flint won by two votes – the smallest majority in any individual constituency election since universal suffrage was introduced.

Flint, although a Labour supporter, apparently had no real interest in a political career. He was persuaded to stand in the Ilkeston division by Derby MP J H 'Jimmy'Thomas, one of the cabinet members who had followed MacDonald into the National Government.,

It was claimed that Jimmy Thomas persuaded Flint to stand in Ilkeston to relieve electoral pressure on himself in Derby. George Oliver by this stage of his career was an effective politician and an assured speaker who would constitute less of a danger to MacDonald fighting to keep his seat than being free to speak and canvass for Official Labour elsewhere.

The campaign, effectively an internecine civil war, was bitter, with Jimmy Thomas greeted with shouts of 'Judas' when he spoke for Flint in the Ilkeston campaign.

After the polls closed it became obvious that the Ilkeston election was very close. After no definite result had been reached in the early hours of the morning, the Returning Officer decided to call a halt to the count, which was resumed later in the day.

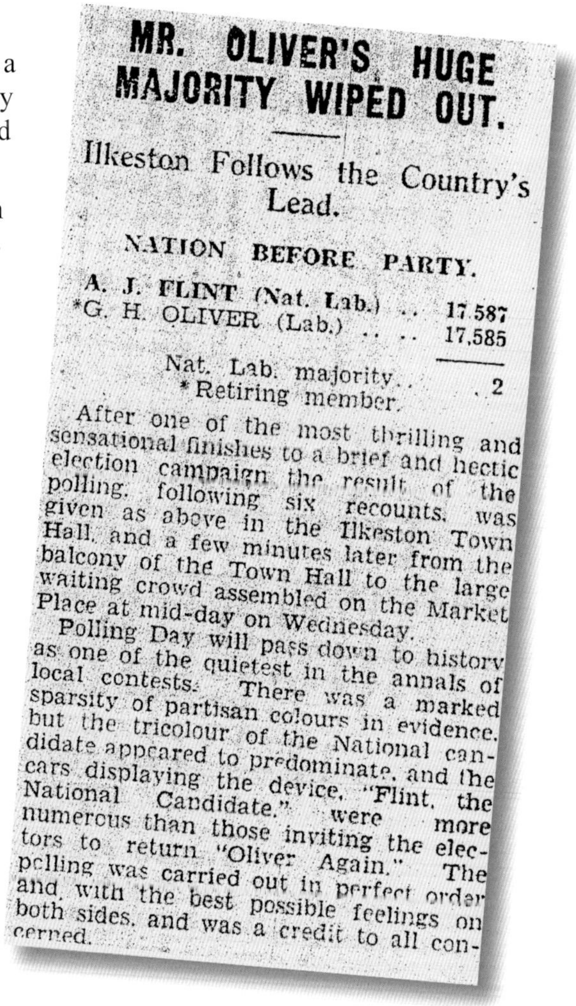
MR. OLIVER'S HUGE MAJORITY WIPED OUT.

Ilkeston Follows the Country's Lead.

NATION BEFORE PARTY.

A. J. FLINT (Nat. Lab.) ..	17,587
*G. H. OLIVER (Lab.)	17,585
Nat. Lab. majority..	2

*Retiring member.

After one of the most thrilling and sensational finishes to a brief and hectic election campaign the result of the polling, following six recounts, was given as above in the Ilkeston Town Hall, and a few minutes later from the balcony of the Town Hall to the large waiting crowd assembled on the Market Place at mid-day on Wednesday.

Polling Day will pass down to history as one of the quietest in the annals of local contests. There was a marked sparsity of partisan colours in evidence, but the tricolour of the National candidate appeared to predominate, and the cars displaying the device, "Flint, the National Candidate," were more numerous than those inviting the electors to return "Oliver Again." The polling was carried out in perfect order and, with the best possible feelings on both sides, and was a credit to all concerned.

The headlines in the *Ilkeston Advertiser* following the 1931 General Election, when a National Government headed by former Labour leader Ramsey MacDonald was returned. Ilkeston's sensational election result was the low point of the career of George Oliver, who stayed loyal to the Labour Party (*Ilkeston Local Studies Library*).

When the count was resumed, Flint was eventually declared to be elected. Oliver was gracious in defeat before retiring with his faithful supporters to the Co-op Hall. Abraham Flint said the circumstances of the poll were exceptional - 'I might almost say historic'.

There had, he added, been no bad blood between himself and George Oliver, who were 'the best of friends'.

During the campaign, which the local press reported as having been 'one of the quietest in the annals of local contests, with a sparsity of partisan colours', Flint received a letter of support from Sir Walter Foster's daughter.

Abraham Flint was chosen by the National Government's parliamentary managers to make his maiden speech by seconding the 'Loyal Address' at the opening of the first session in 1931. It was his first and final distinctive act in the House.

By the next General Election, with the Official Labour Party on the brink of a modest comeback, Flint sensed that he had little chance of retaining the seat and announced that he would not be a candidate. He continued his practice at the Bar, became a Circuit Judge in Nottingham and served in World War Two as a major in the Royal Artillery. He died in 1971.

During his spell out of Parliament, George Oliver worked as a barrister for the Transport and General Workers Union.

Flint's instincts about the likely outcome of the 1935 General Election proved to be sound. George Oliver, opposed by just one candidate, for the National Government, romped home by 10,601 votes.

The National Government, by now led by the Conservative Stanley Baldwin, maintained a comfortable majority, although Official Labour, led by Clement Atlee, almost trebled its 1931 score, winning 154. The National Liberals and mainstream Liberals won 54 seats between them, Ramsey MacDonald's National Labour again totalled 13, while the Independent Labour Party, led by James Maxton, won in three constituencies.

Normal service had been resumed in Ilkeston in what was to be the last General Election, because of World War Two, for ten years.

George Oliver eventually became regarded as leaning towards the more moderate wing of the Labour Party. At the party's annual conference in 1939, he moved the expulsion from the party of Aneurin Bevan and three other left wing members because of their involvement in the 'Popular Front' movement, which attempted to build an alliance with the Liberal Party, the Communist Party and some anti-fascist Conservatives.

When Labour achieved its first ever majority government at the landslide election of 1945, Oliver was given ministerial office, as Parliamentary Under-Secretary of State at the Home Office, leaving the government two years later.

The 1950 boundary changes mentioned earlier in this chapter, bringing Alfreton and other mining centres into the Ilkeston constituency, gave Oliver one of the safest Labour seats in Britain. At the 1951 General Election his majority of 30,398 was a very far cry from his despairing two-vote defeat in 1931. He stood down at the 1964 General Election, but lived to be 95.

Long Eaton's radicalism was usually at odds with the conservatism (with small and large c) of the South Derbyshire rural area with which the town found itself united for parliamentary purposes in the second half of the 19th century.

Candidates for both Conservative and Liberal parties were drawn from the ranks of landed gentry, brewers and mill owners, with the sequence only being broken in 1929, when Derbyshire South's first Labour MP, David Pole, son of a ship's captain from the Shetland islands, was elected. Pole served for just two years.

One of Derbyshire South's most prominent MPs, who also represented South East Derbyshire after boundary changes, was the former railwayman Arthur Joseph Champion, usually known as Joe. He was first elected for South Derbyshire at the 1945 general election, with a thumping majority of nearly 23,000 votes.

He then held the South East Derbyshire seat until losing to his Conservative opponent in 1959 by just 12 votes. In the last year of Clement Attlee's Labour Government, he served from April to October 1951 as Parliamentary Secretary to the Ministry of Agriculture and Fisheries. After taking his seat in the House of Lords, he was a Minister without Portfolio from 1964 to 1967 in Harold Wilson's government.

He was made a life peer on 11 May 1962, as Baron Champion, of Pontypridd in the County of Glamorgan and in January 1967 was appointed as a Privy Counsellor. He died in Pontypridd aged 87.

The gloriously side-whiskered, frock-coated candidates of the 19th and early 20th centuries, of whichever party, would probably have looked askance at the line-up in Erewash for the 2005 General Election.

The victorious Labour candidate, Liz Blackman, might have raised a few Victorian and Edwardian eyebrows, having

Factors including religious affiliation still mattered in local and national politics in the first half of the 20th century. Irishman James Frayne was elected to Long Eaton Urban District Council in 1924 and nine years later, in 1933, became the first Roman Catholic to become chairman of the authority. He is seen addressing a public meeting in the town in the early 1930s *(Author's Collection).*

been selected from an all-woman shortlist, although the Conservative and Liberal Democrat would have been regarded by their predecessors as at least coming from a recognisable political tradition.

Equally, the political viewpoints of the anti-European Union candidates, the television presenter Robert Kilroy-Silk for Veritas, a splinter group from the United Kingdom Independence Party and Geoffrey Kingscott (the chronicler of Gladstone's visit to Trent Station) for UKIP itself, would no doubt have been accepted by most as legitimate.

But what can be said about the British National Party nominee, who secured almost a thousand votes?

William Edward Hopkin, Nottinghamshire County Council Alderman, member of Eastwood Urban District Council for 45 years and a close friend, confidante and loyal champion of D H *Lawrence (Nottinghamshire County Council and www.picturethepast.org.uk).*

Or, stretching credulity to the limit, David Laurence Bishop of The Church of the Militant Elvis, who received the backing of 116 fellow devotees of the King of Rock'n'Roll?

Local government politics in the valley through the years, although failing to attract the national spotlight which on occasions has shone brightly on Members of Parliament , have thrown up their fair share of characters. In 1931, the year of the epic battle between Abraham Flint and George Oliver, the Ilkeston Borough Council elections were contested in the town's North, Granby and South wards, with nominated candidates in the Victoria, Market and Old Park wards being returned unopposed.

Standing on a political party ticket in a local government election in that era was less usual than today. The local press list of those standing for election in the contested wards had no mention of political affiliation Looking at the descriptions of the individual candidates however offers some hints as to their political preferences.

In one ward a miner opposed a butcher, whilst elsewhere the contest pitted a silk fabric manufacturer against a housewife and a land agent against an erector. The three candidates returned unopposed were all professional men, a chartered mechanical engineer, a barrister and a solicitor.

Across the River Erewash in Eastwood , one of the most active and effective figures in public life was William Edward 'Willie' Hopkin, a prominent figure in both the political and social spheres , an early influence on D H Lawrence, and regarded as a member of the author's 'set' in the context of the author's life whilst still living in the valley

Hopkin (1862-1951) was renowned for keeping 'open house' for intense debates and discussions on politics and other topics, and Lawrence attended these during some of his most formative years. He married twice, firstly to ardent feminist Sallie Potter , who died in 1923 and secondly , in 1925, to Olive Slack..

Willie and Sallie Hopkin befriended the young Lawrence and remained loyal confidants throughout his life, championing the author at a time when he was unpopular in Eastwood.

Hopkin was a member of Eastwood Urban District Council for 45 years and was also a member of Nottinghamshire County Council, with his many years of service recognised when he was made an Alderman. His contributions to public life also included service as a school governor and a magistrate.

The debt that the author owed in many respects to the Hopkins is reflected in many of the letters which form part of the Lawrence Collection at Eastwood Library. His affection for Willie and Sallie is also evident from the inscriptions on the signed first editions of his works he presented to the couple over the years, which also form part of the library collection.

By 1951 women had held important positions in national Government, but had yet to penetrate the corridors of power at Long Eaton Urban District Council. This photograph of the elected members and chief officers, taken in the Festival of Britain year of 1951, was solidly male. *(Author's Collection).*

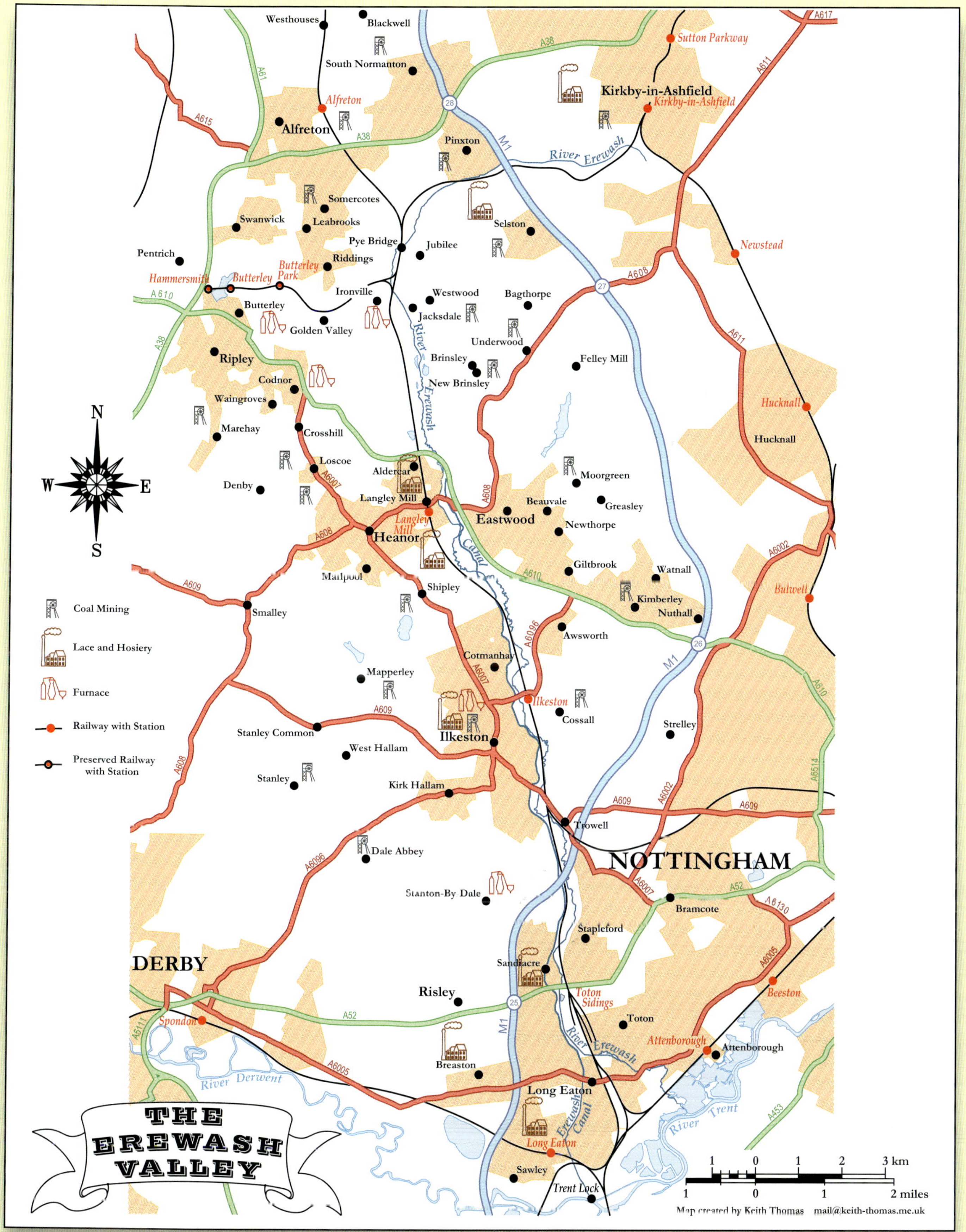
THE EREWASH VALLEY
Westhouses
Blackwell
South Normanton
Alfreton
Kirkby-in-Ashfield
Sutton Parkway
Pinxton
River Erewash
Somercotes
Swanwick
Leabrooks
Selston
Pye Bridge
Jubilee
Pentrich
Riddings
Butterley Park
Hammersmith
Butterley
Newstead
Ironville
Westwood
Bagthorpe
Jacksdale
Golden Valley
Underwood
Ripley
Brinsley
New Brinsley
Felley Mill
Codnor
Waingroves
Marehay
Crosshill
Hucknall
Loscoe
Aldercar
Denby
Langley Mill
Moorgreen
Beauvale
Greasley
Eastwood
Newthorpe
Heanor
Erewash Canal
Giltbrook
Watnall
Marlpool
Shipley
Kimberley
Nuthall
Bulwell
Smalley
Awsworth
Cotmanhay
Mapperley
Ilkeston
Cossall
Strelley
Stanley Common
West Hallam
Stanley
Kirk Hallam
Trowell
Dale Abbey
NOTTINGHAM
Stanton-By Dale
Bramcote
Stapleford
DERBY
Sandiacre
Toton Sidings
Beeston
Risley
Toton
Spondon
Attenborough
River Derwent
Breaston
Long Eaton
River Trent
Sawley
Trent Lock
N
S
W
E
Coal Mining
Lace and Hosiery
Furnace
Railway with Station
Preserved Railway with Station
A38
A61
A615
A610
A608
A6007
A609
A6096
A6002
A611
A617
A6514
A52
A6005
A6130
A453
A5111
M1
28
27
26
25
1 0 1 2 3 km
1 0 1 2 miles
Map created by Keith Thomas mail@keith-thomas.me.uk

Rural tranquillity. Looking across the Erewash Wetlands nature reserve between Jacksdale and Aldercar, to the pastures on the eastern slopes of the valley (*Author*)

The dramatic Crich Stand, the memorial to the Notts and Derby Regiment, The Sherwood Foresters, overlooks the Erewash Valley from its towering ridge (*Author*)

Jacksdale's war memorial, featuring the former pit village's unknown soldier, is captured through the spokes of the wheel of the mining memorial (*Author*)

The meandering stream. The River Erewash near Aldercar (*Author*)

Looking north from the terraced streets of Eastwood to the landscape immortalised by D H Lawrence as 'The Country of My Heart'.

The regular lines of fairly recent woodland and a steeply sloping pasture betray the fact that this is a restored pit tip, near Brinsley (*Author*)

The ruins of Beauvale Priory near Eastwood stand close to an attractive adjoining modern farmhouse (*Author*)

One of the area's most attractive and historic parish churches, All Saints at Sawley, stands close to the banks of the River Trent (*Author*)

Ancient Erewash. The Hemlock Stone, which stands between Stapleford and Bramcote (*Author*)

A rural section of the Pinxton Arm of the Cromford Canal near Jacksdale is still watered (*Author*)

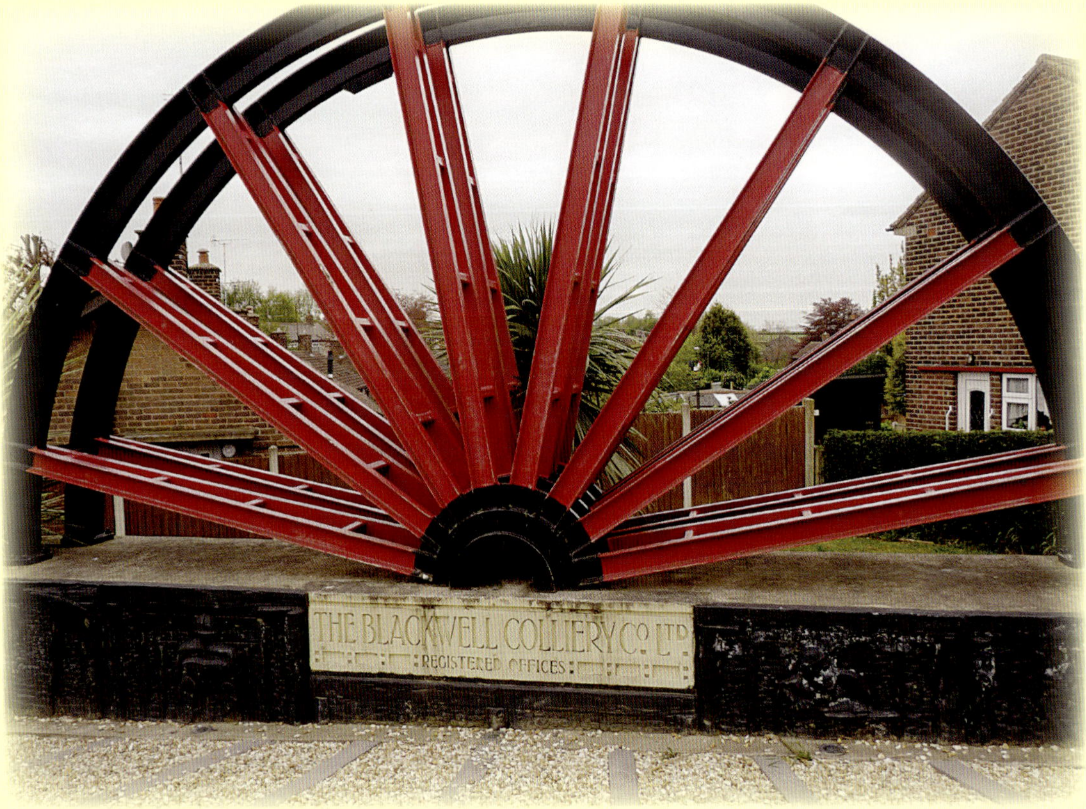

Every village in the coalfield areas commemorates those who toiled underground. Blackwell, in the upper Erewash Valley, is no exception to the rule. (*Author*)

Industrial decline. The sad sight of a derelict brewery, once operated by Hardy and Hansons, at Kimberley (*Author*)

Industrial Adaptability One. Harrington Mill at Long Eaton, the largest tenement lace mill ever built, is no longer home to lace making. Instead it provides space for a wide variety of trades and has a waiting list for potential tenants (*Author*)

Terry Cooke is a skilled upholsterer maintaining the skills for which Long Eaton is internationally famous

Industrial Adaptability Two. Cluny Lace of Ilkeston replaced its modern machinery with traditional Levers Lace machines, some a century old, to re-establish itself in a niche market for high quality decorative lace. Pictured are twisthand Ian Palfreyman and Cluny Lace director and leading historian of the industry, Sheila Mason.

Industrial History. The 70ft high monument to William Jessop Junior, a partner of the The Butterley Company, near Codnor Park and Ironville, is no longer accessible to the public. It is pictured in holiday mood, complete with swingboats, circa 1908. The view illustrates the Whit Sunday walk, when local Sunday Schools walked in procession to the monument (Stuart Saint www.codnor.info)

Sir Barnes Wallis, inventor of the 'bouncing bomb' of RAF Dambusters fame, is commemorated on the sign of the pub named in his honour, in Ripley (*Author*)

Erewash Heritage One. Erewash Museum Collections Officer Kate Crossley displays the carefully preserved banner of the Women's Section of Ilkeston Labour Party (*Author*)

Erewash Heritage Two. One of the private owner railway wagons once operated by the Stanton company is prominently displayed in Ilkeston (*Author*)

Erewash Heritage Three. Former Butterley Company housing in Ironville (*Author*)

Tradition Preserved. The Derbyshire art of well dressing is practised in two Erewash Valley industrial villages, Waingroves and Swanwick. Pictured at Waingroves Methodist Church in 2017 are Barry and Margaret Bailey and John Grace (*Author*)

Rural Erewash. The parish church and dwelling house which share a common roof, at Dale Abbey (*Author*)

Urban tranquillity. A narrow boat moored by the Erewash Canal, off Station Road in Ilkeston (*Author*)

Erewash at Play One. Long Eaton Carnival's street parade passes through the town's Market Place (*Tim Fryzer-Smith*)

Erewash at Play Two: Ripley Fair in the town's Market Place, with the Town Hall in the background (*Author*)

Sporting Erewash One: Young fans await the start of Alfreton Town's final National League home match of the 2016-2017 season, against Nuneaton Town (*Author*)

Sporting Erewash Two: Ilkeston Town's New Manor Ground celebrated its 25th anniversary in 2017. Pictured is the distinctive Clocktower Stand (*Author*)

Sporting Erewash Three: Cricketing giants caught for posterity in Kirkby-in-Ashfield. Former mineworkers Harold Larwood (bowling) and Bill Voce (crouching for a catch at mid-wicket) face Australian legend Don Bradman (batting) in a recreation of the 1932-33 Australia-England test series. The 'bodyline' bowling of Larwood and Voce threatened to shatter friendly relations between Australia and the Mother Country (*Author*)

Midland Railway architecture at Butterley railway station, on the Midland Railway Centre's preserved line. The station buildings were originally at Whitwell, near Chesterfield but were carefully taken down and re-erected at Butterley (*Author*)

Narrow boats moored at a boatyard on the Erewash Canal, close to Trent Lock (*Author*)

Rail's Modern Image One: A freight train shakes the platforms at Ilkeston's new railway station in the spring of 2017 (*Author*)

Rail's Modern Image Two. Trams of the Nottingham Rapid Transit System pass just outside the western terminus of the line at Toton (*Author*)

Trent Lock, the area's waterways junction. The entrance to the Erewash Canal is at the bottom left of the picture, with the Cranfleet Cut diverging from the River Trent in the foreground. The Trent itself flows under the railway bridge carrying the Midland mainline from St Pancras. The river flows across a weir which boaters avoid by taking the Cranfleet Cut (*Author*)

Chapter Six

The Valley that Punched above its Sporting Weight

'The road was crowded with colliers travelling on foot to see the match between Notts and Aston Villa ... no goals at half-time, two-none for Notts at the finish. The colliers were hugely delighted, especially as Flint, the forward for Notts, who was an Underwood man well known to the four comrades, did some handsome work, putting the two goals through'. – Strike Pay.

For just a brief moment in time, in the era of gas lighting and hansom cabs, a football team from the Erewash Valley held its own with the future giants of the professional game.

A couple of decades later, in the sunlit Edwardian summer before the disaster of World War One, cricketers playing on a modest miner's welfare ground in the north of the valley established a world record that still stands today.

Further enhancing the sporting reputation of the district was its brief reign as one of the international hot spots for a style of cycle racing now long disappeared.

During this all-too-short period of sporting success in the late 19th and early 20th centuries, the Erewash Valley punched well above its weight.

Since that time, the remorseless concentration of high achievement in the big cities has meant that sensational sporting headlines have become rarer in the valley towns. But for decades the district's prized status as a venue for first class cricket, the occasional exploits of its football teams in the FA Cup, and a late 20th century flowering of two and four wheeled motor sport kept the names of Erewash Valley towns in the nation's sporting consciousness.

One arena in particular, the Recreation Ground at Long Eaton, staged not only professional football, county championship cricket, and international cycle racing but, after being re-developed in the 1920s into a stadium, became known across the world for a great variety of activities, including speedway, stock car racing, trotting and professional boxing.

The Rutland Recreation Ground in Ilkeston saw County Championship cricket from 1925 to 1994, with many of the greatest names in the sport playing for or against Derbyshire.

Football

Long Eaton Recreation Ground was a venue used by the legendary Long Eaton Rangers Football Club, who in the late 19th century pulled off one of the greatest giant-killing acts in the early history of organised football by beating West Bromwich Albion in the final of the Birmingham Senior Cup.

During that era the competition was one of the most prestigious, involving the first teams of some of the biggest names in the sport. On May 7 1887 a reported five thousand spectators, a big attendance at the time, assembled for the final, which was played at the Wellington Road ground in the Perry Barr area of Birmingham, then the home of Aston Villa.

West Brom were hot favourites to win the match, having defeated Villa, Derby County and Stoke to reach the final for the second season running. Yet after the 90 minutes were completed, the Albion team and their fans were in a state of shock, with the side from the small Erewash Valley town running out winners by a single goal.

The Birmingham Senior Cup victory was not the sole triumph for the Rangers, a club which for a short time played at the highest level of English football.

Long Eaton Rangers Football Club, winners of the Birmingham Senior Cup in 1887 beating West Bromwich Albion 1-0 in the final The team is pictured in front of the Pavilion at the Recreation Ground, Long Eaton, where the club played from the ground's opening in 1885. Back row, left to right, T Hardy, G H Smith, F Start, G Whittaker (trainer), J Plackett, J Wiseman, T S Vessey. Middle row, l-r, J Orchard (captain), B Bestwick (umpire), Joseph Orchard (President), B Stevenson. Front row, l-r, F Gelsthorpe, W Smith, A Smith. The scorer of the winning goal in the cup final, George Clay Winfield, was absent when the photograph was taken. *(Derbyshire Local Studies Libraries and www.picturethepast.org.uk).*

True competitive football dates back to the start of the FA Cup in 1871-72, and the Football League started operations in 1888-89, with twelve clubs drawn from Lancashire and the Midlands. The original members included Derby County, but the one club per town rule meant that the Rams' bitter modern-day rivals Nottingham Forest were excluded, in favour of neighbours Notts County.

A second professional league competition, the Combination, also operated in that season, with its members including Long Eaton Rangers. The badly-run Combination was replaced for the 1889-90 season by the Football Alliance, a genuine rival to the fledgling Football League. Twelve clubs, the same number as in the League, were accepted into Alliance membership, again drawn from the north of England and the Midlands, and including the Rangers.

The list of opponents visiting the Recreation Ground at Long Eaton during the course of the season makes impressive reading, and included Nottingham Forest, The Wednesday (later to become Sheffield Wednesday), Newton Heath, better known in later years as Manchester United, and Small Heath, the forerunner of Birmingham City FC.

Sadly, the Rangers finished bottom of the league, winning just four out of their 22 matches, but they at least secured local bragging rights with a 5-3 victory over Nottingham Forest at the Lenton Gregory Ground in Nottingham.

At the end of the season Long Eaton Rangers dropped down from the Alliance to what was at the time another major football competition, the Midland League, where they were joined at various times by Ilkeston Town (and later Ilkeston United), Heanor Town and Alfreton Town. The Midland League of this era included teams such as Sheffield United, Lincoln City, Doncaster Rovers, Barnsley and Mansfield Town.

Both Long Eaton Rangers and Ilkeston Town distinguished themselves in the competition, finishing runners-up in 1890-91 and 1898-99 respectively. The Rangers enjoyed nine seasons in the Midland League, dropping out in 1899. Ilkeston Town joined the league for the 1894-95 campaign before being expelled from the competition during the course of the 1902-03 season. Near neighbours Heanor Town spent five seasons as members of the Midland League in the last decade of the 19th century.

Long Eaton Rangers helped mould the career of Amos 'Jammer' Smith, the man now recognised as Derby County's first 'superstar'. Smith, who had also featured for another Erewash Valley club, Sawley Rangers, played in Derby's first-ever game in September 1884, which the Rams lost 6-0 at Great Lever.

Football in Long Eaton experienced some fallow years after the disappearance of the Rangers. As the years progressed the Midland League became increasingly dominated by the reserve teams of Football League clubs, including at various times Derby County, Sheffield Wednesday, Sheffield United and Leicester.

Nevertheless, Erewash Valley clubs did return briefly to the competition in the 1920s and Ilkeston, Heanor and a team called simply Long Eaton were joined for a couple of seasons by Alfreton Town.

The Midland League declined in status during the 1950s and lost many of its leading clubs to other competitions. It staggered on with an influx of sides from the north east, including Blyth Spartans and North and South Shields, before folding in 1960 when its most successful side in recent times, Peterborough United, was elected to the Football League.

The Primrose Hill ground at Blackwell in the upper Erewash Valley, where Derbyshire's Arnold Warren and John Chapman set a world record for a 9th wicket partnership in 1910, scoring 283 against Warwickshire. The ground was formerly the sports field for the village's Miners' Welfare Institute. This is the building just to the right of the centre of the picture, outside the boundary wall. The taller building next door is former colliery offices *(Author)*.

Revival came in 1961, with Ilkeston Town, Heanor Town, Alfreton Town and a new club from Long Eaton (United) all in membership. The new Midland League was never to attain the status of the old competition but it provided success for Ilkeston, champions in 1967-68 and Alfreton Town, who achieved the honour in 1969-70, 1971-72, 1973-74 and 1976-77.

Across the Nottinghamshire border Eastwood Town was for many years an amateur team which competed with distinction in the FA Amateur Cup (now the FA Vase). The Badgers, named for their black and white striped kit, later turned semi-professional and won the Midland League in 1975-76.

When non-league football was re-organised on a pyramid basis in 1982, the Midland League again disappeared (only to be once again resurrected in the second decade of the 21st century). The Erewash Valley's principal clubs – Ilkeston, Long Eaton, Heanor and Alfreton have since that time played in a variety of competitions. Alfreton, with a spell as members of the National League (effectively the fifth tier of English football) rose higher than any valley team since the heyday of the Football Alliance and the original Midland League.

High spending on wages and then the withdrawal for various reasons of investors meant both Ilkeston and Eastwood going bust and then re-emerging lower down the football pyramid, a fate shared by Eastwood's fellow Nottinghamshire side, Hucknall Town, based in the neighbouring Leen Valley.

Ilkeston FC, formed after the Town club was liquidated, themselves went into liquidation in 2017. Notts County owner Alan Hardy came to the rescue reviving the Ilkeston Town name and ensuring football at the New Manor Ground in season 2017-2018, albeit at a much lower level than that to which the fans had become accustomed.

Erewash Valley clubs over the years have also performed well in the FA Cup, starting with Long Eaton Rangers' narrow 2-1 defeat at home to future cup winners Wolverhampton Wanderers, in 1890-91. Heanor Town's list of opponents in the FA Cup in the early years of that competition is long and distinguished, and includes Aston Villa, Nottingham Forest and Southampton.

In 1927 the site of the Recreation Ground at Long Eaton, one time home to Long Eaton Rangers FC and the scene of a County Championship cricket match between Derbyshire and Lancashire in July 1887, was transformed into a greyhound stadium. The main grandstand takes shape in front of the Pavilion Hotel *(Long Eaton Local Studies Library)*.

Long Eaton Stadium in 1928, after completion. There were seven wooden grandstands in all, with a claimed capacity for the ground of 10,000 spectators *(Author's Collection).*

Ilkeston Town were renowned cup fighters in the 1950s, with visits to the old Manor Ground by Peterborough United and Rochdale drawing attendances of up to 9,000 – possible in the days before stricter health and safety rules were tightened and it became forbidden for spectators to stand on grass and cinders.

Nevertheless it was not until much later that Ilkeston achieved success in the competition. The Robins drew away at Scunthorpe United in the second round of the FA Cup in 1997 before narrowly losing the replay.

In the 1999-2000 season Ilkeston claimed a first-ever league club scalp, beating Carlisle United at the New Manor Ground, followed by a second round draw at home against Rushden and Diamonds. Another replay defeat once again cost the Robins the chance of an appearance in the third round and a money-spinning tie against Premiership or Championship opposition.

On the Nottinghamshire side of the Erewash, Eastwood Town reached the first round proper of the FA Cup for the first time in the 1999-2000 season, losing 2-1 away at Exeter City.

In 2008-2009 the Badgers had an exceptional run in the competition, becoming the only Erewash Valley side to reach the third round of the FA Cup. Eastwood played eight games, including two replays, to reach that stage, including overcoming Wycombe Wanderers at Coronation Park in the second round.

Then the Badgers' luck ran out. Dreams of Manchester United or Arsenal visiting Coronation Park disappeared when the draw matched them against fellow non-leaguers Kettering Town. Eastwood lost 2-1 away from home.

In the FA Amateur Cup Coronation Park hosted ties against some of England's top amateur sides, including competition winners Enfield and Wealdstone. In the FA Vase, which succeeded the Amateur Cup, the Badgers reached the quarter final in 2003-4, losing to Colne after a replay.

Many footballers whose list of clubs includes sides from the Erewash Valley have enjoyed long and successful careers at the very top of the game, notably Gary Birtles, who began his career at Long Eaton United. Birtles was a carpet fitter, signed by Nottingham Forest for a bargain basement £2,000 from Long Eaton, who became part of the legendary Forest team which won back to back European Cup (now Champions League) titles.

The stadium at Long Eaton was ravaged by fire in 1948. Some of the greyhounds kennelled at the arena died in the blaze *(Author's Collection).*

He scored more than 70 times in some 200 games for Nottingham Forest under the inspiring management of Brian Clough and Peter Taylor, and ensured a place in the club's history by playing in the Reds' European Cup victories in 1979 and 1980.

Capped on three occasions for England, Birtles had two spells at the City Ground, with a less successful period at Manchester United sandwiched in between. He is now a television commentator.

Long before the European Cup became the ultimate prize and footballers became glamorous television performers, one player achieved something like the fame (and notoriety) later to become the preserve of George Best, Paul Gascoigne and the like. William Henry 'Fatty' Foulke, a professional cricketer and footballer in the late 19th and early 20th centuries, was renowned for his great height, 6 feet 4 inches, and weight, reaching a reputed 24 stone at the end of his career.

He played cricket for Derbyshire but won his fame as a goalkeeper (what else) for Sheffield United, helping the Blades to win a Football League Championship and two FA Cup finals. He later played for Chelsea and Bradford City and won one international cap for England.

Ilkeston's professional football clubs have come and gone over the years. This is the Ilkeston United version of 1913-14, the last completed season before World War One. The picture was taken at the old Manor Ground in the town, which is now occupied by Dunelm Mill. The dressing rooms that can just be seen in the top left hand corner of the picture survived until the last match at the ground. A new grandstand, erected in the mid-1950s replaced the structure seen in this image, and was also standing at the end *(Derbyshire Local Studies Libraries and www.picturethepast.org.uk)*

Alfreton Town FC was formed in 1959 from the merger of two local sides and joined the Central Alliance League (North). In 1960 Alfreton set a record for their ground when 5,023 spectators (pictured right) watched a game against local rivals Matlock Town *(Courtesy of Alfreton Town Football Club).*

One of the first black footballers to play for an Erewash Valley team was Lloyd Lindbergh "Lindy" Delapenha (1927–2017) . He was the first Jamaican to play league football in England, representing Portsmouth, Middlesbrough and Mansfield Town, and later signed for Heanor Town. When he returned to Jamaica he became director of sports at the Jamaica Broadcasting Corporation and helped bring international football to the island *(The Gleaner).*

Foulke's link with the Erewash Valley was the fact that he was discovered by a Sheffield United scout whilst playing for village side Blackwell in a Derbyshire Cup tie at Ilkeston Town's old Manor Ground. His enduring link to the modern game lies in the claim that the eternally popular chant aimed by fans at the more rotund of footballers, 'who ate all the pies', was first directed at Foulke.

In the days before footballers became millionaires, the Erewash Valley clubs once specialised in recruiting players at the end of their Football League careers.

One of the best-known recruits to the lower level of football was Reg Harrison, who played 254 games (52 goals) for Derby, mostly at Division One level in the years following World War Two and was a member of the Rams FA Cup winning squad in 1946. Harrison both played for Long Eaton and managed the club, and later became manager at Alfreton.

Another member of Derby's FA Cup winning team, Jim Bullions, was later associated with Alfreton Town.

Colin Walker from Long Eaton worked as an office boy at Derby before being signed as a professional by the Rams. In 1946 it was his task to collect a parcel from the railway station containing the club's allocation of Cup Final tickets before the tie at Wembley against Charlton Athletic.

He walked the not inconsiderable distance from the station back to the Baseball Ground past hundreds of people totally unaware of what he was carrying - slips of paper for which many of them would have given their right arm.

Walker's career began on a high, appearing as an 18-year-old for the Rams in front of 48,000 spectators at Manchester City's then Maine Road ground. After making a number of first team appearances his career was interrupted by National Service and a knee injury. He eventually drifted into non-league football, being tempted to South Derbyshire side Gresley Rovers by the club's manager, former Rams legend Sammy Crookes.

In later years Colin recalled that he had been offered a contract by Nottingham Forest, then a Division Three side, at £4 a week. He turned it down, reasoning that the money he received from Gresley, plus his wages from a job in industry, made it hardly worthwhile to play full-time professional football!

Cricket

Less than two months after Long Eaton Rangers' footballing triumph over West Bromwich Albion, the Erewash Valley again featured on the national sporting map. For the first and only time Derbyshire County Cricket Club staged a first class County Championship match at Long Eaton, against Lancashire, on the Recreation Ground.

The Red Rose county won a low-scoring game, played on what was described as a 'fierce' wicket, by a margin of 54 runs.

The game was completed in two rather than three days and whether because of the standard of the wicket, or perhaps the consequent loss of a day's gate money - a serious matter for a

Bill Bestwick from Tag Hill, Heanor, who achieved Derbyshire's best-ever bowling performance in 1921. Bestwick may well have played for England, but his reputation was damaged when he killed a man in a fight in a pub. The coroner's court recorded a verdict of justifiable homicide *(Heanor and District Local History Society).*

Derbyshire's team for the first County Championship match to be played at Ilkeston, in July 1925, photographed in front of the Rutland Recreation Ground pavilion. Back row, l-r, Hutchinson, Elliott, Shardlow, Horsley, Bowden. Front row, l-r, Leslie Townsend, Lee, Cadman, G R Jackson, E F Loney, Morton. Jackson and Loney were amateurs *(Ilkeston Local Studies Library)*.

perennially hard-up Derbyshire club - this was to be the first and last appearance of first class cricketers in a competitive game in Long Eaton for some 80 years.

Subsequent county matches in the town, starting in the mid-1970s and played on the attractive Trent College ground, were one-day, non-first class games, in the Sunday afternoon John Player League.

It was 22 years after the Long Eaton championship game that Derbyshire ventured again into the environs of the Erewash Valley. The county found the playing conditions more congenial at Blackwell, a mining village to the north west of the valley, playing seven County Championship games on the Welfare Ground between 1909 and 1913.

One of those games found a prominent niche in cricket's history.

Derbyshire's games against Warwickshire were regarded right up to the 1950s as important local derbies and were eagerly awaited by members and supporters. At lunch on the final day of the 1910 match at the Primrose Hill ground in Blackwell, still the home of local cricket in the upper Erewash Valley, Derbyshire were struggling. The home side had lost eight second innings wickets and were still far behind Warwickshire's first innings score.

With the weather perfect for cricket, a comfortable win for Warwickshire looked certain. The Derbyshire secretary W T Taylor, who served the county for more than 50 years as player and official, later recalled: "I knew that Warwickshire, in view of their strong position, were hoping to catch an early afternoon train.

"During the luncheon interval I had a conversation with their fast bowler, Frank Field and remarked, 'you look like catching your train all right, Frank'.

"His reply was, 'I'm not so sure about that, Mr Taylor. These chaps (the Derbyshire ninth wicket pair of captain John Chapman and England bowler Arnold Warren from Heanor) are pretty good bats, you know.'

Mr Taylor added: "How right he was. Chapman and Warren put on a world record partnership for the ninth wicket of 283, which still stands today and Warwickshire had to be content with a draw."

A full house at Ilkeston for Derbyshire v Notts in the County Championship in August 1928. The view is taken from the southern end of the ground, with the 'popular ' side of the ground, a large concrete terrace with wooden benches, full to capacity. The pavilion is out of sight at the top left hand corner of the photograph and the scoreboard is similarly off the bottom right hand corner of the shot. *(Ilkeston Local Studies Library)*.

All our own work! K G Viljoen (Orange Free State) with 152 runs, and H B Cameron (Transvaal) with 132, established a new ground record fifth wicket stand of 262. The match was Derbyshire v the touring South Africans in May 1935 *(Ilkeston Local Studies Library).*

The pair scored their runs in less than three hours, Chapman making 165 and Warren 123.

Derbyshire did not return to Blackwell after World War One, settling down to a pattern of playing the majority of home games at either the County Ground in Derby (situated in the centre of what between the wars was still Derby's racecourse) and Queen's Park in Chesterfield.

Then, in 1925, Derbyshire established a long-time Erewash Valley home at Ilkeston, with the Rutland Recreation Ground hosting at least one County Championship match – and sometimes as many as three or four - each year until 1980. After an interval, first-class cricket returned to the Rutland Ground in the 1990s but ended for good when the 'Rec' was 're-developed' by the local council.

In total the ground hosted 93 first-class matches and 16 one day limited over games. Most first class counties visited Ilkeston over the years, although the money-spinning Derbyshire-Yorkshire game was jealously guarded by Chesterfield.

A significant proportion of the first-class games at Ilkeston (including the very last, in 1994) were against neighbouring Nottinghamshire. The game drew big crowds to the end, including a Rutland Ground record for a day of some 10,000 spectators in 1948.

The highest team score on the ground was the 529 for 7 total posted by Derbyshire in 1952, whilst the lowest was the 54 recorded by Middlesex in 1977.

The rising demand in the modern era for better spectator and hospitality facilities began to count against Ilkeston. The ground had no cover for spectators, who were mainly accommodated on a vast concrete terrace on the town side of the arena, equipped with simple wooden benches with no backs – hardly the height of comfort for a long day's cricket watching.

The Pavilion, situated at the northern end of the ground, had a few rows of somewhat more comfortable seating, and there was a highly attractive wooden scoreboard at the opposite end. Apart from these minimal facilities, there were grassy banks around the rest of the field, ideal for a warm summer's day.

Ilkeston was the epitome of a cricket out-ground, was liked by spectators and, during the time when the County Ground at Derby was out of bounds to the county club, a valuable asset to Derbyshire.

Although lack of modern facilities obviously contributed to Ilkeston's demise as a first class cricket ground, the final straw came when Erewash Borough Council cut the spectator terrace in two and constructed an ugly shed to accommodate indoor tennis courts on half of the space.

In addition, the seats were removed from in front of the Pavilion and the scoreboard was demolished. The side of the ground opposite the truncated remains of the terrace now hosts an athletics track.

The stylish former Yorkshire and England batsman Phil Sharpe moved from Yorkshire to Derbyshire for the 1975 and 1976 seasons. He is seen batting for his new county in front of the Ilkeston pavilion *(Derby Telegraph)*.

The Town Ground, Heanor, is certainly one of the longest-established sporting venues in Derbyshire, hosting both football and cricket. The small venue was used successfully for John Player Sunday League matches in the 1980s but eyebrows were raised when it was announced that Derbyshire would play a Championship game there in 1987, especially as the visitors would be Hampshire, including the fearsome West Indies fast bowler Malcolm Marshall.

Derbyshire won what, predictably given the short boundaries, proved to be a high-scoring encounter, with three declarations. Hampshire scored 349-2 in their first innings, with unbeaten centuries for batsmen Mark Nicholas and David Turner. Derbyshire replied with 314-7 declared, including 91 for skipper Kim Barnett.

When Hampshire batted again, captain Mark Nicholas again declared and set Derbyshire a challenging target of 297 in 59 overs. The home team reached their winning total with just two balls to spare, largely due to an innings of 106 by Bruce Roberts.

Top class cricket had in the meantime returned to Long Eaton in the 1970s, with the tree-lined ground at the town's public school, Trent College, used for John Player League matches.

Ilkeston still sees league cricket of a fairly high standard, as the home of Ilkeston Rutland, members of the Derbyshire Premier League. Sadly, it is highly unlikely that first class cricket will be staged in the town, or in the Erewash Valley as a whole, ever again.

Before the re-organisation of club cricket into leagues based on counties, top local competitions often crossed county boundaries. In the Erewash Valley the premier competition for many years was the Notts and Derby Border League, which originally consisted mainly of clubs from along the tram route which ran from Ripley to Nottingham, via Codnor, Heanor and Langley Mill, and was immortalised by DH Lawrence in his short story *Tickets Please*.

The Rutland Recreation Ground was the ideal venue for school sports. This photograph shows the start of the father's race at Kensington School's sports event in the 1930s. One father has a pipe in his mouth and two others are lighting cigarettes! *(John Bush and www.picturethepast.org.uk)*.

The Notts and Derby Border League was composed of clubs mainly from along the tram (later trolley) bus route from Ripley to Nottingham. This is the Butterley team of the late 1940s, when matches attracted large crowds. Spinner Norman Else (second from left in the front row) broke bowling records and was on occasions awarded a ground collection *(Norman Else)*.

Many players of great ability played in the Border League. Former Nottinghamshire captain and England batsman Reg Simpson topped the league's batting averages in 1938, at the start of his career. Locally-born players also enjoyed some spectacular successes. Norman Else, later to enjoy a distinguished career as a head teacher, played in the immediate post World War Two era for his local side, Butterley United.

A slow bowler, at times unplayable, Norman features in the Border League's records with analyses of 9 for 46 and 9 for 45. He remembers the large crowds that attended the league's matches in his era, and the fact that players who scored a fifty or took five wickets were rewarded with a collection taken among the crowd.

"It was a great feeling to go home with your cricket bag full of copper, threepenny bits and sixpences", he recalls.

Until the start of county premier leagues, Sandiacre played in the Notts Amateur League, together with clubs from Eastwood and Kimberley. Today Selston Town is the only Nottinghamshire side to play in the Derbyshire County League, which also includes clubs from Staffordshire.

Nottinghamshire County Cricket Club, based at the magnificent and historic Trent Bridge ground, made somewhat less use of out-grounds than their Derbyshire neighbours, and no first class cricket has been played on the Nottinghamshire bank of the Erewash Valley.

Derbyshire's modest cricketing fame has been built mainly around the county's ability to produce top class fast and fast-medium bowlers. The legend grew over the years that the club secretary had only to shout down a pit shaft in the coalfields of either the Erewash Valley or North East Derbyshire for a pace bowler, 'boweller' in the local dialect, to appear and cause an overnight sensation on the county grounds of England and Wales.

Derbyshire's best-ever bowling performance was produced by Bill Bestwick, born in 1875 at Tag Hill, Heanor, who first worked down the pit at nearby Coppice Colliery at the age of eleven. Bestwick turned professional for his native county in 1898 (continuing to work down the pit in the close season) and produced some sensational performances, often in tandem with another county legend, Arnold Warren, born just down the road in Codnor.

One of the most attractive grounds in Derbyshire is at Sandiacre, with excellent facilities including a modern pavilion similar in design to its wooden predecessor. Sandiacre have played in leagues in both Nottinghamshire and Derbyshire *(Author)*.

Selston Town Cricket Club play on the former Miners' Welfare Ground, which is now the village hall and sports ground for the village. Selston is the only Nottinghamshire club playing in the Derbyshire County Cricket League *(Author)*.

Bill holds the record for the best-ever bowling performance in a single innings by a Derbyshire player, ten wickets for 40 runs, before lunch, against Glamorgan at Cardiff in 1921, when he was aged 46. All in all he captured nearly 1,500 wickets between 1898 and 1926.

Bestwick's performances might easily have led to a place in England's test team, but what has been described as his 'unpredictable nature' and his liking for drink counted against him. In 1907, after a night's drinking, he killed a man in a fight. The inquest into the death took place the following day and a verdict was returned of justifiable homicide.

Arnold Warren might not have been a better bowler than Bill Bestwick, but his considerable superiority over his fellow Erewash Valley man when it came to batting and fielding won him an England cap in the Ashes test against Australia at Headingley, Leeds, in 1905.

Warren took five wickets for 57 runs in the first innings of a drawn match, dismissing the cream of Australia's batsmen and taking the especially prized wicket of Victor Trumper in both innings. Warren was never selected to play for England again.

Three generations of the Beet family, grandfather George and his son George Junior, both born in Somercotes, and George Junior's nephew Gordon, born in Heanor, played for Derbyshire at intervals between 1910 and 1961. George Beet Senior appeared in the Derbyshire eleven at the same time as another Erewash Valley man, fast bowler Fred Root, also from Somercotes.

Beet took many catches off the bowling of Root, leading to the legend 'caught Beet bowled Root' appearing in the county score books.

A contemporary of Bestwick and Warren around the turn of the 19th and 20th centuries was William Storer, usually known as Bill, who scored nearly 13,000 runs for Derbyshire and achieved more than 430 dismissals as a wicket-keeper.

Storer, who was born at Ripley, was reputed to stand up to the wicket to the bowling of Bestwick and Warren. His best score in first-class cricket was 216 not out against Leicestershire in the 1899 season and he was the first professional to score two hundreds (against a strong Yorkshire side) in a match. In addition he was a competent leg spinner, taking 232 first class wickets at 33.89.

He toured Australia for England, making his debut in the 1897 Test at Sydney and played against the tourists at home, his last Test coming at Trent Bridge in 1899 when he was also named a Wisden cricketer of the year. Storer was also a footballer, playing for Derby County. His brother Harry Storer also played cricket for Derbyshire and football for the Rams.

When Derbyshire won the County Championship in 1936, three men from the Erewash Valley played in the victorious side.

Denis Smith, born in Somercotes, was the mainstay of his county's batting line-up during the 1930s, when the county also finished second and third during the decade. He played for England in two Tests against the South Africans in 1935 and later became an uncompromising county coach. His career aggregate of runs and his 30 centuries for the county were both Derbyshire records until beaten by Kim Barnett in the 1990s. Smith was a Wisden Cricketer of the Year in 1936.

The second test player from the Erewash Valley in the 1936 Derbyshire championship winning side was Leslie Fletcher Townsend, from Long Eaton. Townsend did not play cricket in his youth and was only attracted to the game by watching the Nottinghamshire star batsman George Gunn.

Along with Smith he was the indispensable backbone of Derbyshire's batting during the Championship-winning campaign. He was the county's leading all-rounder between the wars and at his peak probably the most deadly bowler on a sticky wicket Derbyshire ever produced, owing to his perfect length and ability to turn the ball back from the off.

Townsend played in four tests for England. He later emigrated to New Zealand and became a leading coach in Auckland, helping to produce many test cricketers.

The third Erewash Valley man to feature in the Derbyshire championship winning side was Leslie Townsend's brother Arnold, also born in Long Eaton. Arnold was a right-handed batsman and played 200 innings in 117 first class matches with an average of 23.13 and a top score of 142 not out, being described by Wisden as being "the epitome of [Derbyshire's] patient watchful batting".

Nottinghamshire's list of cricketing immortals and test players is, like the county's record in the County Championship and other competitions, far more impressive than their Derbyshire neighbours. But for some reason the Nottinghamshire bank of the Erewash has produced considerably fewer cricketers for Notts than the Derbyshire bank has for the Peak County.

Nottinghamshire's legendary bowling duo of Harold Larwood, born in Nuncargate near Sutton in Ashfield and Bill Voce, from Annesley Woodhouse, near Kirkby in Ashfield, both came from similar mining communities to Derbyshire's Bestwick and Warren, on the fringe of the the Erewash Valley and, together with the immortal Don Bradman, their opponent in the infamous 'bodyline' test series, are commemorated by statues in Kirkby town centre (see photograph in colour section, on page 98).

The honour as the best-known product of the valley to play cricket for Notts falls to one of the Trent Bridge club's greatest characters, cricketer and footballer Mordecai Sherwin, who was born at Greasley, near Eastwood in 1851. Sherwin, like Fatty Foulke, played in goal (for Notts County) and like the Sheffield United man was heavily built, at around 17 stone.

As a cricketer, he was a wicket-keeper, playing in three tests for England in Australia in 1886/7. He captained Notts in 1887 and 1888 and was named as one of the Wisden cricketers of the year in 1891.

A publican by trade, Sherwin became an umpire after retiring as a player, and stood in one test match. Despite his seventeen stone, Sherwin was noted for his nimbleness, both between the posts and behind the wicket. During his time as a player, it was the custom for teams to entertain each other to dinner after games. At one banquet Sherwin was reported to have obliged the company by singing 'Oh dem golden slippers' and delighting his fellow players with a jig and a somersault.

It has been claimed that the name of Arthur Conan Doyle's most famous character, Sherlock Holmes, was inspired partially by Mordecai Sherwin, and partially by Frank Shacklock.

It was not until many years after Mordecai Sherwin's retirement that the Nottinghamshire side of the Erewash Valley produced another outstanding cricketer/footballer. Arthur Jepson, born at Selston, was a right-arm fast-medium bowler for Nottinghamshire between 1938 and 1959, taking 1,050 first-class class wickets, qualifying him as one of the top ten most prolific bowlers in the club's history. He then spent 26 years as an umpire, presiding over four Test matches.

In his footballing career he played for Port Vale either side of World War II and at the end of hostilities played in the game's top flight for Stoke City. In the latter days of his career he managed Long Eaton United.

Rugby

For generations rugby failed to make much of an impression on the Erewash Valley, with the area often considered to be too far north for the Union code and too far to the south for professional rugby league.

The position has changed considerably in more recent times, with the Union game probably benefitting from the much higher profile the game has enjoyed in the media since the advent of professionalism.

Three Derbyshire clubs play within the boundaries of the Erewash Valley, the senior of which, somewhat confusingly, is Amber Valley, whose ground at Pye Bridge is close to the River Erewash and some distance from the River Amber from which it takes its name!

Ilkeston RFC play at the former Stanton Ironworks Institute – 'the Stute' as it is popularly known, whilst Long Eaton

Rob Cook of Long Eaton RFC runs with the ball during the club's Midlands Vase Final victory.

RFC, founded in 1968, have their own developing facilities on the council-owned West Park.

Long Eaton's 1st XV were the 2016/17 champions of the Rugby Football Union's Midlands Division 4 East (North) having remained unbeaten for the entire season. In the same season the club was also winner of the RFU Midlands Junior Vase.

The Rugby League code has constantly attempted to expand its appeal beyond its traditional heartlands of Lancashire, Yorkshire, Cheshire and Cumbria.

A serious attempt to establish the 13-a-side professional game was made in 1984 when the Mansfield Marksman club was established, with a place in the Rugby Football League's second division.

Mansfield Town's Field Mill ground was the venue, with the town being selected for an attempt to spread the league code because of its position in the heartland of the Nottinghamshire coalfield and its proximity to Yorkshire.

The club name reflected the Marksman lager produced by the main sponsor, Mansfield Brewery. The side won its first home game against Wakefield Trinity, in front of a crowd of more than 2,000, but it found life a struggle and crowds plummeted to just over 300 spectators.

Mansfield Marksman lost £90,000 in the first season, could no longer afford the rent at Field Mill and moved home closer to the Erewash Valley, to Alfreton Town's ground at North Street. An opening crowd of 290 did not bode well and a further move soon followed, to Lowmoor Road at Kirkby in Ashfield.

In 1989 the club, re-named Nottingham City RLFC, moved to the Harvey Haddon Stadium in the city, but the side won only seven games in four years and were eventually relegated from the Rugby League.

A new club, Nottingham Outlaws, was formed in 1999 and in 2015 won the championship of rugby league's Conference League South.

Greyhound Racing

By far the most controversial sport to establish a firm footing in the Erewash Valley in the 20th century was greyhound racing, regarded by the great and good as an unmitigated evil.

Whippet racing was a firm favourite in mining communities, and in relatively recent times the dogs were raced on a flat section of ground close to the River Erewash at Gallows Inn, between Ilkeston and Trowell.

Professional cycle racing was staged at Long Eaton Recreation Ground in the 1880s, with competitors from as far afield as the United States. The machines, which resemble penny farthings, were designated as high wheel racers *(Long Eaton Local Studies Library)*.

Mechanised dog racing on an oval circuit came to Britain from the USA in 1926, at Belle Vue Stadium in the Gorton area of Manchester.

The Recreation Ground at Long Eaton soon caught the eye of greyhound racing promoters and a substantial stadium was constructed, with seven wooden grandstands offering accommodation for 10,000 spectators.

Long Eaton became the first dog track in the area by default, when plans to build a stadium in Nottingham were defeated by the opposition of church leaders. T G Hine, a leading Anglican layman in the county, chairman of the Nottinghamshire Football Association and a member of the autocratic Football Association itself, did not mince his words when leading the opposition to 'the dogs'.

Hines declared that greyhound racing was 'a vicious thing – the most vile thing that has come on earth in my opinion'. On a national level future Prime Minister Winston Churchill added his disdain, dismissing the sport as being 'little better than animated roulette'.

The sport proved popular enough in Long Eaton to warrant the opening of a second venue for greyhound and whippet racing in the town, close to the original stadium, on a 40-acre site close to where the River Erewash forms the Derbyshire/Nottinghamshire boundary and where Long Eaton becomes Toton.

The Nottingham Road venue was short lived but the well-appointed Stadium thrived and eventually, like its predecessor The Recreation Ground, became a multi-sport venue.

It survived a disastrous fire in March 1948 that destroyed most of the grandstand accommodation and the clubroom, and badly damaged the greyhound kennels and other facilities, killing eleven dogs. The alarm had been raised by passers-by who noticed smoke coming from the kennel area. Together with the fire-fighters, members of the public did their best to try and liberate the fire-maddened animals, some of which bit their rescuers.

Greyhound racing continued at Long Eaton until the stadium's demise in 1998. Long Eaton's major rivals for punters were the greyhound tracks in Nottingham (where the sport survives today) and Derby, but with dog racing so popular in mining communities across the country, it is perhaps surprising that tracks were not opened in Erewash Valley population centres such as Ilkeston, Heanor, Ripley and Eastwood.

The Heanor/Eastwood area was served for a brief period by a circuit on the county boundary at Langley Mill. Sometimes known as the Victory Track, greyhound and whippet racing began in April 1930 over distances of 330 yards and 500 yards, with hurdle events also featuring. The track, close to the New Inn at Langley Mill, had a very short life, closing during 1931.

Longer-lived was a dog track at Somercotes, convenient for the Ripley and Alfreton areas. Owned by the Alfreton & District Greyhound Company Limited, in the persons of Harry Hill, Len Meredith, Ted Callaghan and Charlie Hall, the circuit opened in September 1954.

Facilities included a pavilion and a shelter for the bookmakers and the 370-yard circuit had racing distances of 270 and 480 yards. The track itself was grass with sand and peat moss on the banked bends, and the dogs followed an inside hare. Racing was on Monday and Friday evenings, with trials for the dogs held after racing.

The site of the greyhound stadium, which also accommodated a football pitch in the centre of the racing circuit, is now part of an NHS Distribution Service Depot.

Speedway

Dirt-track racing, or speedway, began at Long Eaton Stadium in 1929 but failed to attract sufficient spectators to continue past 1930. When the sport boomed after World War Two promoters moved to revive the motor cycle sport.

Although the Stadium was in a residential area, any objections were overcome largely due to the continuing dislike church and civic leaders shared for greyhound racing.

When Long Eaton Urban District Council met in 1949 to consider an application for planning permission for speedway, several councillors were clearly influenced by the possibility that a successful speedway team might mean the end of greyhound racing at the Stadium.

The consensus of opinion was that the moral depravity of greyhound racing and the constant yapping of the dogs kennelled on the site was a nuisance. Motorbikes, it was felt, could be the lesser of the two evils!

Speedway's apparent superiority was confirmed when a delegation of councillors and the sanitary inspector attended a meeting at Leicester's Blackbird Road circuit.

The delegates were duly impressed, with one councillor declaring that he had been delighted to see `such a respectable

Long Eaton's speedway team, the Archers, competed in the sport's top division for three seasons 1965-67. The team's teenage star, Ray Wilson (left) is seen on the way to a win over four times World Champion Barry Briggs of New Zealand, in the individual Silver Sash match race competition at the Station Road stadium *(John Sumpter of JMS Photography).*

crowd, so enthusiastic and with no gambling allowed'. He did not think a cleaner sport had ever been seen.

Speedway nationally enjoyed a boom period in the aftermath of World War Two, with eleven million people attending matches in 1948. An attempt was made to obtain a licence for Long Eaton in 1949 but this was not forthcoming until the following season, when a team known as the Archers, in a nod to Robin Hood, raced a season of friendly matches.

The Archers gained admittance to the National League Division Three for 1951, racing fixtures against teams from much larger towns and cities, such as Wolverhampton, Swindon, Cardiff, Ipswich and Exeter, finishing next to bottom of the league.

Almost two decades later, in 1984, the Long Eaton team, by now re-named the Invaders, achieved the track's greatest ever success, winning the National League (second tier of the sport) championship. Here the riders leave the starting gate in a home league match against the Edinburgh Monarchs *(Author's Collection).*

The competition changed its name to the Southern League for 1952. Long Eaton's results were generally better but the crowds were insufficient to show a profit for the promoters at a time when the sport was subject to a punitive entertainment tax rate.

The result was that the team withdrew from the league midway through the season, with the final match against Wolverhampton being watched by some 3,800 spectators. A few unlicensed 'pirate' fixtures were run at the Stadium in 1954, with some of the riders taking part being subsequently banned by the Speedway Control Board.

The sport went into decline in the mid and late 1950s, only to be revived in 1960 by the creation of a new competition, the Provincial League. Long Eaton was entered into the PL in 1963 and 1964 by former rider Reg Fearman and the venture was reasonably successful.

Speedway was riven by a major dispute in the winter of 1964-65 which was eventually settled by an inquiry held by a former Attorney-General, Sir Hartley Shawcross. The two leagues operating in the UK at the time, the National League and the Provincial League merged into one 18-team competition, the British League.

Long Eaton opened the 1965 season with a crowd of more than 5,000 to see the Archers race against Reg Fearman's old team, West Ham. A succession of injuries to Archers riders saw the Erewash Valley club finish bottom of the league.

With steady if unspectacular support Long Eaton raced on in the British League in 1966 and 1967, producing young local talent in the form of Ray Wilson, the son of team manager and ex-rider Ron Wilson, and all-round Derby-based motorcyclist Norman Storer. Five-times World Champion Ove Fundin of Sweden rode in several matches for the Archers in 1966.

The fans. A group of Long Eaton speedway supporters pause for refreshments on the way to the 1967 World Championship final at the old Wembley Stadium. The front windows of their coach display blow-up pictures of the two Long Eaton riders who qualified for the final, Swede Anders Michanek on the left and Ray Wilson on the right *(Phil Wells).*

The 1967 campaign was Long Eaton's most successful season from a results point of view, with the team spearheaded by Ray Wilson and a new Swedish star, Anders Michanek, who eventually became World Champion.

It was a shock for the local fans when promoters Fearman and Wilson transferred the track licence to Leicester for 1968 sensing, correctly, that the crowd potential was much higher at that venue. Long Eaton lay fallow for a year, but was then revived to stage British League Division Two racing.

From that point, until the closure of the stadium and its sale for housing development forced the end of speedway after the 1997 season, Long Eaton teams raced in the second tier of British speedway. The team's greatest success came in 1984, when the championship of the second tier came to the town.

Stock Car Racing

Although stock car racing is generally associated with the United States, the version introduced to Britain in 1954, which allowed a significant amount of contact between stripped down and heavily armoured saloon cars – railway sleepers were initially used as bumpers – actually originated in France.

The sport was an instant success at Long Eaton, with crowds of more than double those which had attended speedway. The stock cars, which as the sport developed became more sophisticated, raced at the Stadium continuously until the venue closed, staging many top meetings, including World Championship semi-finals.

Stock Car Racing at Long Eaton Stadium *(Author's Collection).*

Two other forms of short-circuit motor sport, at extremes of the spectrum, were also staged at Long Eaton. Hot rod racing banned non-accidental contact between the competing cars, whereas banger racing was entirely based on clashes between the vehicles and their drivers.

Kart racing, now very often the route into Formula One motor racing for young drivers, was also staged at Long Eaton.

Cycle Racing

High-speed racing on two wheels, with close contact between the riders, had been a major attraction at Long Eaton as far back as September 1888.

What the fans witnessed in 1888 was pedal power in action, with star cyclists such as the American champion Stillman G Whittaker setting world records in against-the-clock and other events, riding machines which in some respects resembled penny farthings but which were known as high wheel racers.

Whittaker, who rode all over the world at top-class velodromes nevertheless rated Long Eaton as his favourite British circuit.

The fans

The Long Eaton Stadium's clubhouse boasted a large, pot-bellied cast-iron stove which threw out a tremendous heat, particularly useful in the case of dog-racing, which was a year-round sport.

It also provided physical comfort for the professional gamblers who gathered around it for high-powered poker sessions in midweek, providing ample evidence to the councillors and churchmen who so strongly disapproved of gambling.

The author was told by the manager of the Stadium that the venue essentially attracted three different types of spectators.

Speedway racing attracted the sporting enthusiasts, who backed their team in the same way as football fans. Stock car racing was a family night out for the enjoyment of thrills and spills.

The manager added: "The typical spectator at a Friday night dog meeting is a working man in a flat cap and muffler, cigarette hanging off his bottom lip, and with his wage packet hanging out of his jacket breast pocket!

Sadly, with the stadium now a housing estate, fans of all the sports featured at the venue must look elsewhere for their pleasure.

Chapter Seven

Chapel, Church, Co-op and Culture in the Valley

'The [Co-operative] Women's Guild ...was a little club attached to the Co-operative Wholesale Society ... which met in the long room above the grocery shop of the Bestwood Co-op. The Guild was called by some hostile husbands, who found their wives getting too independent, the clat-fart shop, that is the gossip shop'.
– Sons and Lovers.

One of the many traits traditionally shared by the nonconformist chapels and the co-operative movement was an abiding taste for a lavish tea party.

In their heyday of the late 19th century and early 20th centuries, at gatherings of the Methodists, Baptists, Congregationalists and other denominations, and equally at social events organised by the many co-operative societies which flourished in the valley's towns and villages, the tea urn was almost as vital a piece of kit as the pulpit in the chapel and the cash till in the Co-op store.

Both chapel-goers and co-operators had little taste for more intoxicating beverages. *My drink is water bright, from the crystal stream,* was a popular refrain and water was certainly valued, particularly when boiled and poured over some fragrant leaves, preferably sold by the Co-operative Wholesale Society.

If the colliers and other working men preferred, after a shift at the coal face or furnace side, to slake their thirst with beer, at least one of the most popular drinks consumed underground was cold tea.

Both the nonconformists and the co-operators could be fiercely evangelical when it came to the demon drink.

Just before the outbreak of World War One in 1914, a quarterly meeting of the members of the Long Eaton Working Men's Co-operative Society voted by an overwhelming majority to reject a motion calling on its board of directors to take out a wine, spirit and beer licence, 'with beer to be sold in not less than one dozen half pint bottles'.

Methodism. Although John Wesley, the founder of Methodism, remained a member of the Anglican church for the rest of his life, he was barred from preaching in many of the established church's pulpits. He preached widely in the open air, to audiences that varied from the convinced to the openly hostile.

Outdoor Preaching. Bob's Rock is a natural sandstone outcrop in Stapleford where John Wesley preached in 1774 (*Nottinghamshire County Council and www.picturethepast.org.uk*)

A Commemorative Chapel. The Wesley Place Methodist Chapel, close to Bob's Rock, the spot where Wesley preached in 1774, was first built eight years later, in 1782. It is no longer a place of worship (*Author*).

Recording the result of the debate on alcohol provision, the Society's chronicler recorded that 'the most pleasing feature was the practically unanimous feeling against touching the liquor traffic in any form'.

Accounts in literature of nonconformist worship, and the associated social programme which formed a substantial part of the life of each chapel, are captured in the Erewash Valley novels and short stories of D H Lawrence and also in the Five Towns novels of Arnold Bennett, set some 50 miles from the valley in the pottery centres of North Staffordshire.

Bennett in particular wrote superb descriptions of the passion of the Methodist and Baptist faiths, particularly during 'revivals' when skilful orators would whip congregations into a frenzy in a bid to save more souls for the Lord.

Neither Lawrence nor Bennett were particular advocates of religion, but they both acknowledged the part that nonconformism in particular played in moulding and often enriching the lives of the working and lower middle classes.

The enthusiasm of those convinced of the moral righteousness of the co-operative movement was equally passionate and came close to religious belief. The Long Eaton society's first historian, Samuel Clegg describes the efforts of a small group of financially hard-pressed working men, many of them employed by one of the town's major employers, Claye's Wagon Works, to band together to become as self-sufficient as possible.

Many of the men were in debt to local tradesmen and Clegg describes their bid to 'escape the thraldom of the huckster', adding: "Their first steps to becoming co-operators reads like the record of a conversion, and the organising of a crusade."

Co-operation: The massive bulk of the Long Eaton Co-operative Society's original Central Premises, now under conversion to apartments. The clock tower remains a dominant landmark in the town (*Author*).

A substantial staff line up outside an early Ilkeston Co-operative Society store in the town's South Street. A job 'on the Co-op' was highly prized in 19th and 20th century Britain. Local societies were regarded as good employers (*Erewash Museum*).

Alfreton's Watchorn Memorial Methodist church was built by Robert Watchorn (1859-1944), a local man who worked down the pit from the age of eleven. He later emigrated to the United States and amassed a fortune, spending part of it in endowing the church, a park, housing and a memorial library in his native town (*Author*)

Samuel Clegg was headmaster of the local secondary (later grammar) school. His daughter Mary married Frederick Attenborough, at one time a teacher at the Long Eaton County School, as it was then known, and their children included the late Lord Attenborough (the actor and film director Richard Attenborough) and Sir David Attenborough, the broadcaster and naturalist.

Both Richard and David inherited much of their grandfather's crusading zeal.

To later generations the passionate response of working people to the appeal of the fathers of nonconformism such as Methodism's John Wesley and the Baptist leader and active politician John Clifford, born in the village of Sawley, may be difficult to comprehend.

It becomes much more understandable when set against the background of an age when the financial and social gulf between the well-to-do and the mass of working men and women was a veritable chasm, and when there were no welfare benefits, just charity doled out, often grudgingly, on a parish level, to ease the lot of the less fortunate.

Through much of the 18th and 19th century the established Church of England was in a deep trough, with absentee clergymen and, with notable exceptions, not much evidence of a social conscience.

Wesley remained a member of the established church

Like Robert Watchorn, his nonconformist counterpart, John Clifford (1836-1923) left school early and worked as a child in a lace factory in Long Eaton. He came to the attention of the Baptist Church locally and was educated for the ministry, taking charge of his own church in London at the age of 22. He became a church leader and politician with an international reputation. His adoption of passive resistance as a campaigning tactic was said by Gandhi to have been one of his early influences.

Stapleford man Ted Perfect has spent a lifetime working both for the Methodist church and for the wider Co-operative movement. Ted is photographed with (left) the certificate stating that he has been a lay preacher since 1955 and, on the right, a print commemorating the founders of co-operation, the Rochdale Pioneers of 1863, several of whom were active Methodists (Author).

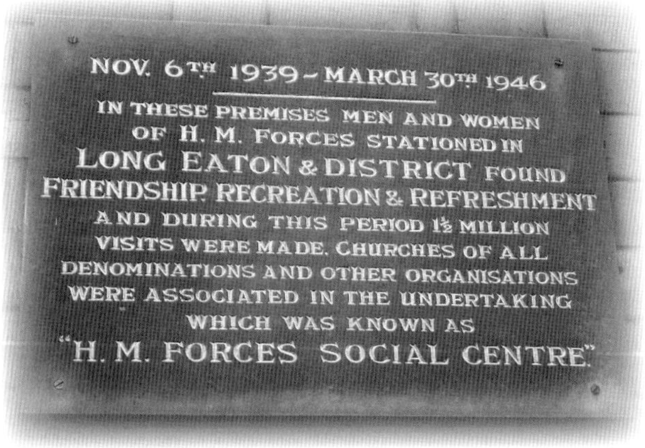

Service to the Community One: Serving the community has always been a big part of the creed of both nonconformism and co-operation. The Station Street Baptist Church premises at Long Eaton housed a social club for the armed forces during World War Two (*Author*).

throughout his life, insisting that Methodism sat comfortably within the Anglican tradition. He was a son of an Anglican cleric and a graduate of Christ Church College, Oxford.

John Clifford became not just a respected nonconformist divine but also an active politician.

He was born in 1836 and started work at the age of 11, as a 'jacker-off' in the Long Eaton lace trade, splicing the cotton on the bobbins in order to maintain an unbroken thread. Throughout his life he remembered the drudgery of the work and was an active campaigner for better conditions for working people.

After becoming a Baptist, he began to preach and eventually, at the age of 22, became pastor of the Praed Street Baptist Church in London. Clifford revived a congregation in decline and remained in post for 57 years, amassing several university honorary degrees, including an honorary doctorate awarded by an American institution.

In the Baptist Church Clifford rose to the highest positions, including the Presidency of the National Baptist Union and the Baptist World Alliance, being received on one occasion at the White House by President Taft of the USA. He was a prominent campaigner against the Boer War and advocated passive resistance to the Education Act of 1902.

This legislation enraged nonconformists, who objected to paying the element of taxation used to support denominational religious teaching in schools.

Clifford, although well established in London by the time the Long Eaton Working Men's Co-operative Society was established in 1868, kept in touch with trade conditions and the lot of workers in his home area.

Shopkeepers in Long Eaton, some of whom were probably experiencing difficult times themselves, did not welcome the competition they faced from the fledgling Co-op. Two bakers and a publican from the town broke into the new Society's first tiny shop, smashing windows and damaging a sign.

Service to the Community Two: When floods struck Long Eaton, a common occurrence in the 1920s and 1930s, the local Co-operative Society donated bags of coal to members to help them dry out their homes (*Author's Collection*).

Starting out to offer reasonably-priced provisions and household necessities, the Co-op societies of the Erewash Valley steadily branched out to a point where they could literally meet all the cradle to grave needs of their members. The gentlemens' outfitting department in Ilkeston was having a sale in 1930 (*Peter Wiles and www.picturethepast.org.uk*).

Branches in outlying districts of towns and in rural villages were part of the Co-op's policy of taking co-operation to as wide a public as possible. The Ripley Society's branch in the colliery village of Waingroves appears to have had a delivery via the horse and cart to the left. Co-op policy was always to feature the staff in publicity photographs (*Stuart Saint www.codnor.info*)

When brought before the town's magistrates, the trio pleaded that their action had been 'a mere joke' and a 'gentlemanly spree'. The magistrates seemed to agree with the culprits' lawyer, merely ordering the defendants to settle the matter out of court and pay for the damaged caused.

Opposition to co-operation also took more subtle economic forms, with developers forming cartels to prevent prospering co-operative societies from buying land, as their activities developed into farming and allied activities.

The co-operative societies as first constituted in the Erewash Valley made sure that their titles proclaimed their guiding principles; the Selston Industrial and Provident Society, the Ripley Provident, Industrial and Co-operative Society, and the Long Eaton Working Men's Co-operative Society leaving their communities in no doubt as to their intentions.

They were joined by the Pinxton, Codnor Park and Ironville, Langley Mill and Aldercar, Ilkeston and Stapleford and Sandiacre societies, together with several smaller and very localised organisations that usually quickly merged with their larger and more viable brethren.

It was a Butterley Company worker called George Atkin who suggested to his workmates the idea of starting their own shop. Thirty of the men met together and drew up rules for their society, with the first store being opened in two rooms of the home of one of the workers, Patrick Parkin.

The larger towns of the valley had large department stores. This is the Long Eaton society's Emporium, pictured on opening day in 1935 (*Derbyshire Local Studies Libraries and picturethepast.org.uk*).

The Co-op societies operated farms and dairies and delivered milk, fruit and vegetables and coal, members buying tokens in advance and then leaving them on their doorsteps to be picked up by the delivery men. A Langley Mill and Aldercar horse-drawn milk float proceeds steadily along Station Road in Langley Mill, near the cricket ground (*Heanor and District Local History Society*).

Initially known as the Butterley Co-operative Society, the enterprise enjoyed steady growth but quickly recognised that the centre of its operation should be in the adjacent market town of Ripley. The society's title was changed to reflect this recognition, in 1872.

The Ripley society prospered, opening branch stores in Codnor, Alfreton, Somercotes, Swanwick and Riddings. The imposing central premises in Ripley opened in 1903 and by 1910 membership had reached nearly 15,000.

The Long Eaton society's first stores attracted shoppers from far afield in south Derbyshire, west Nottinghamshire and north west Leicestershire. When evidence showed that enthusiastic co-operators were walking several miles from villages such as Breaston, Draycott, Shardlow, Kegworth, Long Whatton, Sutton Bonington, East Leake and Gotham, the society moved to first deliver to these areas by horse and cart and later to open branch stores.

By the late 1920s Long Eaton's annual sales, which had totalled less than £2,000 in the first year of operation, were heading past the million pound mark.

In later years the Long Eaton Society dropped the 'Working Men's' part of its title, realising that its customer base had widened to include families from a much wider spectrum of society. The Ilkeston Society in turn added a quite modern sounding word, 'Consumer', to its company description.

The Erewash Valley societies, as they grew in both size and confidence, greatly expanded their range of services. The larger town branches brought grocery, butchery and greengrocery departments under one roof (although still divided into separate units) and the societies established bakeries, dairies, coal yards and, in centres such as Ripley, Ilkeston and Long Eaton, opened department stores, selling furniture, carpets, electrical goods, gifts and fashions, giving even quite modest towns something of a metropolitan air.

Chapels and the Co-op alike celebrated milestones and enjoyed processions. This is the Long Eaton Co-op Golden Jubilee celebration in 1919, held a year later because of the continuing Great War (*Derbyshire Local Studies Libraries and picturethepast.org.uk*).

Langley Mill Baptist Church Sunday School on parade on Station Road (*Heanor and District Local History Society*).

A major inducement to shop at the Co-op – for all classes of society – was the practice of paying a dividend of so much in the pound on purchases - sometimes as high as two shillings and sixpence (twelve and a half pence) in the pound.

One of the minor accomplishments of which D H Lawrence boasted in later life was his ability to remember his mother's co-operative society membership number, which it was necessary to quote when making a purchase. It is perhaps one of the few things, apart from an Erewash Valley childhood, that the present writer has in common, not just with Lawrence but with many thousands of British people born around the middle of the 20th century.

The dividend accrued by the member could be redeemed for cash at certain times of the year. At Ilkeston the enthusiasm for the payout has passed into local folklore. Large crowds are remembered to have gathered outside the central co-op premises, waiting for the time when the commissionaire pulled aside a barrier and allowed members to gallop up the staircase to the waiting clerks and cashiers.

Not for nothing was the ceremony known as 'Ilkeston Races'.

The Co-op dividend payment was for many years an important part of the family budget. When families did virtually all their shopping 'at the stores', the amount of cash to be collected in dividend could be substantial.

The 'divvi' helped a young mother to be to buy a cot, perambulator, maternity clothes and other essentials, all purchased, of course, from the co-op, generating yet more dividend for the future. At the other end of life's journey, the co-op, with the help of dividend, furnished everything required for a respectable funeral, including the cooked ham which was an essential feature of the high tea that followed the interment.

In between times the dividend paid for school uniforms, wedding dresses, gifts and even helped towards a mortgage for a house. The co-op was truly the eternal provider and many a domestic crisis was eased by the fact that dividend money had been set aside for a rainy day.

Long before the slogan 'cradle to grave' had been adopted as the semi-official mission statement of the National Health Service, the lifelong commitment to service the phrase embodied had been put into practice by both the nonconformist chapels and the co-operative movement.

From the mid-19th century onwards Roman Catholic places of worship, forced underground since the Reformation, were established, largely to cater for the Irish workers who flocked to the Erewash Valley's industries. The Ilkeston parish of Our Lady and St Thomas of Hereford for many years organised a pilgrimage to the ruins of Dale Abbey (*Father Peter Harvey*).

At first there was considerable suspicion of the Roman Catholic Church in a staunchly nonconformist area but gradually the RC community came to play a full part in local life. Pictured is a stall staffed by parishioners from St Francis of Assisi, Long Eaton, during the town's annual carnival (*Author's Collection*).

Somehow, where the Co-op was concerned, it never seemed quite the same when in the 1960s and 1970s dividend was replaced by the movement's own trading stamps – blue rather than green.

One man from the Erewash Valley who typified the links between nonconformism and co-operation is Edward Perfect of Stapleford, a co-operative employee, a political activist in the Co-operative Party, and a Methodist lay preacher.

His story begins a long way from the Erewash Valley, in the Australian gold mining town of Kalgoorlie, where his parents were prospectors. He was brought to England and Nottingham as a child and in the mid-1950s spent two years studying at the Methodist training school, Cliff College, in Derbyshire.

He later worked for the Nottingham Co-operative Society – later the Greater Nottingham Society – from 1956 to 1994, also serving as a director and playing a major part in the movement's democratic aspect. During his career he was at one time deputy manager of the large department store in Long Eaton.

He received an award from the Co-operative Party in 2016 for his outstanding contribution to the co-operative movement.

Ted Perfect became a Methodist lay preacher in 1955 and is still accredited today. He has no doubts about the major influence nonconformism exerted upon the co-operative movement.

"The movement began with the Rochdale Pioneers, who set up the first society in 1844. More than half of the original Pioneers were active Christians and Methodists.

"In addition to providing the practical necessities of life, the co-operative movement , just like the nonconformist churches, helped the underprivileged educationally and morally and gave them a sense of belonging."

Ted has lived for many years in Stapleford, not far from Bob's Rock, the sandstone outcrop where John Wesley is believed to have preached in the open air in

Through all the upheavals of the centuries the established churches of the valley continued to play their part in the life of the towns and villages. St Mary's in Ilkeston would in earlier days have been at the heart of fairs and other celebrations. Today it continues to tower over the town's famous Charter Fair, held each Autumn and originally staged on a Saint's Day (*Author*).

The strength of nonconformism in the past is demonstrated by the numbers taking part in a Christmas concert at the Wesleyan Methodist Chapel on Heanor Road (Chapel Street), Codnor in the 1930s. (*Aubrey Ratcliffe and Stuart Saint www.codnor.info*).

1774. Close to Bob's Rock is the former Wesley Place Methodist Chapel, named to commemorate Wesley's visit to the Nottinghamshire town. Originally built in 1782, Wesley Place ceased to be a place of worship in 1975..

Like that of the Co-op, the reach of the nonconformist chapels has shrunk somewhat since the heyday of the two institutions.

In many parts of the valley the older, and in some places absolutely cavernous chapel buildings, intended for congregations in the hundreds rather than in the tens, have been sold off and replaced by modern, purpose-built and easier to maintain facilities, which have retained not just a spiritual role but a position as the focus for many community activities.

In the case of the co-operative movement, the place of the all-embracing local societies has been taken by much larger units, organised on what is virtually a national scale, and trading under the banner of the Co-op, using effective slogans such as 'Good with Food' , offering what is claimed to be a much more ethical system of banking and retaining a democratic system of one member one vote for electing representative bodies.

Most valley communities of any size still have a co-op store, usually of medium supermarket size. In some of the smaller towns and villages it forms the most significant and valued retail outlet.

The co-ops' continued to sponsor activities of a more secular nature, in the fields of entertainment and education, right up until the latter part of the 20th century. These are the members of the Ilkeston Co-operative Women's Guild, pictured in 1958 (*Derbyshire Local Studies Libraries and www.picturethepast.org.uk*).

The Ilkeston Co-operative Society Youth Group had a substantial membership in this photograph, taken in the 1950s (*Erewash Museum*).

The role of both chapel and co-op in the Erewash Valley of the not-so-distant past cannot be over-stressed. Before the establishment of free and compulsory state education for children from five to 13, in 1870, both movements, together with the established Church of England and, from the mid-19th century onwards, the re-established Roman Catholic Church, taught poorer children their letters and numbers and, through their charitable efforts, helped to prevent absolute destitution and actual starvation.

The churches and chapels of the valley had a role in not only helping to sustain ordinary people before the advent of the welfare state, but also in brightening their lives before the era of shorter working hours, cinemas, theatres and, eventually, home entertainment.

Again, there were many common factors. The churches and chapels encouraged choral singing, both for worship and for the popular performances of oratorios, such as Handel's *Messiah.* At the same time, the co-operative societies formed senior and junior choirs to compete in regional and national contests, alongside drama groups, debating societies, women's guilds, youth and sports clubs.

The chapels in particular were noted for their Anniversaries, which would see a dais erected at the front of the church, on which would assemble the Sunday School children, in ascending ranks according to age groups to sing and recite during a special and eagerly awaited service, inevitably followed by a tea!

Church teas were substantial events, but when the Co-op decided to mark a special event with a special repast, it really went to town.

The Long Eaton Society's celebrations for its golden jubilee had to be postponed from the actual anniversary in July 1918 to the following year, due to the continuing war with Germany. When the event eventually took place the society worked with the town's Sunday Schools (again the church/co-op connection) and provided tea for no fewer than 6,500 children.

With an eye for detail typical of local newspapers of the time, the *Long Eaton Advertiser* reported that the children consumed 87 pounds (in weight) of tea, 294 pounds of sugar (!) 427 pounds of butter, 66 gallons of milk, 156,300 assorted cakes and buns, 2,400 fancy cakes, 1,260 pounds of slab cake and 1,280 pounds of bread.

(For the benefit of the younger generation, a pound in the old Imperial system of weights, is roughly 453 grams).

A nonconformist church that typifies much of what has been necessary to survive and flourish in modern day society is Waingroves Methodist, near Ripley.

Part of the Mid-Derbyshire Methodist Circuit, which embraces 30 individual churches across the centre of the county, including a dozen or so in the Erewash Valley, the church building is modern and well suited not just to the needs of both traditional and contemporary worship but also to its role as the centre of community life for all age groups.

A feature of the community activities is a table tennis club, affiliated to the English Table Tennis Association, which provides qualified coaching to all ages and abilities and fields teams in the Derby & District Leagues.

Waingroves is one of just two Erewash Valley villages (Swanwick is the other) which has adopted the Derbyshire and Staffordshire Peak District tradition of well dressing.

Organiser Margaret Bailey explains the story behind the birth of the ancient custom in the village.

"Local man Reg Maund was a great enthusiast for well dressing and he spent time in the Peak District village of Wormhill learning as much as he could about the tradition. We told Reg we wanted to do a well dressing for Waingroves but, sadly, just as we were about to organise the first dressing, he went into hospital and never came out again.

"As a tribute to Reg the frame that holds our main dressing proclaims that it is 'Reginald's well'.

The older religious denominations enjoyed their special festivals. The Roman Catholic churches of the valley united for pilgrimages to the ruined Carthusian Priory at Beauvale, once home to the earliest English martyrs who refused to renounce their faith after King Henry VIII's split with Rome and destruction of the monastic system.

The sole remaining vestige of Dale Abbey is the great East Window, standing in splendid isolation in a field. The abbey was successfully established in the 12th century as a Premonstratensian House after two previous attempts to established a religious foundation had failed, was also previously a place of Catholic pilgrimage, commemorating a vision of the Blessed Virgin Mary experienced by a baker in Derby, who was told to go to a place called 'Depedale' and there serve God in hunger, thirst, coldness and nakedness.

The hermit lived in a cave, hollowed out of rock, which can still be seen today.

A further connection between popular entertainment and the churches can be found in the surviving charter fairs and village 'Wakes' that still flourish today. In most cases they owe their timing in the calendar to their links to the patron saints of the village churches.

One of the most successful forms of 20th century popular culture was the cinema. Each autumn at fair time the iconic art deco Scala Cinema in Ilkeston, still thriving today, appears to be overwhelmed by the fairground rides and stalls (*Author*).

King Henry III granted a charter in April 1252 to the Lord of the Manor, Hugh de Muskham, and the townspeople of Ilkeston, giving the right to hold a market on the Thursday of every week and an annual two day fair on the Assumption of The Blessed Virgin Mary in August. Today, the original Thursday market has been joined by a Friday and Saturday market, while the annual fair now takes place, still in the hill top market square and down the surrounding streets of the town, during the third week of October.

At the official opening of the fair each autumn the original charter is read to the crowds which gather in front of the town hall, After the formalities are over, the mayor of Erewash and other VIPs attempt to hold on to their civic dignity whilst riding the dodgem cars.

In the earlier part of the 20th century Ilkeston Fair retained another religious connection. Part of the fair stayed in town after the rides closed on a Saturday night, to operate on the following Monday evening for a charity carnival.

On the Sunday a service was held on the galloping horses, utilising the ride's fairground organ, under the auspices of one of Britain's best-known travelling showmen, Pat Collins.

Collins, born on a fairground, created his business, Pat Collins Ltd, in 1899, after he had established a round of fairs in the Black Country based, like Ilkeston, on traditional charters and feast days.

One of the greatest and most enduring figures in British pop music history, Cliff Richard and his group, The Shadows, made their professional debuts in Ripley in 1958.They performed as Harry Webb (the singer's real name) and The Drifters. The Drifters became The Shadows to avoid a clash with the American group of that name. A plaque on the wall ofThe Regal, then a dance hall, now a club, marks the historic occasion (Author).

He was a major force in making travelling fairs a respectable business, serving not only as President of the Showman's Guild of Great Britain but also as the Mayor of Walsall and as Liberal MP for that division in the 1920s.

The firm Collins founded in Victorian times is still associated with Ilkeston Fair in the second decade of the 21st century.

Having devoted much of this chapter to tea, with more than a passing mention of the distaste felt for alcohol by the chapels and the Co-op, those twin bastions of Erewash Valley life, it is time to redress the balance and turn the focus onto licensed premises.

Just as in the Victorian/Edwardian era described by D H Lawrence, the working man (and in recent years increasingly the working woman too) continues to enjoy a drink in a public house or a social club.

Unlike in the era described in *Sons and Lovers,* when beer and whisky were the colliers' staples, the drink of choice is just as likely to be lager or wine as ale brewed in Kimberley by the twin breweries of Hardys and Hansons (later to merge into one concern), by Shipstones at Basford or Home Ales at Daybrook, both in the Nottingham suburbs.

Despite holding their own at a time when many brewers were forsaking traditional beer in favour of fizzy keg products such as Double Diamond and Watneys Red Barrel, the local brewers eventually succumbed to the increasing rationalisation of the industry.

This was ironic, given that the real ale trend championed by CAMRA, the Campaign for Real Ale, in the 1970s grew in strength in the 1980s and 1990s and was given a boost by the creation of literally hundreds of independent micro breweries.

In 1978 Shipstones, with an estate of more than 500 pubs, was acquired by Greenall's of Warrington, which was in the process of expanding through the take-over of breweries from neighbouring areas – a familiar process across Britain in that era.

For several years Greenall's continued to brew in Nottingham, but in 1990 announced that it was ending all beer production and becoming a retail company only. At the time, it looked like the beginning of the end for the Shipstone brand established in 1852.

Although Shipstones beers continued to be produced for a while under licence at breweries in Burton upon Trent, the day arrived when it became impossible to walk into a pub and ask for a pint of 'Shippos'.

Next in line for takeover was the equally proudly independent Home Brewery Co Ltd, first registered in 1890. The brewery, with its distinctive Art Noveau building in Daybrook, and an estate of more than 400 public houses, was taken over by the expanding Scottish & Newcastle Breweries in July 1986.

As with Shipstones, the Daybrook brewery was retained for some years, finally closing in 1996.

Hardy and Hansons were the third of the Nottinghamshire brewing trio to lose their independence. The company had been formed in 1930 by the merger of long-established friendly rival breweries, Hardys and Hansons.

The former rivalry was emphasised by the presence on Derby Road at Ilkeston (as no doubt in many other areas) of a former Hansons pub, the Horse and Jockey, on one corner of a narrow side street and a one-time Hardys house, the now closed Miners Arms, opposite – both still proclaiming their original ownerships on their facades.

The Kimberley Brewery survived as an independent until 2006, when its brewing facilities and all of its public houses were sold in a multimillion-pound deal to Greene King brewery of Bury St Edmunds. In this instance, unlike with Shipstones and Home Ales, there was to be no continuation of brewing under new ownership. Greene King ended the brewing tradition in Kimberley, quoting cost effectiveness, and sold the Kimberley site.

There is further irony to be found in the takeover of Kimberley Ales by Greene King.

In the early days of CAMRA, Greene King were unquestionably regarded as one of the 'goodies' in the brewing industry, ranking as a regional independent. Indeed, it must be said in fairness that the company produces some fine beers to this day, including ales brewed in Suffolk to the original Kimberley recipes.

Today, however, the CAMRA Good Beer Guide reflects the fact that Greene King has expanded tremendously in recent decades, taking over other breweries besides Kimberley, and a large number of public houses and hotels.

The guide now gives Greene King, and another former regional independent brewer, Burton-on-Trent's Marstons (now merged with Banks of Wolverhampton) a new status, that of 'new nationals', occupying a place in the middle ground of the industry between truly independent breweries and what CAMRA describes as the 'global giants' of Carlsberg, Heineken, Molson Coors etc.

A huge change from the *Good Beer Guide* of 1980 that I would have consulted to see which Erewash Valley pubs were included in its listings is the size of the section devoted to independent breweries. Today, some thirty long-established family breweries still exist and thrive across Britain and have a special place in the hearts of real ale fans.

They have been joined, as hinted at earlier in this chapter, by literally thousands of smaller independents, some now rivalling the old time companies in size, and far outstripping the literal description of 'micro'. Derbyshire and Nottinghamshire at the time of writing have some of the best of the new independents in Britain, over 40 west of the River Erewash and more than 20 on the east bank.

The Erewash Valley itself is well represented, with independents in Ripley, Heanor, Marlpool, Stanley Common/West Hallam, Stapleford and, fittingly, Kimberley itself.

Riding the crest of the great and growing popularity of traditional ales, the old names have also returned. Kimberley, acknowledging Greene King's continued brewing of ales following the original recipes, has never really gone away.

Shipstones beer was re-launched in 2013, the work of Nottingham brewery expert Richard Neale and Colin Brown, a former brewer at the original Shipstone brewery. They started small, brewing a bottled ale and selling it through pubs and independent distributors in the region.

In 2015 Nick Whitehurst, who grew up in the shadow of the Home Brewery's company's landmark brewery in Daybrook, revived the brand after taking on the licence from Heineken.

In addition to the news of the return of the Erewash Valley's best-selling 20th century brands, the CAMRA Good Beer Guide includes details of recommended pubs from one end of the valley to the other.

The River Erewash itself, much cleaner now than in the past, itself plays host to the first community event of each New Year, the Toton Duck Race. Crowds line the banks in chilly conditions to watch the ducks float downstream (*Tim Fryzer-Smith*).

Micro breweries have now been joined in the valley by micro pubs, which have often been opened in former shop premises. One of those with a strong reputation for the quality of its ale and its atmosphere is the Burnt Pig Ale House in Market Street, Ilkeston.

On the other side of the coin, a considerable number of public houses in the area have closed their doors over the past three or four decades, victims of social change, perhaps notably the trend towards consuming at home the alcoholic drinks bought much cheaper from supermarkets which are, unfairly in my view, exempt from aspects of the high taxation which pubs must pay.

If some pubs have closed because of simple economics, others have been forced to put the bar towels on the pumps for the last time for much stranger reasons.

In the early 1980s I often walked or drove the short distance from West Hallam to the former mining village of Mapperley, for a pint in the Royal Oak, or the Candlestick as the pub was better known – a name bestowed upon the house in the days before gas or electric lighting, said to derive from a candelabra carried from room to room by the landlady of the day.

The pub had been a favourite gathering place for local miners in the heyday of the coal industry in the West Hallam/ Mapperley/Shipley area and the custom of pulling pints when the pit blower sounded ready for the rush of thirsty men was observed here as elsewhere.

The Candlestick had a loyal and devoted clientele. Sadly, its long history, with the licence believed to date from as far back as the 16th century, came to an end in the autumn of 1984, when it was closed for health and safety reasons due to methane gas seeping into the cellar.

Another great source of entertainment in the valley were the Miners Welfare Institutes and other sports and social clubs attached to companies, including the former Stanton and Staveley facilities in Ilkeston.

Despite the demise of the British coal mining industry, CISWO, the Coal Industry Social Welfare Organisation is still very active and highly valued. CISWO is a national charity supporting former miners and their families, giving help and advice to alleviate disadvantage arising from disability, ill health or financial hardship.

One of the most visually obvious effects of CISWO's continued existence is through the continuation, despite the end of the industry, of Miners' Welfare clubs and institutes, of which a dozen or so are situated in the Erewash Valley, from Blackwell and Pinxton (Derbyshire) and Jacksdale (Nottinghamshire) in the north of the valley to Langley Mill (Derbyshire) and Greasley (Nottinghamshire) further south.

In some cases the premises and sports facilities of former welfare institutes have been taken over by parish councils, notably at Selston. Here the former institute itself is now a very active village hall, whilst the excellent sports facilities still play host to football, cricket and bowls.

One former Methodist Chapel in the valley which has escaped demolition and has been tastefully restored as an event venue is the former 'Chapel on the Bridge', built in 1886 next to the Erewash Canal in Sandiacre.

Used by a motor factor for many years after closure in the 1960s, it was purchased by the Reid family, Colin and Debbie and their daughter Alison, and magnificently and tastefully restored to its old glory for its new life as Springfield Hall, holding up to 200 guests for weddings and other special occasions.

The former 'Chapel on the Bridge' in Sandiacre (*Reid Family*)

The magnificently restored interior of the building in its new role as Springfield Hall (*Reid Family*)

Chapter Eight

A Valley at War

'The war had brought the roof down over her head. She had married Clifford Chatterley in 1917 .. they had a month's honeymoon. Then he went back to Flanders; to be shipped over to England again six months later, more or less in bits'. – Lady Chatterley's Lover.

The role played by the people of the Erewash Valley in the two global conflicts of the 20th century embraced not only military heroism and innovation, but also both technological achievement and unremitting toil in keeping the wheels of British industry turning.

Despite the manpower demands of the mines, blast furnaces, foundries, and other vital wartime industries, and the staffing needs of the then intricate railway system that carried the raw materials and finished products, the valley contributed thousands of men and women to the armed forces in both world wars.

In a proud military tradition dating back in recorded form to the Napoleonic wars, the decorated men of the valley include no fewer than eight holders of the Victoria Cross, the highest and most prestigious award for gallantry in the face of the enemy that can be awarded to British and Commonwealth forces, together with countless recipients of other medals recognising outstanding courage.

World War Two represented total war, drawing in men, women and children of all backgrounds.

The Erewash Valley represented a huge concentration, in a relatively small and in many parts still largely rural area, of vital extractive and manufacturing industries and a system of communications vastly important to the overall war effort.

The direct effects of enemy action in 1939-45 against this considerable industrial base were curiously insignificant. Just one high explosive bomb and six incendiaries were reported as having hit the 400-acre Stanton complex during the period, and the huge railway yards at Toton, the marshalling point for much of the coal needed to provide power and fuel industry, and the iron ore required for war material production, told a similar tale.

Stanton works, pictured in later years across the greens of the Erewash Valley Golf Club, played a major role in Britain's war effort between 1939-1945 (*Author's Collection*).

Stanton, an organisation with a worldwide reputation for its ability to adapt to changing conditions, produced armaments in both the century's conflicts, with the company's 6,000-plus employees going to war in a big way in 1939.

Working with the Ministry of Supply a new plant was constructed which, in four years, cast 875,000 bombs, a total weight of 175,000 tons of loaded bombs for the Royal Air Force, together with the production of gun barrels, torpedo body forgings and armour-piercing shells.

The firm's concrete plant played a major part in protecting the civilian population, building thousands of pre-cast air raid shelters. The concrete arm of the company also embraced necessary innovation.

With timber for railway sleepers in short supply, Stanton experimented with the production of a concrete alternative. This proved a success and more than a million were produced, keeping the lines of communication open to the specially-built war munitions factories.

The Erewash Valley Roll of Honour in the two centuries since the defeat of Napoleonic France includes many thousands of ordinary men and women who have served their country in time of conflict in an immense variety of capacities often scarcely recognised, in addition to those whose heroism has gained them notice and, all too often, a place on the war memorials in local towns and villages.

The Roll of Honour has been constantly expanded in recent years, as more and more stories come to light with the passing of men and women, too modest to proclaim their achievements in public during their lifetimes but whose contributions emerge after their deaths.

A man born in the Erewash Valley played a starring role in the most famous of the RAF's wartime attacks on the German heartland, whilst an adopted son of the valley, a German-born Jew, made a vital contribution to the defeat of the Nazi regime as part of the celebrated code-breaking team at Bletchley Park.

Amidst a multitude of heroes, celebrated and unknown, there almost inevitably has to be a villain.

One of the valley's most prominent politicians, the man charged with responsibility for Britain's military policy in the crucial years leading to the outbreak of World War One in 1914, was in fact first cast as hero of the South African war, later being castigated for his political actions and forced to resign his ministerial office.

He was then acclaimed as a hero for his bravery on the field of battle but later in life, was execrated again for his declared support for Hitler.

Although men from both the Nottinghamshire and Derbyshire banks of the Erewash undoubtedly took the King's Shilling to enlist in the British Army and the Royal Navy in the years before the rise of Napoleon Bonaparte and his eventual nemesis at the hands of the Duke of Wellington and his armies, the recorded history of local men at war largely dates from this time.

The outstanding memorial in the quiet village churchyard in the attractive Nottinghamshire village of Cossall, on a hilltop above the River Erewash, stands in honour of three local men who fought with Wellington at Waterloo.

Two, John Shaw and Richard Waplington of the Life Guards died on the battlefield. The third, Thomas Wheatley of the Light Dragoon Guards, survived the battle and died in the almshouses at Cossall, where he is buried, apparently below the joint memorial stone.

The next conflict in which Erewash Valley men distinguished themselves was the Crimean War, a conflict fought from October 1853 to March 1856 in which, after a bitter struggle, the Russian Empire was defeated by an alliance of France, Britain, the Ottoman Empire, and Sardinia.

The causes of the war involved the decline of the Ottoman Empire and the unwillingness of Britain and France to allow Russia to gain territory and power at Ottoman expense.

After inconclusive actions, the British and French allies decided to attack the core of Russian strength in the Black Sea at Sevastopol on the Crimean peninsula. After an eleven-month siege, carried out under brutal conditions, Sevastopol fell and Russia, faced with the prospect of invasion by the allies, sued for peace.

The honour of the Erewash Valley was upheld in the Crimean campaign by two local men, from very different stations in life.

Drury Lowe was a member of a family once known for its extensive coal mining interests in the Erewash Valley and its environs, and which still today holds its seat at Locko Park, near Stanley, in Derbyshire.

The memorial in Cossall churchyard to the local men who fought at the Battle of Waterloo (*Author*)

Lowe joined the 17th Lancers in 1854, served in the Crimea at the battle of the Chernaya River and was present at Sevastopol when the stronghold fell. He saw service in 1858-59 during the Indian Mutiny, rising through the commissioned ranks and, after assuming the surname of Drury-Lowe as a result of an inheritance, was promoted to Lieutenant –Colonel.

He commanded the regiment for 12 years, notably at Ulundi, the last pitched battle of the Anglo-Zulu War and, at that time of frequent colonial campaigns, also served with distinction in the 1882 Anglo-Egyptian War.

He was publicly thanked for his services in the House of Commons, knighted as Sir Drury Drury-Lowe, and became Inspector of Cavalry at Aldershot, being promoted to Lieutenant-General in 1890. He died in 1908.

The martial temperament of the inhabitants of Cossall is marked not only by the church yard memorial to the heroes of Waterloo but also by the nearby grave of Henry Ash, a village boy who served as a sergeant in the 11th Prince Albert's Own Hussars.

Ash gained distinction by serving throughout the Crimean conflict as orderly to the British military commander, Lord Raglan. Henry Ash died in December 1880, aged 58 years.

The Crimean War was one of the first conflicts to use modern technologies such as explosive naval shells, railways, and telegraphs and one of the first to be documented extensively in written reports and photographs.

The notorious charge of the Light Brigade and the appalling conditions suffered by the British wounded and sick meant that the war became increasingly unpopular with the British public and led to a demand for a more professional attitude towards the mounting of military campaigns by the Army.

It also made the name of Florence Nightingale, who lived at Holloway in Derbyshire's Derwent Valley, and transformed hospital conditions for the soldiers, pioneering modern nursing techniques.

The Crimean War was closely followed by the Indian Mutiny, a fairly widespread but ultimately unsuccessful rebellion in 1857-58 against British rule in India by Indian troops, known as sepoys.

The mutiny broke out in the British East India Company's Bengal army, with the pretext for revolt ostensibly the introduction of a new Enfield rifle. To load the weapon the sepoys had to bite off the ends of lubricated cartridges.

The inscription on the Waterloo Memorial at Cossall (*Author*).

Walter Richard Parker VC is honoured in Stapleford (*Author's Collection*).

A rumour was circulated that the grease used for lubrication was a mixture of lard from both cows and pigs, therefore insulting the beliefs of both Hindu and Muslim soldiers. In reality, the increasing westernisation of Indian life and the arrogance of the British rulers was the cause of great discontent.

The Victoria Cross had been introduced in January 1856 by Queen Victoria, initially to honour acts of valour during the Crimean War.

The Indian Mutiny saw the first occasion on which the medal was won by a soldier from the Erewash Valley, with a second senior officer from the valley reputed to have turned down the award.

The recipient of the VC was Sir Henry Wilmot, who after a distinguished military career became a Conservative politician and represented South Derbyshire, which at the time included much of the area of the Erewash Valley within its boundaries, in the House of Commons.

Wilmot was born in Chaddesden, the son of Sir Henry Wilmot and his wife Maria Mundy daughter of Edmund Mundy of Shipley Hall in the Erewash Valley. He purchased commissions, then a common practice in the British Army, first as Ensign, then as Lieutenant and then as Captain in the 43rd Monmouthshire Regiment of Foot.

In 1855 he transferred to the Rifle Brigade and later was on the staff of Brigadier General Hope Grant. It was while assigned to the staff that he fought in the Indian Mutiny; on March 11 1858 at Lucknow, , along with Private David Hawkes and Corporal William Nash, the incident occurred which led to him being awarded the Victoria Cross.

The citation for the award described how Captain Wilmot's company was engaged with the enemy near the Iron Bridge in the Indian city. He found himself at the end of a street with only four of his men, opposed to a considerable body.

One of the four British soldiers was shot through both legs and became utterly helpless: the two other enlisted men lifted him up, and although Private Hawkes was severely wounded, he carried him for a considerable distance, exposed to the fire of the enemy.

Captain Wilmot took his men's rifles and covered the retreat of the party to safety.

Wilmot later served in the Oudh campaign in India of 1858-9 and the Second China War. He subsequently held appointments with the Derbyshire Rifle Volunteers and was a Deputy Lieutenant of Derbyshire. He sat as a Member of Parliament from 1869 to 1885 and was also an alderman of Derbyshire and chairman of the County Council.

A memorial in Stapleford town centre to another of the Erewash Valley's eight Victoria Cross winners, Walter Richard Parker. The memorial is highly reflective and difficult to photograph (*Author*).

Colonel Shaw, born in Ilkeston, was a World War One sniper who lived not only to tell the tale but also to celebrate his 100th birthday. He taught chemistry at The University of Nottingham and his explosives lectures were legendary (*Author*).

The man who reportedly declined the Victoria Cross for bravery in the Indian Mutiny undoubtedly ranks as the Erewash Valley and Derbyshire's greatest soldier.

James Outram was the son of the renowned civil engineer and founder of The Butterley Company, Benjamin Outram of Butterley Hall, Butterley, Derbyshire.

When his father died James and his mother moved to Scotland, where the young man attended Marischal College, now the University of Aberdeen before gaining an Indian cadetship. In 1820 he became adjutant to the 12th Regiment of the East India Company's Army.

Five years later he was sent to Khandesh, where he trained a light infantry corps formed from the Bhils, a tribe from the area's densely forested hills. Outram was popular with the tribe because of his hunting skills and attracted huge personal loyalty.

On the outbreak of the First Afghan War in 1838 he was appointed extra aide-de-camp on the staff of Sir John Keane, and went to Afghanistan, where he carried out various raids against Afghan tribes and performed an extraordinary exploit in capturing a banner of the enemy.

Serving in the Indian province of Sindh, he heroically defended the British Residency at Hyderabad against eight thousand Baluchi tribesmen.

In 1854 Outram was appointed British resident at Lucknow, in which capacity two years later he carried out the annexation of Oudh and became the first chief commissioner of that province.

Appointed in 1857, with the rank of lieutenant-general, to command an expedition against Persia during the Anglo-Persian War, he defeated the enemy with great slaughter, and conducted the campaign with such rapid decision that a peace settlement was quickly agreed.

He returned to India in time for the Mutiny and was appointed to command the two divisions of the Bengal army occupying the country from Calcutta to Cawnpore.

Hostilities had forced the British general Henry Havelock to fall back on Cawnpore. A swift advance was needed to save the besieged British

Arnold Warren, the Derbyshire and England fast bowler from Codnor, aged 40 in 1915, was not eligible for military service in World War One, but persisted in his bid to serve his country on the battlefield as he had on the cricket field. He was eventually accepted into the Royal Garrison Artillery by lying about his date of birth. He served in France and was seriously wounded by a shell in 1917, not being finally discharged until 1919. He experienced pain from his wounds for the rest of his life and had an Army disability pension (*Stuart Saint www.codnor.info*)

British troops experienced horrendous conditions at Gallipoli, where Walter Parker of Stapleford won his VC. The troops pictured here are recovering from frostbite, in a shelter apparently insulated with Huntley and Palmer cartons (*Author's Collection*).

garrison at Lucknow but when Outram arrived at Cawnpore with reinforcements he gave up the honour of leading the relief column to Havelock, whom he admired greatly.

Outram went even further, ignoring his rank and volunteering to serve under Havelock in the ensuing campaign. During the advance he commanded a troop of volunteer cavalry, and in the final action before Lucknow led a charge through what was later described as 'a very tempest of fire'.

His voluntary cavalry officers and men unanimously recommended that Outram should receive the VC but he declined the honour, on the grounds that he was ineligible as the general under whom they served.

Outram then resumed overall command and held Lucknow until the arrival of another force under Sir Colin Campbell, carrying out the evacuation of the Lucknow residency.

In the second capture of Lucknow by British forces and Indian soldiers loyal to the Company and the Crown, Outram commanded the attack to retake the residency. In the words of Sir Colin Campbell, he 'put the finishing stroke on the enemy'.

After the re-taking of Lucknow, Outram was promoted to lieutenant-general. In 1858 he received the thanks of both houses of Parliament, and in the same year was made a baronet, with an annuity of £1000.

He returned to England in 1860, his health shattered, and died in 1863. He was buried in the nave of Westminster Abbey, where the marble slab on his grave bears the epitaph The Bayard of India.

Pierre Terrail, seigneur de Bayard (1473 –1524) was a renowned French soldier whose conduct won for him the reputation throughout the centuries since his death as 'the knight without fear and beyond reproach' (le chevalier sans peur et sans raproche).

James Outram's memory is recalled by statues in London and in Calcutta (now Kolkatta).

Casualties throughout World War One were terrible and some streets and neighbourhoods suffered great loss of life. In Hamilton Road, Long Eaton, is this memorial to the men of one street. It is carefully maintained by the British Legion (*Author*).

They also served: The Chilwell shell filling factory explosion on July 1 1918 killed 134 people and injured a further 250. Unidentified bodies from the blast are buried in the churchyard of St Mary's Attenborough, pictured here (*Author*).

After the horrors of the Crimea and the shock of the Indian Mutiny, Britain's military activities were confined to relatively small-scale colonial conflicts, fought by a small professional army assisted by native troops, raised locally in Africa and Asia.

Anglo-Dutch rivalry in Southern Africa occupied more than a century from Britain's initial capture of Holland's Cape Colony in 1795. The First Boer War was fought from December 16 1880 until March 21 1881 and was sparked by the annexation for Britain of the South African Republic (Transvaal Republic) in 1877.

The Boers eventually rose in revolt and enjoyed considerable military success, including the battle of Majuba Hill, where the British were outperformed by the highly mobile Dutch marksmen.

William Gladstone's government effectively capitulated and the peace treaty gave the Boers self-government, under a theoretical British oversight.

The Second Boer War began on October 11 1899 and lasted for some two and a half years. Great Britain eventually defeated two Boer nations in South Africa - the old enemy in the form of the Republic of Transvaal, and the Orange Free State.

The British, at first both over-confident and under-prepared, defeated the Boers in the field but were then faced by the type of guerrilla warfare at which their opponents excelled.

The solution, corralling the Boers into restricted areas and detaining their non-combatants into concentration camps ensured that Britain had no international support outside its own Empire, and much public opinion at home was also hostile.

The conflict led to the award of the second Victoria Cross to an Erewash Valley man, Harry Churchill Beet. Beet was born in Nottinghamshire in 1873 but was later associated with Long Eaton, where he lived at Sawley Road,

The incident for which he won the VC occurred at Wakkerstroom on April 22 1900. In the cat and mouse warfare typical of the South African conflict, men of Number Two Mounted Infantry Company, the First Battalion of the Derbyshire Regiment, together with two squadrons of Imperial Yeomanry, were forced to retire from their position near a farm, uncomfortably exposed to Boers who held a commanding ridge. Corporal Burnett, Imperial Yeomanry, was left on the ground wounded.

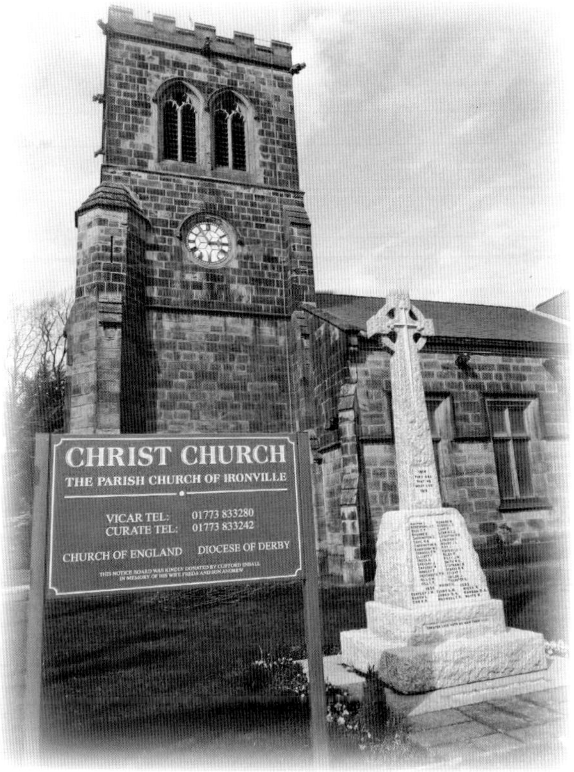

Christ Church, Ironville, built by The Butterley Company to serve its company town, contains the village war memorial. Many of the dead would have worked for the company. (*Author*).

One of the most attractive of the Erewash Valley war memorials is at Kimberley (*Author*).

He was spotted by Corporal Beet, who remained behind whilst the main body of British groups carried out a strategic retirement. Beet placed Burnett under cover, dressed his wounds and by keeping up a constant fire prevented the Boers from approaching the farm.

When it grew dark Beet was joined by a Doctor Wilson of the Imperial Yeomanry and together they managed to evacuate Burnett to safety, despite coming under very heavy fire from the enemy. The citation for Beet's VC recorded that he had been exposed to fire during the whole afternoon.

On his return home in October 1902 Beet was photographed with other local South African war veterans outside the Regent Inn in Long Eaton town centre (later known as The Hole in the Wall).

The men were invited to attend a Welcome Home Banquet at The People's Hall in the town. The event was designed, in the words of the official invitation, 'in order that your fellow townsmen may meet you to express their hearty appreciation of the services you rendered to your country in connection with the late South African war'.

In the photograph some of the men are already back in civilian life. Beet, pictured wearing a bush-type slouch hat, continued his military career and after initially being promoted to sergeant was eventually commissioned, achieving the rank of captain.

He emigrated to Saskatchewan, Canada, and fought in Europe with the Canadian Expeditionary Force in World War One. He died in Vancouver in 1936.

The Welcome Home Banquet staged in Long Eaton marked the change in attitude towards Britain's fighting men. Although a military career was an accepted part of life for the aristocracy and upper middle class, joining the colours had generally been seen as something almost shameful by lower middle and respectable working class families.

The Duke of Wellington, whose troops at Waterloo included the three Cossall men commemorated on the village memorial, notoriously said of his men:

'Ours (our army) is composed of the scum of the earth - the mere scum of the earth', adding: 'I don't know what effect these men will have upon the enemy, but, by God, they frighten me'.

One of the Cossall three, Thomas Wheatley, was pointed out to the Iron Duke by his commanding officer. When told where Wheatley came from, the Duke is said to have replied: 'He is a good soldier

Perhaps the most distinctive valley war memorial is at West Hallam, where a machine gun crew appears to be directing their weapon at the parish church of St Wilfred (*Author*).

but he comes from a riotous county (Nottinghamshire at the time was in the grip of Luddite riots, designed to smash machinery believed to be destroying the county's extensive system of home-working in the textile trades).

The advent of World War One, with mass voluntary enlistment, followed by conscription meant that, for the first time, virtually the entire population of Britain, rich or poor, had direct links with the armed forces.

Kipling's put-upon Tommy Atkins in the poem written in 1890 was no longer someone to be avoided until the drums begin to roll, but everyone's husband, father, son or brother.

World War One produced five Victoria Cross holders with Erewash Valley connections, including one of the legendary fighter aces of the conflict.

In his short life – he was killed in action before his 21st birthday - Albert Ball was awarded not just the Victoria Cross but also three Distinguished Service Orders and the Military Cross. He became the first aerial ace to become a British national hero.

Ball was the son of a Nottingham man who rose from a humble background as a plumber to become a successful business man, Lord Mayor of the City and a Knight of the Realm. His son was educated at Long Eaton's Trent College, and on the outbreak of war was commissioned as a second lieutenant in the Sherwood Foresters, later transferring to the Royal Flying Corps in 1915.

He gained his pilot's wings in January 1916 and after initially flying reconnaissance missions in France transferred to Number Eleven Squadron, a fighter unit. After a period on home establishment, Ball was posted to Number 56 Squadron, which deployed to the Western Front in April 1917. He crashed to his death in a field in France on May 7.

His death caused a wave of national mourning and posthumous recognition, which included the award of the VC for his actions during his final tour of duty. The famous German flying ace Manfred von Richthofen (ironically a member of the family of DH Lawrence's wife Frieda) remarked upon hearing of Ball's death that he was "by far the best English flying man."

At the time of his death Ball was the United Kingdom's leading flying ace, with 44 victories, and by the end of the war was still its fourth-highest scorer.

The first Erewash Valley Victoria Cross of World War One had been awarded in March 1915 to 21-year-old Wilfred Dolby Fuller, from Greasley, near Eastwood.

Fuller was serving as a lance-corporal in the First Battalion, Grenadier Guards, during the Battle of Neuve Chapelle in France, when he saw a party of the enemy trying to escape along a communication trench.

He ran towards them and killed the leading man with a bomb. The remainder of the Germans, nearly 50 strong, promptly surrendered to Fuller, seeing no means of evading his bombs. The Greasley man was quite alone at the time of the incident.

Fuller received his Victoria Cross from King George V at Buckingham Palace in June 1915 and in September of the same year, at the express wish of the Tsar of Russia, he was decorated by the King at an investiture in Sheffield, with the Russian Cross of the Order of Saint George, 3rd Class.

In 1916 he married a nurse from Somerset and after his discharge from the Army on medical grounds he joined the Somerset Constabulary. He died aged 54 and is buried at Frome, Somerset.

Walter Richard Parker, a 33-year-old lance-corporal in the Royal Marine Light Infantry, won the Victoria Cross in Gallipoli, where he was acting as a volunteer stretcher bearer.

One night in May 1915 Lance-Corporal Parker went out with a party of non-commissioned officers and men to take ammunition, water and medical stores to an isolated trench, containing some 40 men, some of whom were wounded. There were no communication trenches leading to the position and several men had already been killed in an attempt to reach it.

After crossing an area of about 400 yards swept by machine-gun and rifle fire, Lance-Corporal Parker found himself alone, the rest of the party having been killed or wounded. Despite sustaining serious wounds himself, he successfully reached the isolated trench and was able to assist the other wounded men.

When the trench was finally evacuated early the next morning, he helped to remove and attend the casualties, again disregarding his own wounds.

Decorated by the King: Sergeant William Gregg of Heanor, receiving his Victoria Cross from HM King George V. Gregg was the first British soldier ever to receive the three highest awards for gallantry, also being the holder of the Military Medal and the Distinguished Conduct Medal (*Heanor and District Local History Society*).

Parker never fully recovered from his wounds, and was invalided out of the service in June 1916. The account of his VC award noted that Parker had consistently displayed bravery and energy over a difficult three day period for the battalion's stretcher bearers, when almost every wounded man had to be evacuated over open ground and under fire.

Walter Parker died at the age of 55, at Stapleford and is buried in the local cemetery. A memorial service to him is held annually at Stapleford by the local Royal Marines Association on the Sunday nearest April 30. A paved area in Stapleford town centre named in his honour.

In the spring of 1918, after nearly four years of stalemate on the Western Front, the German High Command found itself facing a dilemma. The collapse of Russia following the Bolshevik revolution had removed pressure on the German army in the east, but in the west the American forces who had entered the war the previous year were building up their strength to bolster the weary French and British forces.

The German commander Erich Ludendorff identified an area of weakness in the allied front line and ordered a massive offensive designed to drive the British out of the war before the American forces were fully operational.

The 1918 Spring Offensive or Kaiserschlacht (Kaiser's Battle), also known as the Ludendorff Offensive, was a series of German attacks along the Western Front. Although much success was enjoyed initially, the offensive proved to be a failure, leading to the ultimate defeat of Germany.

The final three Victoria Crosses awarded to men from the Erewash Valley were won during the Spring Offensive, as the British Army fought desperately to avoid the Germans breaking through to take the Channel ports.

Charles Edwin Stone was born in Street Lane, Denby, and was a coal miner, like his father. His brother Ernest was killed in action in 1917.

On the first day of the Ludendorff offensive, March 21 1918, he was 29 years old and serving as a gunner in C Battery of the 83rd Brigade, Royal Field Artillery.

Gunner Stone, after working at his gun for six hours under heavy gas and shell fire, was sent to the rear to deliver an order. He then returned, under a heavy barrage, to his unit's position and, taking up a rifle, helped to hold up the enemy on a sunken road.

He at first lay in the open under very heavy machine-gun fire and then moved to the right flank of the two rear guns, holding the Germans at bay. Later he was one of a party which captured a machine-gun and four prisoners.

Charlie Stone, who was promoted to the rank of Bombardier, had earlier been awarded the Military Medal for his gallantry. Following

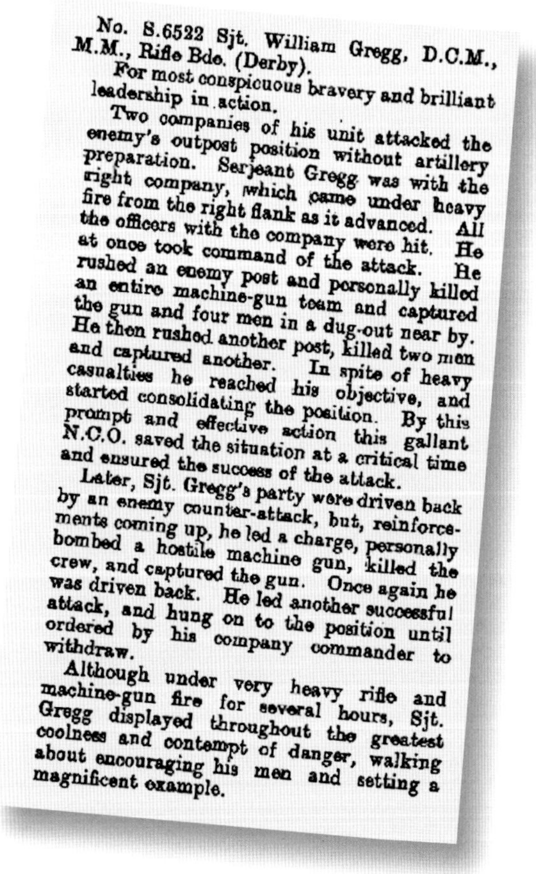

No. S.6522 Sjt. William Gregg, D.C.M., M.M., Rifle Bde. (Derby).

For most conspicuous bravery and brilliant leadership in action.

Two companies of his unit attacked the enemy's outpost position without artillery preparation. Serjeant Gregg was with the right company, which came under heavy fire from the right flank as it advanced. All the officers with the company were hit. He at once took command of the attack. He rushed an enemy post and personally killed an entire machine-gun team and captured the gun and four men in a dug-out near by. He then rushed another post, killed two men and captured another. In spite of heavy casualties he reached his objective, and started consolidating the position. By this prompt and effective action this gallant N.C.O. saved the situation at a critical time and ensured the success of the attack.

Later, Sjt. Gregg's party were driven back by an enemy counter-attack, but, reinforcements coming up, he led a charge, personally bombed a hostile machine gun, killed the crew, and captured the gun. Once again he was driven back. He led another successful attack, and hung on to the position until ordered by his company commander to withdraw.

Although under very heavy rifle and machine-gun fire for several hours, Sjt. Gregg displayed throughout the greatest coolness and contempt of danger, walking about encouraging his men and setting a magnificent example.

Sergeant William Gregg's citation for the award of the Victoria Cross (*Author's Collection*).

the war he worked for many years in the hardening shop at Rolls Royce in Derby. During World War Two he was presented to King George V1 when the monarch visited the works.

In 1924 he had been accorded the honour of turning up the ball at the start of the second day of the Ashbourne Shrovetide Football Match. The first day had been started by the Duke of Devonshire. In 1929, he attended a dinner held in the House of Lords in the presence of the Prince of Wales and Lord Jellicoe, along with other VC winners.

In May 1918, as the Ludendorff offensive continued, two Derbyshire men, William Gregg of Heanor and William Beesley of Church Gresley, both serving in the Rifle Brigade, won the Victoria Cross in the same battle, just two days apart.

William Gregg was aged 28 and a sergeant in the 13th Battalion, The Rifle Brigade (Prince Consort's Own), British when he performed the deed for which he was awarded the Victoria Cross.

On May 6 1918, at Bucquoy, a small village in the Pas de Calais area of Northern France, all the officers of Sergeant Gregg's company had been hit during an attack on an enemy outpost. Gregg took command and rushed two enemy posts, killing some of the gun teams, taking prisoners and capturing a machine-gun.

He was driven back by a counter-attack, but as reinforcements had by now come up, he then led a charge, personally bombed a hostile machine-gun, killed the crew and captured the gun. When driven back again, he led another successful attack and held on to his position until ordered to withdraw.

Gregg later achieved the rank of company sergeant-major and served in World War II with the Sherwood Foresters. He is honoured by his home town of Heanor through the William Gregg VC Leisure Centre.

William Beesley (22) took command at Bucquoy two days after's Gregg's heroic acts. After the Gresley man's platoon sergeant and all the section commanders were killed he single-handedly rushed a German post, shot four of the enemy, took six prisoners and sent them back to his lines.

He and a comrade then brought a Lewis gun into action, inflicting many casualties and holding their position for four hours until the second private was wounded. Private Beesley, by himself, then maintained his position until nightfall, when he returned to the original line with the wounded man and the Lewis gun which he kept in action until the situation became quiet.

The Erewash Valley's hero-cum-villain-cum-hero-cum villain yet again of the period encompassing the years leading up to World War One, the conflict itself and the inter-war era of the European dictators was John Bernard Seely, Liberal Member of Parliament for the Ilkeston Division from 1910 to 1922.

Seeley, an Erewash Valley man, born at Brookhill Hall, near Pinxton, can fairly claim to being on the one hand the most celebrated and colourful member of Parliament ever to have been associated with Ilkeston, and on the other hand certainly the most bitterly criticised.

He became a close friend of Winston Churchill after the two men met in South Africa during the Boer War. Britain's World War Two Prime Minister later recalled: "I met him in South Africa, riding across the veldt. He was Colonel Seely then. I saw him at the head of a column of British cavalry, riding twenty yards in front, on a black horse. I thought of him as the very symbol of Imperial power."

After joining the Imperial Yeomanry, Seeley used his wealth and connections, much in the same way as Winston Churchill, to make sure he was part of the action in the campaigns against the Boer farmers.

He was too impatient to wait for an official summons to join the British forces and arranged private transport to South Africa for himself and his squadron, with the assistance of his uncle Sir Francis Evans, who just happened to be chairman of the Union Castle shipping line, which sailed between Britain and Africa. Seeley was mentioned in despatches, and awarded the Distinguished Service Order (DSO) in 1900.

After winning the Ilkeston seat at a by-election, Seeley had a rapid rise to ministerial rank, serving as Under-Secretary of State for the Colonies under Prime Minister Herbert Henry Asquith, between 1908 and 1911, and was credited with being responsible for much of the work which led to the Union of the South African colonies.

Seeley's next post was as Under-Secretary of State for War from 1911 to 1912, a critical period for the British armed forces as a conflict with the Kaiser's Germany became ever more likely.

He was appointed in 1912 to the top post of Secretary of State for War, with a seat in the Cabinet, a post he was to hold until 1914. Britain had for many decades, as the world's undisputed leading power, stood aloof from European politics.

Basil Hooley, pictured with his wife Dorothy, was a member of the well-known Risley family and the half-brother of the financier Ernest Terah Hooley. He served with the pioneering Tank Corps in World War One and was awarded the Military Cross for conspicuous gallantry whilst commanding a company of tanks in action on the western front. Whilst on leave at Risley in October 1918 he became ill with influenza, which turned to pneumonia, and died three weeks before the Armistice (*Author's Collection*).

Seeley sensed the importance of now forging a military alliance with France, and invited General Foch to attend the British Army Manoeuvres of 1912. He also recognised the potential importance of air warfare and helped develop the Royal Flying Corps (later the Royal Air Force).

At the height of his political powers, Seeley's career at Westminster was brought to a halt when he was held to blame for the mishandling of a crisis in Ireland, which became known as the Curragh Mutiny.

The Liberal plan to give Home Rule to the island of Ireland was due to come into effect in 1914. Welcomed by the Catholic population of the southern counties of Ireland, the idea of self-government was viewed with horror by Protestants in the north.

Officers of the British Army serving at the Curragh Camp in County Kildare, in southern Ireland (then a part of the Empire, sending MPs to Westminster) threatened to resign their commissions rather than be forced to take part in military action against the Protestant Ulster Volunteers threatening to oppose Home Rule by force, unless Ulster was exempted and could remain as part of Great Britain.

During the ensuing political scandal Seeley was considered to have made too many concessions to the Ulster Unionists and their military supporters, and was forced to resign.

His response to his political downfall was to rejoin the army, blazing a trail followed by his friend Winston Churchill two years later, after Churchill, at the time First Sea Lord, had been forced to resign following the military disaster at Gallipoli in the Dardanelles.

At the Western Front Seeley enhanced his earlier reputation for bravery, becoming a major-general and commander of the Canadian Cavalry Brigade, commanding what has been described as an 'assorted bunch of ranchers, clerks, expatriates, Mounties and Native Americans'.

He ended the war as a popular hero, his earlier political disgrace forgotten when, in March 1918, mounted on his charger Warrior, he led one of the final cavalry charges in the history of warfare, against the German army at Moreuil Wood, on the banks of the river Avre in France.

Another member of the Hooley family of Risley, the poet and writer Teresa, sister of tragic war hero Basil, served in the conflict in the Derbyshire Women's Land Army (*Author's Collection*).

Remembrance Sunday has been observed with reverence in the valley since the years following World War One. Two women police officers lay wreaths at the Cenotaph outside Long Eaton's parish church of St Laurence (*Author's Collection*).

Seeley earned the nickname of 'Galloper Jack' for his action, again part of the major German offensive launched in March 1918.

He held his seat at Ilkeston at the General Election of 1918. Seeley's first national contest, because of the war, since he had won the seat at the 1912 by-election. His opponent at the so-called 'Khaki Election' was George Oliver, a former gear cutter for Rolls Royce and a trade union official.

The political climate, in the Erewash Valley and in the country as whole, was changing, with working people switching their political allegiance from the Liberals to the Labour Party and at the next General Election, in 1922, Oliver unseated Seeley.

Seeley returned to the House of Commons two years later, as MP for the Isle of Wight, a seat he had previously held from 1900 to 1906.

A great many political careers end in tears; Seeley's reputation was badly tarnished in the 1930s when, by now ennobled as Lord Mottistone, he spoke favourably of Adolf Hitler.

Marching to the Long Eaton Remembrance Sunday service in the early 1950s. Some of the children watching the parade would have been born during World War Two and many would have had fathers who served in the forces (Author's Collection).

A whole post- World War Two war generation grew up on the story of the Dambusters. The bouncing bomb the RAF squadron used to destroy German dams and disrupt industry was designed by the Ripley-born Barnes Wallis. His genius and the bravery of the RAF crews is commemorated in the Sir Barnes Wallis public house in his birthplace (*Author*).

After Hitler had made a speech in 1935 proclaiming that German rearmament offered no threat to world peace, Seeley told the House of Lords that it should be assumed that the German leader's statement was 'genuine and sincere'.

Seeley added: "I think the noble Lords and all the people who have really met this remarkable man will agree with me on one thing, however much we may disagree about other things — that he is absolutely truthful, sincere, and unselfish."

As late as June 1939 Seeley said: "I am an unrepentant believer in the policy of appeasement" but when World War Two had been in progress for two years, he retracted his earlier support for and confidence in Hitler.

Seeley, who died in 1947, at the age of 79, was described by *The Times* as `a gallant figure in war and politics'. The politician F E Smith, Lord Birkenhead, wrote of him: "In fields of great and critical danger he constantly, over a long period of years, displayed a cool valour."

Memories of Seeley survive in popular culture. Alfred Munnings, a former President of the Royal Academy, regarded his painting of Seeley mounted on his war horse Warrior as his most important work.

Seeley is mentioned in the 2009 film about the life of Winston Churchill, *Into the Storm*, starring Brendon Gleeson as the war leader and Janet McTeer as his wife Clementine. At the end of the film, musing on his defeat in the 1945 General Election, Churchill reads a sympathetic note from 'my old friend Jack Seeley'. Thinking back to their first meeting in South Africa, Seeley tells Churchill: "I feel our world slipping away'.

An autobiography of Seeley, entitled *Galloper Jack*, was written by his grandson, the horseracing commentator Brough Scott.

The end result of modern warfare in the 20th century between sophisticated industrial nations often depended not just on manpower and resources but on which nation or group of allies possessed the best and most innovative minds.

Two men from the Erewash Valley played leading roles in determining that victory should go to the Allied cause.

Sir Barnes Neville Wallis, scientist, engineer and inventor was born at Ripley, where his memory is immortalised in the name of a public house in the town.

He is best known for inventing the bouncing bomb used by the Royal Air Force in Operation Chastise (the 'Dambusters' raid) to attack the dams of the Ruhr Valley during World War II.

The raid was the subject of the 1955 film *The Dam Busters*, in which Wallis was played by Michael Redgrave. Among Barnes Wallis' other inventions were the geodetic airframe and the earthquake bomb.

He originally trained as a marine engineer but later switched to work on airship and then aircraft design. At the outbreak of World War Two he saw a need for strategic bombing to destroy the enemy's ability to wage war and proposed huge bombs that could concentrate their force and destroy enemy targets which were otherwise unlikely to be affected.

After the success of the bouncing bomb, Wallis was able to return to his huge bombs, producing first the Tallboy (6 tonnes) and then the Grand Slam (10 tonnes) deep-penetration earthquake bombs.

Rolf Noskwith of the lingerie firm Charnos, one of the Erewash Valley's most successful and respected business men, was revealed many years after World War Two to have been part of the team of code breakers at Bletchley Park which worked on the German Enigma ciphers and played a major part in the British victory.

They were used on strategic German targets such as V-2 rocket launch sites, the V-3 supergun bunker, submarine pens, and other reinforced structures, large civil constructions such as viaducts and bridges, as well as the German battleship Tirpitz.

Following the terrible death toll of the aircrews involved in the Dambusters raid, Barnes Wallis made a conscious effort never again to endanger the lives of his test pilots. His designs were extensively tested in model form, and consequently he became a pioneer in the remote control of aircraft.

Barnes Wallis' achievements were well publicised during wartime, because of the great morale boost to the British public given by the Dambusters' exploits. Today his memory lives on in his birthplace, commemorated in the Barnes Wallis public house.

The contribution to the winning of the war made by one of the Erewash Valley's most celebrated businessmen, Rolf Noskwith, of the Charnos hosiery and lingerie firm was, by contrast, kept mostly secret, right up to his death at the start of 2017, at the age of 97.

Noskwith, who lived for many years at Sandiacre, was characteristically modest about his role as one of the celebrated codebreakers at Bletchley Park and many who knew the man for his business achievements were unaware of this part of his life.

He worked with the celebrated Alan Turing on the Enigma ciphers used by German U-boats. The success of the small team working in the famous Hut 8 at Bletchley Park has been credited with ending the war up to two years early.

The Noskwith family, who were Jewish, arrived in England from Germany in 1932. Rolf Noskwith's father Charles established Charnos four years later -

The late Slavomir Rawicz, a former Polish Army officer who lived for many years in Sandiacre, wrote *The Long Walk*, a book relating how he and six others had escaped from imprisonment by the Russian secret service after the German-Soviet invasion of Poland and had walked some 4,000 miles across the Gobi Desert, Tibet and the Himalayas to eventually reached British India. In recent years some people have cast doubt on the veracity of the story.

choosing the name from the first letters of his own two names. Rolf attended Nottingham High School before going to read mathematics at Cambridge. As a fan of crosswords and a speaker of German he was the perfect candidate to help break Nazi codes, and he joined Bletchley Park in 1941.

By deciphering the codes the small team helped the Royal Navy thwart much of the U-boat threat. He kept what had happened at Bletchley Park a closely-guarded secret for 30 years, finally commenting: "What was achieved there, no-one knew. We never talked about it. When you think how things are leaked today, it is remarkable that the secrets of Bletchley Park were kept for so long."

Just as the history of warfare is largely written by the victors, it is the victorious politicians, backroom boffins, senior military officers and (deservedly) those decorated for gallantry who tend to be remembered. Those who fought and often died without fanfare tend to live on in the hearts and memories of their immediate families.

For more than two decades after the end of World War Two, the memory of two such unheralded fighting men was recalled each Christmas in the Roll of Honour section of the personal column of a now defunct Erewash Valley newspaper, the *Long Eaton Advertiser*.

On the publication date closest to December 28, the entry commemorated the deaths of two brothers who died whilst serving in the Royal Navy. Illustrated with photographs of the brothers wearing their naval headgear at a jaunty angle, the entry marked the death of Tommy Lockley, killed when the battleship HMS Barham was torpedoed off the Egyptian coast in December 1939, and Ernest Lockley, lost at sea in September 1942 whilst serving in motor torpedo boats.

The entry was always signed, simply, 'Mother'.

The compositors in the *Advertiser* printing department, who included men who had served in the North African desert in WW2 (one had lost a leg at El Alamein) paid their own tribute to the lost brothers, taking great care of the old fashioned photographic blocks, as they took them out of store each year and then set them aside for another long twelve months.

The splendour falls. The ruins of Codnor Castle, in its heyday a powerful medieval fortress, dating back to the late 12th or early 13th centuries, stands on a ridge overlooking the Erewash Valley. It was for some 300 years the stronghold of the powerful De Grey family. The present-day remains represent a three-storey keep and a strong curtain wall and ditch, flanked by round towers. Today the remnants of Codnor Castle are a fragile ruin.

Public access to the privately-owned site is managed by The Codnor Castle Heritage Trust which is working to prevent the castle from falling into further disrepair and to promote it as a site of historical importance (Stuart Saint www.codnor.info)

Selected Further Reading

The books listed below represent but a fraction of the published material which is directly concerned with, or touches upon, various aspects of life in the Erewash Valley. It is rather a list of the books which the author has enjoyed reading, and which have helped to provide an understanding of the ethos of the valley and its people.

General, Industrial and Topographical:

About Britain No 8 East Midlands and The Peak, W G Hoskins, *Collins for the Festival of Britain Office.*

The Face of Britain North Midland Country, J H Ingram, *Batsford.*

The King's England Nottinghamshire, Arthur Mee (Editor), *Hodder & Stoughton.*

The King's England Derbyshire, Arthur Mee (Editor), *Hodder & Stoughton.*

The Buildings of England Derbyshire, Nikolaus Pevsner, *Penguin Books.*

Father's Derbyshire, Cyril Hargreaves, *Moorleys.*

Peakland Days, Roger Redfern, *Robert Hale.*

The Book of Long Eaton, Keith A Reedman, *Barracuda Books.*

Pocket Images Ilkeston, Simon Harvey, *Nonsuch.*

Through Six Decades The story of Co-operation in Long Eaton and District 1868-1928, Gertrude R Lane and Robert Bowley, *Co-operative Wholesale Society Ltd.*

Long Eaton Co-operative Society Ltd A Centenary History, Geoffrey Kingscott, LECS.

Pocket Images Long Eaton, John Barker, *Nonsuch.*

One Hundred Years of Conservatism 1887-1987, John Heath.

Sandiacre Remembered, *Sandiacre Heritage 2000 Group.*

Stapleford in World War Two, Barbara Brooke, Nigel Brooks and Alan Clayton,*Stapleford and Distrrict Local History Society.*

The Iron Dale, Victor Lewis, *The Stanton Ironworks Company.*

Nottingham Lace 1760s-1950s, Sheila M Mason, *Alan Sutton Publishing.*

West Hallam Heritage, Brenda J Hunt, *Moorleys.*

Erewash Valley Portrait, Philip Dalling, *Moorleys.*

Eye Up Mi Duck, Dialect of Derbyshire and the East Midlands, Richard Scollins & John Titford, *Countryside Books.*

Derbyshire Guides from the 1950s to the 1980s.

Official Guides to local authorities in the Erewash Valley from 1950s to the 1980s.

A History of Catholic Nottingham, Martin Cummins, *Regeena.*

From Erewash to Radegund, John Rimington, *Grosvenor House.*

Literature:

The novels and short stories of D H Lawrence (Various publishers/editions)

Means Test Man, Walter Brierley, *Spokesman Books.*

The novels of Alan Sillitoe (Various publishers/editions).

The novels of Eric Malpass.

The Singing Heart, Theresa Hooley, *Frederick Muller.*

D H Lawrence, The Life of an Outsider, John Worthen, *Allen Lane.*

The Intelligent Heart, The Story of D H Lawrence, Harry T Moore, *Penguin Biographies.*

Lawrence In Love, Letters from D H Lawrence to Louie Burrows, James T Boulton, *The University of Nottingham.*

D H Lawrence in the Modern World, Peter Preston and Peter Hoare (Editors), *Macmillan.*

The Country of My Heart, Bridget Pugh, *Nottinghamshire Local History Council.*

A D H Lawrence Album, George Hardy & Nathaniel Harris,*Moorland Publishing.*

Nottingham, A History of Britain's Global University, John Beckett. *The University of Nottingham/Boydell Press.*

Life without Armour, An Autobiography, Alan Sillitoe, *Flamingo.*

The Life of a Long Distance Writer, The Biography of Alan Sillitoe, Richard Bradford, *Peter Owen.*

Letters Volume One 1926 to 1951, John Betjeman/Candida Lycett Green, *Minerva.*

Transport and Communications:

A Regional History of the Railways of Great Britain Volume 9 The East Midlands, Robin Leleux, *David & Charles.*

Forgotten Railways The East Midlands, P Howard Anderson, *David & Charles.*

The Midland Railway, C Hamilton Ellis, *Ian Allan.*

The Midland Line to London, John Palmer, *Grayson Publications.*

The Midland Counties Railway, Mark Higginson, *Midland RailwayTrust.*

London Midland Steam in the East Midlands, J F Henton, *Bradford Barton.*

Rails to Ripley, Howard Sprenger, *Kestrel.*

The Railways of Nottingham (Exhibition Catalogue,1969), *The Railway Correspondence and Travel Society, East Midlands Branch.*

The Mansfield and Pinxton Railway (Article,July & August 1949), *The Railway Magazine.*

Lost Railways of Nottinghamshire, Geoffrey Kingscott, *Countryside Books.*

Lost Railways of Derbyshire, Geoffrey Kingscott, *Countryside Books.*

Last Train from Trent Station, Geoffrey Kingscott, *Kingscott Consultants Ltd.*

Toton Engineman, The Autobiography of a Railwayman, John Henry Woolley,*Steam World.*

Last Days of Steam on the LMS and BR, R H Fowkes, *Halsgrove.*

Rail Centres Nottingham, Michael A Vanns, *Ian Allan.*

Rail Centres Derby, Brian Radford, *Ian Allan.*

The Friargate Line, Mark Higginson, *Golden Pingle Publishing.*

The Great Northern Railway in the East Midlands 3 The Erewash Valley, Alfred Henshaw, *Railway Correspondence and Travel Society (RCTS).*

English Rivers and Canals, Frank Eyre and Charles Hadfield, *Collins.*

The Canal Age, Charles Hadfield, *Augustus M Kelley Publishers, New York.*

Lost Canals of England and Wales, Ronald Russell, *David & Charles.*

Narrow Boat, LTC Rolt, *Sutton Publishing/The Inland Waterways Association.*

Navigable Waterways, LTCRolt, *Penguin Books.*

The Inland Waterways of England, LTC Rolt, *George Allen and Unwin.*

Gateway to the Erewash Canal, *Erewash Canal Preservation and Development Association.*

Sport

Nottingham Post Football Guides – 1940s to 1970s, Nottingham Post.

Canon Football League Players Records. Barry J Hugman, *Book Club Associates.*

Wisden Cricketers Almanacs.

Derbyshire and Nottinghamshire County Cricket Handbooks.

The History of Derbyshire County Cricket Club, John Shawcroft,*Helm.*

The History of Cricket in Long Eaton, Sandiacre & Sawley, Keith Breakwell.

Derbyshire Cricket Grounds A Postwar Survey, Simon Lacey, Chris Higginbottom and Tom Whittington, *Lacey.*

Nottingham and Long Eaton Speedway 1928-1976, Philip Dalling, *Tempus.*

Long Eaton Speedway, Maurice Jones, *Speedway Surveys.*

Classic Speedway Venues, Philip Dalling, *Halsgrove.*